3704363201

D1330144

PARK LEARNING CENTRE
The Park Cheltenham
Gloucestershire GL50 2RH
Telephone: 01242 714333

UNIVERSITY OF
GLOUCESTERSHIRE
at Cheltenham and Gloucester

WEEK LOAN

49766 08/06

FLEXIBLE WEB DESIGN

Creating Liquid and Elastic Layouts with CSS

ZOE MICKLEY GILLENWATER

WITHDRAWN

New Riders

Flexible Web Design: Creating Liquid and Elastic Layouts with CSS
Zoe Mickley Gillenwater

Published by New Riders. For information on New Riders books, contact:

New Riders
1249 Eighth Street
Berkeley, CA 94710
(510) 524-2178
Fax: (510) 524-2221

Find us on the Web at www.newriders.com
To report errors, please send a note to errata@peachpit.com
New Riders is an imprint of Peachpit, a division of Pearson Education
Copyright © 2009 by Zoe M. Gillenwater

Acquisitions Editor: Wendy Sharp
Production Editor: Hilal Sala
Project/Copy Editor: Wendy Katz
Technical Editor: Sheri German
Cover design and production: Mimi Heft
Interior design: Mimi Heft
Compositor: Danielle Foster
Indexer: Karin Arrigoni

Notice of Rights

All rights reserved. No part of this book may be reproduced or transmitted in any form by any means, electronic, mechanical, photocopying, recording, or otherwise, without the prior written permission of the publisher. For information on getting permission for reprints and excerpts, contact permissions@ peachpit.com.

Notice of Liability

The information in this book is distributed on an "As Is" basis, without warranty. While every precaution has been taken in the preparation of the book, neither the authors nor New Riders shall have any liability to any person or entity with respect to any loss or damage caused or alleged to be caused directly or indirectly by the instructions contained in this book or by the computer software and hardware products described in it.

Trademarks

Throughout this book trademarked names are used. Rather than put a trademark symbol in every occurrence of a trademarked name, we state we are using the names only in an editorial fashion and to the benefit of the trademark owner with no intention of infringement of the trademark. Acrobat, Dreamweaver, Fireworks, Photoshop, and Reader are all trademarks or registered trademarks of Adobe Systems, Inc.

ISBN-13: 978-0-321-55384-3
ISBN-10:   0-321-55384-5

9 8 7 6 5 4 3 2 1

Printed and bound in the United States of America

To Cary, my husband and best friend

Acknowledgments

To Wendy Sharp, my acquisitions editor at Peachpit/New Riders, for approaching me in the first place, helping me solidify the concept of the idea for the book, guiding me through the process, and having patience with yet another late author.

To Wendy Katz, my editor, for her incredibly detailed and thoughtful revisions and advice that have made this book much better than it would have been otherwise. Her support and guidance were invaluable, and it was a tremendous pleasure working so closely with her.

To Sheri German, my technical editor, for her painstaking work checking all those code samples and example pages, her help tracking down answers to the tough questions, and—most of all—for her enthusiasm.

To all the people at Peachpit/New Riders in production, marketing, and other departments whom I never worked with directly but who made this book a reality.

To David Fugate, my literary agent, for his guidance and advocacy.

To my friends and family who provided photos of their pets for the example site used throughout the book: Karen Brock and her dog Shelby, Dean Gillenwater and his cat Alley and dog Dutch, Sarah Grover and her cat Nomar, and Laura Sandt and her dog Bailey.

To Stephanie Sullivan and John Gallant, both CSS experts, for getting me into this writing thing years ago. I've learned so much from them and am blessed to have their support.

To all the other CSS gurus and web designers who have inspired and taught me, including Cameron Adams, Holly Bergevin, Doug Bowman, Andy Budd, Dan Cederholm, Ingo Chao, Andy Clarke, Bruno Fassino, Roger Johansson, Eric Meyer, Cameron Moll, Georg Sortun, Russ Weakley, and countless others.

To all my colleagues at the UNC Highway Safety Research Center, for putting up with a sometimes tired, distracted, and stressed version of me over the last several months. Special thanks to my supervisor and friend Katy Jones for her support.

Most of all, to my husband Cary and our mystery baby, both of whom have been there with me throughout this whole process (well, the baby came a little late to the game). I love you both. Cary, I'm humbled by your patience in dealing with the double threat of stressed author and pregnant woman simultaneously. Thanks so much for your amazing support, encouragement, and for taking over cooking duty. I owe you several dinners. And cake.

Table of Contents

Introduction

Take the book you're holding in your hands right now, and resize it so that it's easier to read.

Don't feel bad—I've given you an impossible exercise, but I promise the book will be filled with practical instead of ridiculous exercises from here on out. That's because we're going to be talking about web design, where we're not constrained by the physical limitations of print on paper.

Though both web and print offer opportunities for beautiful and effective design, each has its own strengths and limitations. To create successful web designs, you need to design to the medium's strengths instead of fighting against them. One of these strengths is flexibility. Here, I'm using flexible in the broadest sense—built to adapt to an infinite number of viewing scenarios. Users are ultimately in control of their experience of web sites to a degree beyond what's possible with any other medium. They get to choose—whether or not they do so consciously and willingly—the type of device they view web pages on, how big their screens and windows are, their text sizes and fonts, whether to view still images or Flash animations. Really savvy users can even set up their own style sheets to slightly or dramatically change the visual appearance of the sites they view. Some users don't even "view" web sites—they may hear or feel them instead.

The web medium is also flexible in the narrower sense of the word—web pages and content are not fixed at one particular size. By default, web pages can change in width and height to accommodate the differing text sizes and window widths of the users. This is true of both web pages built with divs and CSS and those built with tables.

Fixed-width web pages—pages that are set at a certain number of pixels decided by the designer—override some of the web's natural flexibility. There are certainly good reasons to build fixed-width designs, as you'll learn in Chapter 1. But the alternatives to fixed-width design can offer a lot of benefit and may work for more types of sites than you may think.

Liquid (or fluid) sites, which resize based on the user's window size, are one alternative. Elastic sites, which resize based on the user's text size, are another. Both types of designs take advantage of the web's natural flexibility and, when done well, can greatly improve the user's experience on your site—all while looking just as attractive as a fixed-width site.

That's what this book aims to teach you: why flexible design is a good thing and how to do it well. You might think with all this flexibility built into the web that it would be a piece of cake to make liquid or elastic web sites. Unfortunately, that's not always true.

Despite the fact that flexibility is built into the web and offers lots of benefits, liquid and elastic web sites remain pretty rare—perhaps because they have their own set of challenges in both the design and development phases that most web designers are not used to. There's not much currently out there that addresses these challenges head-on. This book does.

What You Will (and Will Not) Learn

This book aims to teach you:

* the benefits of each type of flexible layout

* how to choose the appropriate type of layout for your particular content, design, or audience

* which visual elements work well in flexible designs and which to avoid

* how to construct and slice your graphic comps with flexibility in mind

* the (X)HTML and CSS for liquid, elastic, and hybrid layouts

* how to make backgrounds and content work within their flexible layout containers

What you will *not* learn is that fixed-width layouts are evil and you're a horrible person and a hack if you make one—not because my editor made me cut all that stuff out, but simply because it's not true.

The "fixed vs. flexible" debate can be very heated in the web design community; this book does not seek to provide a definitive answer to which is "better." I believe, as do many designers, that both fixed and flexible layouts have their place, with each suited to different types of sites. I use a variety of types of layouts on my sites, including fixed-width.

This book is simply meant to provide more detail on the side of the debate that doesn't get as much coverage—the flexible side. If you do decide that flexible layout is right for your site—and I hope this book will expand your ideas of when it *is* effective—this book aims to teach you how to do it well and without too much trouble.

Who Should Read this Book

This book is meant for professional web designers who already have experience creating web sites from scratch. It won't teach you (X)HTML or CSS; you'll need to have at least an intermediate level of experience in both. I assume that you know enough CSS to be able to create a basic layout with it, but you don't need to be a CSS layout expert, and you certainly don't need to have any experience using it to create flexible layouts.

Even if you intend to continue designing fixed-width sites primarily, there are a lot of design ideas and techniques in this book that you can use to enhance your work. Fixed-width designs still have to account for some degree of flexibility due to the user-controlled nature of the web—how to make your pages elegantly adapt to different user text sizes, for instance, is something every CSS designer should know.

I think this book will be especially helpful to former print designers or web designers used to table-based layout who still struggle to produce pure CSS layouts. It will teach you how to think in the CSS mindset so that designing for CSS becomes natural and you no longer find yourself fighting against inappropriate comps when it comes time to actually build the pages.

Example and Exercise Files

Examples of the web design techniques taught in each chapter are provided on this book's companion web site at www.flexiblewebbook.com. You can use these representative example files as a starting point for your own implementation of the techniques they exhibit, without having to copy down all the code written in the book.

Most of the chapters also contain an exercise portion, providing you the opportunity to implement some of the techniques taught earlier in the chapter in a real page, step by step. Throughout the book, you'll work on building a flexible web site from the design comp to the finished pages. You can download the files for these exercises at www.flexiblewebbook.com as well and use them to work along with as you go through the steps of each exercise.

No web page can look or work the same in every browser, and the example and exercise files for this book are no exception. The files have been tested in the latest versions of the major browsers: Internet Explorer, Firefox, Safari, and Opera. Some of the older but still popular versions of Internet Explorer—7 and 6—are also accommodated in the code, but versions earlier than 6 (including Internet Explorer for the Mac) are not, due to their minuscule browser market share. The content of the files should still be accessible in these browsers, but they're probably not going to look pretty!

Conventions Used Throughout this Book

This book uses a few terms that are worth noting at the outset.

- ◆ (X)HTML refers to both the HTML and XHTML markup languages.
- ◆ IE 6 and earlier refers to Windows Internet Explorer 5.0 to 6.0.
- ◆ IE 5.x refers to Windows Internet Explorer 5.0 and 5.5.

The CSS referred to and used in this book is based on the CSS 2.1 specification, unless otherwise noted. HTML 4.01 Strict is used for the markup examples, but all examples will also work with XHTML 1.1.

All CSS examples shown should be placed in an external style sheet or in the head of an (X)HTML document, while all (X)HTML examples should be placed in the body element of the document. Occasionally, snippets of (X)HTML and CSS will be shown in the same example, one after the other, for the sake of brevity. However, each needs to go in its respective place to work correctly.

Also for the sake of brevity, the ellipsis character (...) is used in some code examples to indicate a removed or repeating section. For instance, the ellipsis in the following code sample indicates that not all the li elements inside the ul are being shown to you:

```
<ul>
    <li>Apples</li>
    <li>Bananas</li>
    ...
    <li>Watermelon</li>
</ul>
```

Some code examples will contain characters or lines in turquoise blue. The highlight means that content has been added or changed since the last time you saw that same code snippet.

Understanding Flexible Layouts

The term "flexible layouts" can mean different things to different people, so let's make sure we're all on the same page before we dive into designing and building them. In this chapter, you'll learn the defining characteristics of each of the main layout types—fixed-width, liquid, elastic, and hybrid— described in the Introduction. We'll focus on the benefits and pitfalls of each so that you can decide which type might be right for your particular site.

Types of Layouts

We can group web-page layouts into three categories based on how their width is set: fixed-width, liquid (or fluid), and elastic. It's also possible to combine these layouts into hybrid layouts by mixing units of measurements; each column of the design can use a different unit. In any of these four types of layouts, any number of columns or aesthetic themes is possible; the type simply establishes how the browsing device determines how wide to make the layout appear to the user.

Fixed-width: Rigid Pixels

Fixed-width layouts are the designs you're most used to seeing—and probably making, since you're reading this book to learn the alternatives. The width of the overall layout of a fixed-width design is set to a value in pixels that's decided by the designer. Usually, the designer chooses a width based on one of the common screen resolutions, such as 800 by 600 or 1024 by 768.

Fixed-width designs are rigid: they don't change size based on any variations in the user's setup (**Figure 1.1**). This can allow you to design a graphically rich site that holds together well and looks consistent across a variety of user setups. If you have done your homework on the target audience of your site, you can design a layout that fits nicely in the majority of users' browser windows, and you can make sure the lines of text are set at an optimal width for ease of reading—at least, if you assume a couple things.

FIGURE 1.1 The same fixed-width layout in two differently sized browser windows.

FIXED-WIDTH DESIGNS ARE NOT EVIL!

This chapter does a fair amount of beating up on fixed-width designs and a lot of singing the praises of liquid and elastic designs. This is simply because that's what the purpose of the book is: promoting and teaching flexible layout techniques, and what they have to offer. But I want to stress that I don't think fixed-width designs are "wrong;" they are definitely appropriate in certain situations, as we'll discuss in more detail at the end of this chapter.

SCREEN RESOLUTION DOES NOT EQUAL BROWSER WINDOW SIZE

The biggest problem with fixed-width layouts is that they essentially depend on you making a guess as to what width will work well for the largest number of your users. Even if your web statistics software can tell you the screen resolution of each of your users—heck, even if you're making an intranet and are certain that only a single resolution will be used—it's simply not the case that screen resolution matches the browser window width all the time. Some people don't browse with their browser window maximized (admittedly a small number, but growing as monitors and resolutions increase in size). Also, some people use browser sidebars that can take away hundreds of pixels from the available width.

Fixed-width designs are always going to result in some segment of your audience seeing a design that is either too wide for their windows (necessitating the dreaded horizontal scrolling) or too narrow (leaving oceans of space on one or both sides of the layout). And based on my experience with user testing, many people get almost as distressed about "wasted space" in their browser as they do about horizontal scrolling!

RESEARCH ON BROWSER WINDOW SIZES

In October 2006, Thomas Baekdal published a very interesting report, "*Actual Browser Sizes*," on his web site, www.baekdal.com. He gathered three months' and five sites' worth of data on both screen resolutions and browser window sizes. The report states that while the majority of the tested users maximized their browsers—or at least came close—a significant number did not. For instance, users with 1024-by-768 resolutions—the most common by far—maximized about 80 percent of the time. His conclusion was that "in order to support 95% of your visitors, you need to design for a maximum size of 776x424px"—even though he found that only five percent of his users had 800-by-600 screens. Check out the full report at http://baekdal.com/reports/actual-browser-sizes.

NOT EVERYONE USES 16-PIXEL TEXT

If you know the size of the text you're working with, you can choose a fixed width to optimize the number of characters that appear on a line, or the line *length*, to aid readability. Print designers do this all the time; Robert Bringhurst's famous book *The Elements of Typographic Style* recommends line lengths of 45 to 75 characters, based on years of research on readability of printed text. More recent research into the readability of onscreen text has shown that longer line lengths, from 75 to 100 characters, result in faster reading speeds (though many of the tested users say they prefer shorter lines).

However, on the web, we can't know our users' text sizes. The default size for browsers nowadays is 16 pixels, and the vast majority of your users will leave their text set at this default. However, some users do change the default, or set up user style sheets to format text in a way that makes it easier for them to read. Even users who leave the text at the default have the option of bumping up the size on a per-page basis if a particular page of text is difficult to read (even text you set in pixels is resizable, except in Internet Explorer 6 and earlier). So, if you optimize line lengths for 16-pixel text, you may be optimizing readability for the majority of your visitors, but not for all. Don't get me wrong; designing for the majority is a good thing. Just don't fool yourself into thinking that "majority" is the same as "all."

Another problem is that these line-length studies don't take into account different disabilities that may lead certain groups to prefer much shorter or longer line lengths. Although I agree that it's often our job as designers to set things up for our users in the best way for them because they don't know what's best themselves, there are times when we need to trust them to be better informed than we are about what will best meet their needs. At the very least, we can optimize the design for what we think will help the majority of our users, but leave open the possibility for individual users to adapt our design to better meet their needs—an advantage that print and more rigid media do not enjoy.

Liquid or Fluid: Adapts to the Viewport

■ **NOTE:** *Viewport* is a generic term for the viewable area of a page in the user's device. It's preferred over *window* because, after all, not every device uses windows (for example, mobile phones).

Liquid layouts, also known as fluid layouts, change in width based on the size of the user's viewport. Liquid layouts built with CSS may or may not have any width assigned to them. If they don't have a width assigned, they will fill up the user's viewport no matter how big or small it is (**Figure 1.2**).

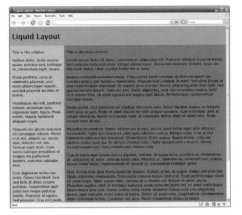

FIGURE 1.2 The same liquid layout changes width based on the browser window size.

If a designer does assign a width to a liquid layout, it will be measured in percentages, not in pixels. The percentage refers to the portion of the viewport it takes up.

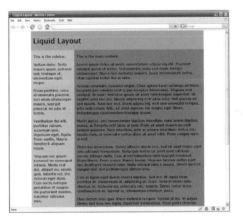

FIGURE 1.3 A liquid layout always adapts to the browser window size, even if you assign a smaller percentage width so that it never takes up the full width of the browser window.

TAKING ADVANTAGE OF SCREEN REAL ESTATE

When a liquid layout changes in size, all of the content within it—and often the background images as well—has to shift around on the page to fill up the space. As long as the content can wrap, this flexibility prevents horizontal scrollbars from appearing and makes full use of the screen real estate available on each user's device.

Once the content can no longer wrap, due to the fixed widths of images and other content, a horizontal scrollbar will finally appear, but this will happen only on the very narrowest of screens or on sites with very large fixed-width content. Using a liquid layout instead of a fixed-width one, it's much less likely that a user will miss important content hidden by a horizontal scrollbar. Also, for users with very large viewports, more content will be visible on the page at once, decreasing the amount of vertical scrolling they have to do.

RESPECTING USER PREFERENCES

A liquid layout allows you to stop guessing at what works for your users and instead let them choose what page widths best meet their needs. There's no longer a need for a "best viewed at 1024 by 768" type of disclaimer on your home page. Even if a user can change his resolution to meet this require-ment, the chances are slim to none that he's going to do so to accommodate your site. He's set that resolution for a reason: either he has no other choice given the constraints of his device, or it's the resolution that he enjoys or finds the most useful (for instance, some users stick with 800 by 600 because it makes everything bigger, which is easier to read). With liquid layouts, you don't need to worry about this anymore. Liquid layouts just work in a larger range of viewing scenarios, respecting users' preferences for how they like to view the web.

IMPROVING READABILITY

■ **NOTE:** One of the main arguments against liquid layout, actually, is that it decreases read-ability due to overly long lines of text on very large browser windows. This can certainly be the case when a liquid layout is implemented poorly or in certain user scenarios. We'll talk more about this chal-lenge later in the chapter.

Horizontal scrollbars are the sworn enemy of readability. After all, scrolling continually back and forth to read across several lines of text does not make for the most enjoyable reading experience. With a liquid layout, horizontal scrollbars almost never happen, because users can size the window however they like to produce lines of text that they find the most comfortable to read and understand. Preferences for line length can vary by age, disability, and browsing device, so leaving widths adjustable can help a much broader range of people read your content efficiently than setting one fixed width might.

DEALING WITH HANDHELD DEVICES

While liquid layouts increase the range of sizes at which your web site can look good and work well, you're still probably going to need to set up a separate style sheet for handheld devices such as mobile phones and PDAs. It's just not possible to design something that works as well at 200 pixels wide as at 1200 (unless you're going for the old-school, plain-text look).

INCREASING ACCESSIBILITY FOR PEOPLE WITH DISABILITIES

Some users have disabilities that make line length even more essential for successfully reading and understanding content. If a user has a visual impairment that requires her to make her text size very large, she may prefer to browse with a very large window to allow more words to fit across each line. In a narrow, fixed-width layout, large text may allow only two or three words to fit on every line, making reading more difficult and resulting in a huge amount of vertical scrolling.

Other types of visual impairments may necessitate the use of screen magnifying software, which shows only a small, highly zoomed portion of the window to the user at one time. People who use screen magnifiers may prefer to make their windows very narrow so that the entire width of each line of text fits within their small, magnified area of the screen and they don't have to keep pushing the magnified view back and forth horizontally to read.

FIGURE 1.4 If the browser window is wide, screen magnifying software may not be able to show the entire line length of text within the magnified overlay, so the user has to push the overlay right and left to read the text (left). If the browser window is narrow, and the text width adjusts accordingly, the entire line of text can fit in the magnified overlay (right), making reading faster and easier.

Line length can also play a role in comprehension. For instance, many people with dyslexia find it easier to read and understand text with short line lengths.

Elastic: Adapts to the Text Size

Elastic layouts change in width based on the text size set in the user's browsing device. A user who has set a larger default text size will see a page where not only is the text bigger, but the entire layout is bigger proportionally than that seen by people with the default text size (**Figure 1.5**). If a user changes his text size while viewing the site, the entire layout width will also change proportionally, either wider or narrower, depending on whether he increased or decreased the text size.

FIGURE 1.5 The same elastic layout in two browser windows of the same size, but using different text sizes.

Like fixed-width layouts, elastic layouts always have a width assigned to them, but that width is set in a unit of measurement called an *em*. If you've used CSS for formatting text, you're probably familiar with ems (but we'll go over this in more depth when we start actually building elastic layouts). One em is equal to the font height, which in turn equals roughly two characters in width, since most characters aren't nearly as wide as they are tall. By setting the width of your layout in ems, you're essentially telling the design to be as wide as a certain number of text characters. That means when the text gets bigger, the whole layout has to widen as well to stay equal to the same number of now-larger text characters. It works in reverse, too, of course: smaller text sizes make the layout narrower.

THE DIFFERENCE BETWEEN ZOOMING AND TEXT RESIZING

In many browsers, you can use the zoom feature to make all pages act like elastic layouts. Zooming is not the same as resizing text, which is a separate browser function. Browser zoom functions scale images as well as text, as if you were truly moving closer into, or magnifying, the entire page. Think of it like changing the magnification on a PDF in Adobe Acrobat or Adobe Reader.

While all layout types zoom when you use a browser's zoom function, elastic ones also zoom when you use the text-resizing function as well as when the user starts out with a larger or smaller default text size. However, images do not change size in elastic layouts, as they do when you zoom a layout using the browser feature, unless you explicitly set them to. We'll cover how to do this in Chapter 9.

BROWSER SUPPORT FOR ZOOMING AND TEXT RESIZING

Resizing text is a good way to put the flexibility of your pages to the test, but not every browser handles it in the same way. Here are the basics on how to resize text as well as zoom entire page layouts in the major browsers.

TABLE 1.1 How to Resize Text or Zoom

BROWSER	HOW TO RESIZE TEXT	HOW TO ZOOM
Internet Explorer 7	View > Text Size or View > Text Zoom, and then choose a size keyword (e.g., Larger)	Ctrl + + (plus sign) to zoom in Ctrl + - (minus sign) to zoom out
Internet Explorer 6 and earlier	View > Text Size, and then choose a text size keyword (e.g., Larger)	Not available
Firefox 3	Ctrl/Command + + (plus sign) to increase Ctrl/Command + - (minus sign) to decrease	Deselect Zoom Text Only (View > Zoom > Zoom Text Only) Ctrl/Command + + (plus sign) to zoom in Ctrl/Command + - (minus sign) to zoom out
Firefox 2 and earlier	Ctrl/Command + + (plus sign) to increase Ctrl/Command + - (minus sign) to decrease	Not available
Opera	Not available on a per-page basis	Ctrl/Command + + (plus sign) to zoom in Ctrl/Command + - (minus sign) to zoom out
Safari	Ctrl/Command + + (plus sign) to increase Ctrl/Command + - (minus sign) to decrease	Ctrl/Command + + (plus sign) to zoom in Ctrl/Command + - (minus sign) to zoom out Available only as part of Mac OS system-wide zoom feature; not built into Safari on Windows.

Elastic layouts are the rarest type of layout because before CSS became usable for page layout, they were simply impossible to create with tables (the page-layout mechanism used before CSS and still in heavy use today). Since many browsers now allow you to "zoom" pages, I don't think that designers will increase their use of elastic layouts, which behave similarly to zooming. Nevertheless, there are definite benefits to elastic layouts.

INCREASED TYPOGRAPHIC CONTROL

Elastic layouts give you more control over where text falls in relation to other design components on the page. In other words, your design proportions stay intact. In a fixed-width layout, if a user increases his text size, the text has to wrap onto more lines and make its container taller (or overflow, which is even worse). Your meticulously crafted headline that fit so perfectly on one line might now be awkwardly broken between two lines, or a piece of text that needed to be near a certain image may have moved. The same thing can happen with liquid layouts when a user narrows her browser window. Elastic layouts can keep the same number of words and characters that appear on each line consistent no matter the size of the user's text or window.

FIGURE 1.6 Dan Cederholm's SimpleBits web site features an elastic design, so as you increase your text size, the text doesn't wrap any differently. Notice that the blurb text at the top of the page keeps the same number of characters on each line when the text is small (left) or large (right).

IMPROVING READABILITY THROUGH STANDARD LINE LENGTHS

With widths set in number of characters per line, you can choose line lengths that optimize readability. As mentioned earlier, line lengths of 75 to 100 characters usually result in increased reading speed (though not necessarily increased comprehension or comfort) over shorter line lengths.

As we saw with liquid layouts, however, not all users prefer the same line lengths. Certain types of disabilities, as well as device limitations and age, may make the line lengths you choose less ideal or downright problematic for

LINE-LENGTH RESEARCH

While more recent research shows that longer line lengths are better for onscreen text than the shorter lengths that have been traditional to print media, it's hard to draw conclusions that are much more concrete than this. I think this is an area where we'll continue to see new standards emerge as we get more extensive research into online reading performance and preference.

The most recent line-length study, "The Effects of Line Length on Reading Online News" by A. Dawn Shaikh, makes an interesting read and provides figures from the conclusions of several older studies. The article was published in the July 2005 issue of the Usability News newsletter (http://psychology. wichita.edu/surl/usabilitynews/72/LineLength.htm). Another good overview of the results of line-length studies through 2002 is "Optimal Line Length: Research Supporting How Line Length Affects Usability" by Dr. Bob Bailey (www.webusability.com/article_line_length_12_2002.htm).

some people. In fact, the most recently published study found that users pre-ferred either the shortest length tested (30 percent preferred 35 characters per line) or the longest length tested (another 30 percent preferred 95 characters per line). Also, many studies have shown that users say they prefer shorter lines even though the testers found they read faster with longer lines.

It's a delicate balancing act: do you trust users to set up the ideal browsing environment for their needs, or, knowing that most users have no idea what line length would be most comfortable or result in the best performance for them, do you optimize it in the way you think will work best for the majority? And if you do choose to use an elastic layout to optimize line length, do you optimize it to the users' preference or to their performance, since it appears they often don't match? There's no right answer, which is why there is no one type of layout that is right for all sites. We'll cover how to choose which one may be best for your site later in the chapter.

INCREASING ACCESSIBILITY

While the readability improvements that we've discussed can affect every-one, they can have an even greater impact on people with disabilities, such as visual impairments that don't warrant the use of a screen reader but do require larger than normal text. People with motor impairments might also use larger text in order to have larger than normal link text, to make it easier for them to "target." And some people, such as those with tunnel vision, might actually prefer smaller than normal text so that more content can fit within their range of vision. Designing layouts that stay proportional at all these different sizes can really help a wide variety of people.

Hybrid Layouts

You don't have to stick with one of the "big three" types of layouts. You can create countless hybrid versions simply by mixing units of measurement or limiting the flexibility range of a liquid or elastic layout.

MIXING UNITS OF MEASUREMENT

Most web layouts are built using the idea of columns, whether or not the columns are explicitly visible in the design. Each column can have its own unit of measurement and be thought of individually as fixed-width, liquid, or elastic. Mix them together, and you've got a *hybrid layout*. For example, a common type of hybrid layout has a fixed-width sidebar with a liquid main content area (**Figure 1.7**).

FIGURE 1.7 The same hybrid layout (fixed sidebar, liquid main column) in two differently sized browser windows. Note that the sidebar is the same width in both windows, while the main content column adapts to fill the remaining viewport space.

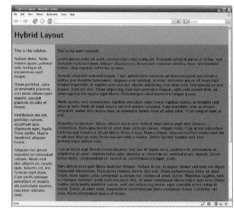

RESOLUTION-DEPENDENT LAYOUTS

A resolution-dependent layout is a page that uses JavaScript to switch the CSS and thus the layout of the elements on the page by detecting browser window size. It's kind of like a fixed-width and liquid hybrid, because although each of the possible layouts might be a fixed width, which fixed width the browser chooses is based on window size. It can keep users from seeing horizontal scrollbars and it makes the best use of the available horizontal space, so the design never looks awkwardly stretched out or squished together.

The problem with these types of pages is that you have to create at least two and possibly several different layouts. It can be quite difficult and time-consuming to create a design that can adapt that radically. But it's certainly a cool effect that can enhance the usability as well as the design aesthetic, if you're up for the challenge.

You can see a number of examples of resolution-dependent layouts linked from http://clagnut.com/blog/1663. Teaching the JavaScript necessary to create such layouts is beyond the scope of this book, but two popular scripts, as well as more information on how the technique works, are freely available at http://themaninblue.com/writing/perspective/2006/01/19 and http://alistapart.com/articles/switchymclayout.

Some day you may be able to use CSS 3's media queries feature to do a similar thing without having to ever get JavaScript involved. See www.w3.org/TR/css3-mediaqueries for more information.

Usually, a design that has even one liquid column is called liquid, even if parts are fixed-width; likewise for hybrid layouts that are partially elastic. We'll stick to calling them hybrid layouts throughout this book and reserve the terms *liquid* and *elastic* for layouts that are 100 percent liquid or elastic.

Hybrid layouts offer many of the advantages of liquid and elastic layouts without some of the disadvantages. But they're sometimes tricky to build due to the math involved—quick, what's 200 pixels plus 80 percent? It's impossible to know, of course—and if you don't know, how can you set the width on the container that's supposed to hold these two elements? Luckily, there are usually ways to avoid or work around these challenges, as we'll go over in Chapter 6 when we build some hybrid layouts.

LIMITING FLEXIBILITY WITH MINIMUM AND MAXIMUM WIDTHS

Another way to create a functionally hybrid layout is to limit the amount of a liquid or elastic layout's flexibility by setting minimum and maximum widths. The CSS properties `min-width` and `max-width` allow you to set limits on how far a flexible layout will expand or contract. When a flexible design hits its minimum or maximum width, it essentially becomes a different type of layout—whatever type corresponds with the unit of measurement you used for the `min-width` or `max-width` value.

For example, you might give a liquid layout a minimum width in pixels to keep the images inside the layout from overflowing when the viewport is too narrow. The page would act like a liquid layout as the window was narrowed, until it reached the `min-width` value, at which point it would snap to that value and no longer budge, now acting like a fixed-width layout.

Even though using `min-width` and `max-width` essentially creates hybrid layouts, they're usually still called by whatever type they would fall into if the minimum and maximum widths weren't there. It's pretty rare that you'll make a liquid or elastic layout without using either `min-width` or `max-width`, or both, so we'll still call these layouts liquid and elastic in order to keep from calling practically everything hybrid.

Challenges of Liquid and Elastic Layouts

We've already gone over the benefits of liquid and elastic layouts. But they're not without their problems as well. Obviously, I think the benefits outweigh the problems, or I wouldn't be writing this book, but I'm not going to lie to you—flexible design isn't always easy. Both types of flexible design present many challenges, which, as you'll learn throughout this book, can be overcome, but are worth knowing before you start. So read on, and don't be discouraged.

Breaking Out of the Grid: Beyond Your Design Comfort Zone

Perhaps the biggest challenge that designers face when building flexible layouts is learning how to design outside the bounds of a predictable, rigid grid. This is really hard for print designers making the transition to the web, since in print design every piece of content and design element has a fixed, precise spot on the page. Web designers who are used to table-based layout often have similar difficulties. Flexible designs are much more unpredictable, and that can make designing them a lot less comfortable.

When you design for flexible layouts, particularly liquid ones, you have to stop thinking of the page as one big grid. You can't depend on this piece of content to fall directly under that design element—sometimes it will, sometimes it won't. In flexible designs, there's no (visible or invisible) underlying grid you have to conform to—it's a *truly* blank page. You add as many independent boxes to it as you wish—boxes that can overlap each other, move, grow. It's tricky at first, but only if you're used to an alternative way of designing. It *can* be learned.

GRIDS IN CSS DESIGN

Grids have actually made a comeback in CSS-based designs, but those grids aren't the ones I'm talking about here. Modern grid-based design focuses on creating a number of "units" of uniform width, with uniform gutters between them, and combining the units into any number of columns. It offers a lot more flexibility than the grids of table-based design, and you can use percentages or ems as the widths of your units and columns to create flexible CSS grids if you want. For an in-depth walkthrough of how to create a CSS grid-based page layout, check out Khoi Vin and Mark Boulton's presentation "Grids Are Good" at www.subtraction.com/pics/0703/grids_are_good.pdf. Tons of other grid articles, examples, and tools are linked from Smashing Magazine's "Designing With Grid-Based Approach" (www.smashingmagazine.com/2007/04/14/designing-with-grid-based-approach).

Saying Goodbye to Pixel Perfection

Not only do you have to get used to the idea of there being no fixed grid to hang onto, you also have to get used to the fact that no two people are necessarily going to see your page exactly the same—and that's OK. Controlling every little detail of the page's appearance to make it look exactly the same across all platforms, browsers, and user setups is known as "pixel perfection." It's actually not achievable even with table-based or fixed-width layouts, as there are always differences between platforms and browsers that we can't control, and the user can always customize her own viewing setup by altering text sizes, creating user style sheets, and changing other device and software preferences.

In flexible layouts, however, the lack of pixel perfection becomes even more apparent, since even more design permutations are possible. We designers tend not to like this idea. We made something look a certain way for a reason! But allowing users some control over the appearance of web pages actually benefits *us*—by increasing usability for *them*. Unlike in print media, where people are stuck with whatever paper size, text size, and other design elements the designer chose, web users can customize their web viewing experience to some degree, and thereby better enable themselves to use our sites effectively to buy products, learn new information, or meet other goals.

Flexible layout is one way we can embrace variable, user-controlled design instead of fighting unsuccessfully against the web's true nature.

LETTING GO OF CONTROL

If you learn to see the lack of pixel perfection on the web as a positive feature instead of a constraint, you'll have a much easier time designing layouts and building pages that work well with this feature. Sure, it's possible to design adaptable web pages while still shaking your fist in anger at the web and its users for being so unpredictable, but it's going to be a lot more painful than it needs to be. John Allsop applies the philosophy of the Tao Te Ching to the web design process in "A Dao of Web Design" at http://alistapart.com/articles/dao. Though published in 2000, the article is still a highly relevant and entertaining way to help yourself come to a state of acceptance.

Convincing your clients that lack of pixel perfection is not only inevitable but good is another matter. In Part 1 of *Transcending CSS: The Fine Art of Web Design*, Andy Clarke makes a convincing case for design differences between browser versions by comparing them to differences seen between HDTV and analog television, or between different versions of iPods. You could argue for design differences due to liquid or elastic layouts using similar analogies.

■ **TIP:** It's perfectly acceptable to optimize your design for a particular width—say, the most common screen resolution of your audience—and still keep it readable, usable, and attractive at other widths. The design doesn't need to look equally good at every single width within its range.

■ **NOTE:** Web developer Christian Montoya has created an entire site, No Resolution, dedicated to showcasing attractive liquid and elastic designs. Go to www.cssliquid.com to get some inspiration for your next flexible design.

■ **NOTE:** Even though it's correct behavior for text to overflow its container by default, IE 6 and earlier did not allow this to happen. Instead, they would expand containers to hold the excess, often causing more disruption in the design than the overflow would have. Thankfully, IE 7 resolved this bug.

Making a Design Look Good Big and Small

You're probably familiar with basic graphic design principles such as balance, contrast, and rhythm. Ensuring your designs fulfill these types of principles is hard enough on the web, where the viewing scenario is so variable, but can be even harder when you aim for flexibility. How do you design something that has balance, for instance, when you don't know where on the page a certain element is going to fall in relation to the others around it?

Some flexible web sites avoid this issue by keeping their designs very plain, with few graphics, or even none. But it doesn't have to be this way. It can take more work, but it is possible to design a layout that looks visually appealing at a variety of sizes. You'll see some examples of well-designed flexible sites in the next chapter, and throughout this book we'll be building a design that has no shortage of graphics.

Dealing with Text Overflows

Text overflow isn't really an issue with elastic design, since the entire layout scales with the text, but it can become problematic in liquid layouts. Even though text can wrap to accommodate a narrower space, at some point it just can't wrap any more—often due to a really long word in a narrow sidebar or text connected with punctuation like slashes—and has to hang outside of its container's side or bottom. Sometimes this results in just the design looking a bit off, but other times that excess text may overlap other elements on the page and become unreadable, causing a serious usability and accessibility problem. Setting minimum widths can make your design less susceptible to text overflow, but there's always some small chance it will happen.

In reality, text overflow can happen in any design, even fixed-width ones, because users can control their text sizes, affecting both the width and height that text takes up. You have to design for variable dimensions of text space no matter what type of layout you're going with, but especially when you're making liquid designs. In the next chapter we'll go over how to create designs that allow for resizable text and avoid text overflows. Later, we'll also learn the CSS to create boxes with scrollbars within the page to adapt to variable-height blocks of content.

Dealing with Horizontal Scrollbars

While horizontal scrollbars rarely occur in fully liquid layouts, they can be a problem in elastic layouts. When you set a width to a particular line length, you're basically telling the design to ignore the viewport width as a constraint. If the user has a larger than default text size, or increases the text size while viewing your site, it's quite common for the width to extend off the viewable area of the screen and produce a horizontal scrollbar. This can be even worse for readability than awkward line lengths, which you were trying to avoid by using an elastic layout in the first place, so what to do?

Luckily, we can set a maximum width on the layout to keep a horizontal scrollbar from ever appearing. This compromises our ideal line lengths, but is usually better for readability than the alternative, so it's a frequently used technique with elastic layouts.

Fitting Fixed-width Content in a Flexible Box

Although text can wrap, fixed-width content can't, including images, Flash and other video content, and tables. Fixed-width content is even more likely than text to overflow when placed inside a flexible container. Depending on the browser, this can result in overlapping content or even cause an entire column to drop out of view. Luckily, the fixed width of this content often makes it easy to pick an appropriate value for a minimum width to apply to the layout and avoid this problem. Generating scrollbars for the piece of overly large content is also an option (that we'll cover in Chapter 6).

Unlike text overflow, overflowing of fixed-width content can occur even in elastic layouts, because even if a user sets a small text size for a very narrow layout, the multimedia content is not going to follow suit. Or, at least, not necessarily—there actually are ways to make non-text content scale along with the text. We'll cover those in Chapter 9.

Increased Design and Testing Time

Many of the problems I've mentioned are preventable to a large degree by planning for them during the design process or adding certain CSS techniques to the page. But obviously, all this takes time. You'll probably spend a little more time both designing and building flexible layouts than you did making fixed-width ones. You'll also need to devote more time to the testing phase. There are just so many more user scenarios possible and, therefore, places where things can go wrong. We'll go over the testing process in Chapter 4.

■ **NOTE:** Even though you might not declare a width for a table or any of the columns within it, you can still consider it fixed-width and unwrappable, because table columns can't wrap below when there is not enough room. Also, each column automatically expands to hold its widest piece of content. The number of characters of the widest word in each column effectively sets the minimum width for that column, with the minimum width of all the columns together acting as the fixed, minimum width of the table.

Browser Shortcomings

Browser bugs and inconsistencies don't add to the fun of any web design project, and there are certainly browser shortcomings that specifically affect flexible layouts. These include:

- Cross-browser differences in rounding sub-pixel measurements
- IE 6 and earlier lack of support for `min-width` and `max-width`
- IE 6 and earlier auto-expansion of width and height
- IE 6 and earlier italics text bug
- IE 6 and earlier em text resizing bug
- IE 6 and earlier (noticing a pattern?) peekaboo bug

Again, there are ways to avoid, work around, or simply live with these problems, and we'll go over each as we run into them throughout the book.

Choosing the Right Layout Type for Your Page

As you've seen throughout this chapter, each design type has its own benefits and challenges. Following are some reasons to choose each of the three design types we've covered. This list certainly isn't comprehensive, since of course I can't anticipate every type of site you'll want to make or audience demographic you'll have to design for. Use your judgment to decide what will work best for your project, using this as a starting point.

I want to emphasize that not only is there no one right way to lay out every type of site, but that even if you do pick a layout type that is really well suited to your particular audience's needs and fits with your content and design, there are still going to be some users who will dislike it. The well-known CSS developer Eric Meyer sums this up humorously in his article "Making Popular Layout Decisions" at www.thinkvitamin.com/features/design/making-popular-layout-decisions.

A NOTE ABOUT HYBRIDS

Although hybrid layouts are not covered separately here (since there are so many variations), they are often the best choice for many projects. Consider the reasons for each of the three types of layouts also as reasons to use a hybrid version of that layout type. For instance, where a liquid layout is deemed appropriate, it's likely that a primarily liquid layout that incorporates fixed-width sidebars would also be appropriate. Use the lists below to help ascertain what primary layout type to use, and then decide if you want to add hybrid features to further enhance the effectiveness of the site. We'll discuss hybrid types in more detail in Chapter 6.

Fixed-width

You might opt for a fixed-width design in any of the following (or similar) scenarios:

- The design contains a lot of large, fixed-width content, such as images, embedded media players, and Flash movies.

   If most of your content will be rigid, it doesn't make a lot of sense to put it in a flexible box. Types of sites that might be much more media-heavy than text-heavy include e-commerce, art, portfolio, and media storage or display. For instance, Flickr (www.flickr.com) makes sense as a fixed-width site because its primary purpose is to showcase large, fixed-width images. Amazon (www.amazon.com), on the other hand, is an e-commerce site that features a lot of images, but almost none of them need to be large. It's easy for text to flow and shift around the small types of images on Amazon's pages, but this isn't the case on sites where images have to stand on their own and take up almost the entire width of the content area.

- The site is for a small group of known users with known setups.

   If you're building an intranet or specialized web application for a controlled group of people, you can optimize the layout exactly and exclusively to those users' needs. If there's still a fair amount of diversity within the group in terms of browsing window size, text size, and other user-controlled web characteristics, you might be better off going with a more flexible layout, but fixed-width layouts are fine when you know you won't be harming usability for some segment of your audience.

- You're a beginning web designer or beginning CSS designer.

  By definition, fixed-width designs are usually easier to build, which is helpful when you're just starting out in web design. It's also easier to stick to them if you're an experienced designer but are in the process of switching from table-based to CSS-based layouts. CSS can be hard enough to learn as it is, so don't bite off more than you can chew with your first couple of layouts. Despite the benefits of flexible layouts, a robust but simple fixed-width layout is going to be much more beneficial to your users than a poorly implemented flexible one.

- You just need to get something small and simple together quickly.

  Sometimes you just need to design a little site for your uncle in two days for a hundred bucks and get it out the door. While flexible layout doesn't have to be fancy or complicated, even seasoned CSS designers may find themselves spending more time on a flexible site than the budget allows. If you know the site isn't going to be high traffic, or is just something temporary, go ahead and throw together a fixed-width site if it helps you get the job done. I'd love for us all to always make sites that are perfectly crafted for the full swath of our target audiences and challenge us to learn new skills and be better designers, but I know we live in the real world.

Liquid

Choose a liquid design in any of the following (or similar) scenarios:

- Readability is of the utmost importance (for example, when a site is text-heavy).

  Certain types of sites are very text-heavy, and many of these will have the user doing a fair amount of reading, instead of just completing a quick task and leaving. Readability is often very important on news and magazine sites, portals, search engines, and blogs, as well as sites that feature legal, bureaucratic, or educational information, such as corporate, non-profit, government, and training sites.

- The site is a web application and based on user-generated content.

  In a web application, users have definite tasks they want to get done and ways they want to do them, and they often expect an even greater level of control than they would in regular (non-application) sites. Add to that the fact that many web applications rely on the users themselves providing or creating the content, such as text documents, bookmarks, or financial data, and you can have some angry users on your hands if you try to lock them down to working with their text in a very rigid way. Obviously, this doesn't apply to all web applications or user-generated content sites—I've already mentioned how Flickr makes sense as a fixed-width site—but even graphically oriented web applications might benefit from being flexible. For instance, think of how frustrating it would be if Google Maps (http://maps.google.com) featured a single-size map that may or may not fit your screen, or if the image editor in Picnik (www.picnik. com) didn't resize with your window.

◆ Your audience includes a particularly wide variety of browsing setups.

Almost all sites have a fair amount of diversity in their audiences, but some lend themselves to even more of it than others, and thus require even more flexibility. For instance, I've worked on several sites targeted to schools, and I know how wildly varied the capabilities of their computers—and thus their screen resolutions and browsers—can be. Such varied user setups among the audiences of these sites make flexible layouts good choices.

Don't be too quick to write off this criterion because you think your audience's diversity is fairly limited. We don't and can't really know the full scope of who is using most of our sites and how. Even the limited information we can glean from web-server statistics can be deceiving, as it can set you up for a self-fulfilling prophecy. For instance, you believe you don't need to cater to Mac users because they're not using your site, as evidenced by the web stats, but maybe they're not using your site precisely because you're not catering to them.

◆ You're required to or want to comply with accessibility guidelines.

Liquid design is certainly not a requirement of the U.S. government's Section 508 accessibility law, but there are lots of ways you can enhance accessibility above and beyond Section 508, and flexible design is one of them. For instance, making text and its containers resizable is part of both the Web Content Accessibility Guidelines (WCAG) 1.0 recommendation, which is used by some countries as their accessibility regulations, and the 2.0 working draft. For the details of WCAG, see www.w3.org/ WAI/intro/wcag.php.

◆ You like a good challenge.

I guess I'm a web-design geek, but I think giving myself a design and construction challenge is fun. For me, it's exciting to try to put together a layout that looks great at a bunch of different sizes. It pushes me to be more creative with my designs, instead of just reaching for my comfortable old design tricks to mindlessly put together a fixed-width quickie site. I learn new CSS tricks and get more confident in my work each time I build a new flexible site. That's not to say that fixed-width designs are inherently easy to make—I marvel in envy at the beautiful, graphically rich work of many CSS designers—but that flexible design is yet another avenue for refreshing your designs, pushing your boundaries, and expanding your skill sets.

Elastic

All of the reasons listed above for choosing liquid layouts are applicable to elastic layouts as well. However, there are a few additional reasons you might consider an elastic layout:

- The site contains many large data tables.

  Tables are unique in that they're made up of text, so they can get bigger (unlike images) but they can't be wrapped (like images). Table cells will get as small as they possibly can for the content inside them, but after that, the table columns won't start wrapping onto multiple lines if the design is too narrow. Instead, the table will just hang out the side, which is never very attractive and often quite unusable. If your site has a lot of tables in it, like the data-heavy government sites and web applications I've worked on do, it makes sense to place those tables in a container which will also resize when the table text does: an elastic container.

- Typography or the proportions of design elements is very important.

  If the design of your text influences its meaning, such as where line breaks fall in a poem, then elastic layouts can help preserve that design no matter what text size the user has.

How to Design Flexible Layouts

Creating flexible layouts isn't just a matter of what CSS to use. You need to start out with a design comp or mockup that can be successfully turned into a liquid or elastic layout. Not every design can. Since design comps are static images, not changeable web pages, many designers fall into the trap of designing graphic elements that can work at only one size, or with a particular font size, or only if they appear at a certain point on the screen. When you learn how to stop designing in this way and start thinking in terms of the eventual flexible CSS, you'll have a much easier time creating flexible layouts that are attractive and robust enough to stand up to several different user scenarios. In this chapter, you'll learn how to identify design features that are—and are not—flexible-friendly, as well as how to change those that aren't—sometimes only slightly—to work in a liquid or elastic layout. We'll also start to work directly on the pages of the example site that we'll be building throughout the book.

Design Principles for Flexible Layouts

There are a number of guidelines for flexible designs that you can simply memorize and always keep in mind when designing your own layouts. Many of these are not only applicable to creating liquid and elastic layouts, but also to creating fixed-width layouts that you want to make more adaptive to user preferences such as font size. They're a good primer to designing for the unique strengths of the medium—that is, specifically for the web, rather than for print.

Many of you don't get to design your own layouts, but instead have graphic designers—most of whom don't know how to actually build web pages, at least not with CSS—creating the design comps that you then turn into real pages. This isn't an ideal scenario, because it's really important that the designer understand how the eventual product will be created to be able to successfully design something that's compatible. If your designer knows how to make CSS layouts but simply chooses not to because the two of you have a good division of labor going on, you probably won't run into many problems. But if you're working with designers who aren't also (X)HTML and CSS developers, you've probably experienced a lot of frustration in try-ing to translate their work to the web. These graphic designers would be the ones to benefit the most from this chapter (maybe you can leave a copy of this book on their desks, with a nice big bookmark in this chapter), but you can also use it to your own advantage. Many of the problematic design fea-tures you'll see demonstrated here don't require much change to work with flexible layouts—it's just a matter of knowing what that change should be.

We'll walk through the main dos and don'ts of these design principles—those you should avoid and those you should plan for and incorporate from the beginning.

Avoid: Fixed Heights for Anything Containing Text

Not designing for fixed widths might seem like the first thing we ought to cover. After all, variable widths are what flexible layouts are all about. However, fixed heights are just as problematic for flexible designs as fixed widths, since a change in the width of a text box affects how many lines the text takes up (in a liquid layout) or its overall height (in an elastic layout).

Avoiding fixed heights should be the mantra of web designers the world over, whether they are making flexible CSS layouts or not. You simply can-not know what size text any of your users have specified, and so you can't design any block containing text to be a particular height. If you do, you're setting yourself up for overflowing and overlapping text.

Designing for flexible heights also makes a good deal of sense when you consider that text on the web changes frequently. How often have you had a client say, "That's perfect! The web site is complete! But just change this block of intro text, and if we can just change a few words here, and we forgot to add our tagline here…"? Leaving heights flexible ensures that you can always add or subtract a certain amount of text from an area of the page without having to completely overhaul the design or change any of the (X)HTML or CSS.

Of course, every good design principle needs some caveats. Most of the time, you're not going to be able to design for infinitely expanding heights. There is always going to be some font size which is so extreme that text overflows its box or causes some other interference in the design. Your job is simply to design for as wide a range of flexibility as possible.

Also, you can sometimes assign heights to boxes with the em unit of measurement, so that as the text grows, the height of the box grows to match. To do this, you'll need to make sure that the width of the box is elastic as well. Using em heights doesn't usually work on boxes that are meant to be liquid, since resizing them wraps the text onto more lines, which the em height hasn't accounted for.

You can quickly test to see whether a fixed-width web page could be made liquid by increasing the text size in your browser, since this also has the effect of wrapping the text onto more lines. For instance, here's the banner area of the fixed-width site www.greg-wood.co.uk at the default font size (**Figure 2.1**).

FIGURE 2.1 At the default font size, the text fits well inside the graphic banner on www.greg-wood.co.uk.

When you increase the font size a few times, you'll see that the text, which used to be on three lines, now spans six (**Figure 2.2**). It's overflowed out of the fixed-height box and is overlapping the text below. Because some of the overflowed text is white, it blends in with the background of the page and has disappeared completely. Right now, this page isn't liquid-compatible.

FIGURE 2.2 The overflowing text indicates that this banner is not currently set up to change in height or width to accommodate text-wrapping changes that would occur in a liquid layout.

RESIZING TEXT IN YOUR BROWSER

Every browser lets you resize text, but each does it a little differently. Here's a quick rundown on how to do it in the major browsers. See your browser's help files if you need more information.

- Firefox 3: Choose View > Zoom, and check Zoom Text Only. Once this option is selected, using the keyboard shortcuts for zooming will change the text size instead of zooming the entire page: press the Ctrl key on Windows or the Command key on Mac with the plus key to increase the font size or the minus key to decrease the font size. Alternatively, you can hold down Ctrl or Command and use your mouse's scroll wheel to make text bigger (if you scroll down) or smaller (if you scroll up).

- Firefox 2: Choose View > Text Size, and then choose Increase or Decrease. You can also use the same keyboard shortcuts described for Firefox 3.

- Internet Explorer 7 and 8: Choose View > Text Size, and then select from the five size keywords listed (Medium is the default). The keyboard shortcuts for resizing text in Firefox will zoom the layout in IE, instead of resizing text only, so be careful. Also, text set in pixels as the unit of measurement cannot be resized in any version of IE.

- Internet Explorer 6 and earlier: Same as IE 7. Since zoom does not exist in versions of IE prior to version 7, the keyboard shortcuts do nothing.

- Safari: Choose View > Make Text Bigger or View > Make Text Smaller. The keyboard and scroll-wheel shortcuts described for Firefox work in Safari as well.

- Opera: There's no way to change text size on the fly, only universally through your preferences.

However, there's actually nothing about this banner design that couldn't be made liquid. The illustration on the right side of the banner doesn't take up the whole height, but instead has a solid background color above it. This background color could easily be expanded as the text spanned more rows and increased the height of the banner—you'd just need to slice the graphics differently and change the CSS a bit.

Another common example of this would be boxes with rounded corners or otherwise decorative borders, such as those shown on www.dynamixnew-media.com (**Figure 2.3**). The "Economic Pack" and "Our product" boxes contain images of text, but the other boxes shown in Figure 2.3 contain real text. Since these boxes haven't been built to be flexible, the real text overflows when it is resized, just as it would if the entire design was allowed to get narrow and wrap the text onto more lines (**Figure 2.4**). But the straight portions of the sides of these boxes could instead be created out of tiled background images (the default behavior of background images is to repeat over and over again to fill the available space) to create boxes with expandable dimensions. We'll go over how to do this in Chapter 8.

FIGURE 2.3 At the default text size, the text fits well inside the "tags" and "news" boxes with rounded corners on the Dynamix New Media home page.

FIGURE 2.4 When you enlarge the text, the rounded corner "container" boxes don't increase in height.

Many other designs, however, could not be adapted to liquid so easily. They would require not just CSS adjustments, but actual changes to the design. There's a big difference between not designing for flexibility and simply not *building* for it. We'll be mainly focusing on the former in this chapter.

So where are the examples of sites that weren't designed for flexibility, instead of just not being built for it? This principle of no fixed heights is the basis for many of the concepts we'll discuss next, so the way you choose to work around it in your design depends on why you are implementing a fixed height to begin with. We'll go over each of the design reasons for fixed heights, as well as their possible workarounds, in the next few sections.

NOT DESIGNING FOR FLEXIBILITY IS OK

Remember that there's nothing wrong with not designing for flexibility, since fixed-width layout is a perfectly acceptable option for web design. Thus, none of the example screenshots from real web sites I'm showing throughout this chapter should be seen as "bad" design. They're simply not "flexible-friendly" design, and in most cases they weren't meant to be. As long as they still allow for some degree of flexibility in allowing somewhat variable text sizes, I have no bone to pick with any of them. Despite being built for fixed-width layouts, they're still useful for learning about flexible-friendly design, as this chapter aims to teach you how to adapt your normal fixed-width design conventions to work in liquid or elastic layouts.

Avoid: Irregular Shapes

One of the reasons why people design fixed heights as well as widths for blocks containing text is that the text blocks are laid on top of background image shapes that aren't straight and regular. A common example of this is when the background of a text box is made to look like some object from real life, such as a sticky note or patch of fabric. Or the irregular shapes may be more abstract, such as the paint splotch backgrounds used throughout the web site for The Lippincott at www.thelippincott.net (**Figure 2.5**).

FIGURE 2.5 With an irregularly shaped background image, such as the orange and green paint splotches here, you almost always have to stick with a fixed-width as well as a fixed-height text block.

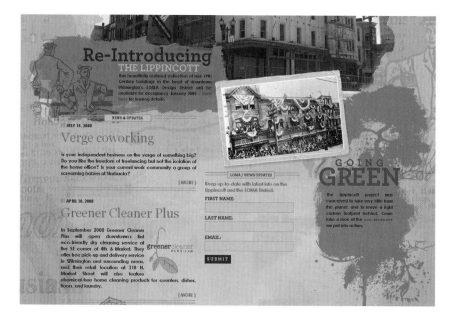

These paint splotches fit beautifully with the weathered look and the theme of renovation used on the site, but they're not flexible shapes. Because these shapes don't have straight, up-and-down edges, there's no way to tile a portion of either image to create an expandable box. Often, you would not want irregular shapes like these to expand, as they would no longer look like the object they are supposed to be imitating once they did. The Lippincott is a classic example of a design that not only wasn't built to be flexible, but was never designed to be flexible in the first place.

Irregular shapes don't come only in the form of graphic background images sitting behind the text itself. If the irregular shape just borders the text area, it can be problematic. For instance, look at the ribbon graphic on http:// scrapbookyourmemories.myshopify.com (**Figure 2.6**). Since it doesn't have a straight edge, it can't expand or contract in width through tiling, so the text block below can't change width either. The negative space that the ribbon graphic creates for the text area, just by bordering it, creates an irregular shape to the text area that thus can't change in width.

FIGURE 2.6 The lack of a straight portion of the ribbon graphic makes it impossible to tile the graphic to be flexible in width, so the text block below it can't expand or contract in width either.

This doesn't mean that all shapes in flexible designs have to be straight-edged rectangles. You might be able to create a hybrid design, where the irregular shape forms a fixed-width column beside another flexible column. Even in fully flexible designs, irregular shapes that don't contain text, and that don't create negative space for text that thus becomes irregular, are fine. Also, irregular shapes can work as long as they have portions that can be tiled, either because those portions are straight or they have some regular pattern. For instance, the banner area of the liquid site www.simonwiffen. co.uk has an irregular border along the top edge, but resizes just fine because the graphic that makes up this irregular border can tile (**Figure 2.7**). This same technique is used for the irregularly shaped footer of the site as well.

FIGURE 2.7 Because Simon Wiffen has designed the irregular edge on the banner of his site to be able to tile, the banner can expand and contract in width.

■ NOTE: We'll cover a technique to create a curve that straightens out in the middle in Chapter 8.

Another example of an irregular shape that can expand is on the inner pages of the elastic site for the design agency Neurotic (http://en.neuroticweb.com/web-design). The purple box that frames the top of the layout is curved, which normally would mean that it couldn't expand in width. However, the middle of the curve straightens out, so this straight portion of the image can be tiled to allow the irregular shape to expand and contract (**Figure 2.8**).

FIGURE 2.8 A tiny straight piece in the middle of the curved purple shape tiles to create a flattened-out portion of the curve, allowing the overall shape to expand and contract in width.

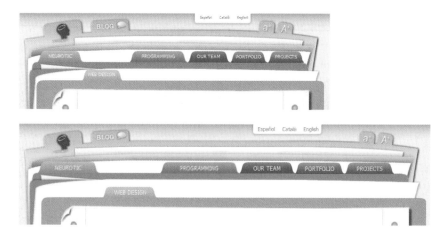

Avoid: Text Matched with Images That Can't Expand

■ NOTE: The "images that can't expand" part of the heading for this section may sound confusing—don't all images have set dimensions? Not necessarily. You'll see what this means in just a bit.

Another very common reason for designing fixed-dimension text blocks is to accommodate the fixed dimensions of an accompanying image. I'm not talking about inline images here—the kind that are stuck within an article with the text flowing around them. I'm talking about images in places like banners or feature boxes where you lay text either on top of an image or right beside it, and want the text to match the image in height or width.

In both the text-on-top and text-to-the-side scenarios, you run the risk of text overflowing, overlapping onto an unreadable portion of the image or page, or simply becoming misaligned with the image in an aesthetically un-pleasing sort of way. We saw an example of overflowing text due to attempted alignment with an image back in Figure 2.2. However, that was a case of the design not being *built* for flexibility, while many others are not designed for it.

Take the banner graphic on www.etondigital.com (**Figure 2.9**). It has a similar layout to the one from greg-wood.co.uk: a horizontal band with a block of text on the left and a graphic, matching in height, on the right. This time, though, there are a lot more graphic elements involved. The graphic on the right is an irregular shape, made to look like two pieces of paper; it overlaps the edges of the horizontal band and has a drop shadow. The band itself has a gradient instead of solid color background, as well as rounded corners and a background image aligned at the bottom. While it would be possible to build the band in a way that would allow it to grow in height to accommodate wrapping text on the left in a liquid layout, it would be quite difficult and messy. It would also result in the pieces-of-paper graphic no longer perfectly filling the height of the band, since the irregular graphic can't contain a tiling portion to expand and contract to match the height of the adjacent text.

FIGURE 2.9 All the graphic elements in this banner have to appear in precise relation to each other and the to accompanying block of text, making it very difficult to let the text resize or wrap differently, as would be required in a flexible layout.

Whether or not your design of text with images can be made flexible is largely dependent on your choice of images. To design for flexible layouts, then, what type of images do you need to pick? You'll need to pick images or design imagery that can expand (hence the title of this section). Here are a few ways how.

IMAGES THAT ARE MASKED

Images like those in the banner on the Usolab home page (www.usolab.com), where the subject matter of the image is cut out (or masked out) and sitting on top of a solid color or simple pattern background, are generally great for matching up with text, since you can create as much space around them as needed for the text (**Figure 2.10**). Just be sure you make the area around the masked images big enough for the text to sit in at many different wrapping points and text sizes. Ideally, the block will expand with the text. When you narrow the Usolab site to just under 800 pixels wide, the text overlaps the images below, making it much more difficult to read and not very attractive to look at (**Figure 2.11**). It's because of a fixed height again. The banner area could have been built with a flexible height, with the image portion anchored at the bottom, allowing more or less color to show above it.

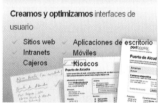

FIGURE 2.10 Masked-out images, like the pieces of paper in the Usolab banner, are usually very good for pairing with text because you can create as much space around them as needed for the text.

FIGURE 2.11 Because the block containing both the images and the text is fixed in height, the text overlaps its accompanying images when resizing the window forces it to wrap onto additional lines.

So, masked images can be great, as long as they provide enough space for the text. They need to allow the box they are in to expand and contract as needed, showing more blank color around them for the text to sit in as it changes in size. And they need to look good with the text, even if they don't match up exactly in height. Luckily, this is almost always the case with this type of image, as you're not trying to match up a rectangular image with a rectangular block of text.

For instance, the photo of the woman in the banner of the Sesame Communications web site (www.sesamecommunications.com) has its background masked out so that her picture appears on top of a simple gradient (**Figure 2.12**). This allows the photo to slide along the length of the banner based on the user's viewport size, creating a variable-width area for the text to sit in beside it. There's a minimum width in place that keeps the photo from appearing too far to the left and leaving no room for the text.

FIGURE 2.12 This masked-out photo looks fine even when not matching the text perfectly in height, and also has plenty of empty space beside it to allow the text to expand into as needed.

IMAGES THAT CAN SHOW MORE OR LESS OF THEMSELVES

Some images only make sense or look good if they are cropped in a very particular way. Others can look good cropped at several different points, showing more or less of the image. If you can use the latter type of images, you'll have a much easier time matching up text with images in flexible layouts.

The case studies featured on the Erskine Corporation home page (www.erskinecorp.com) each include an image that spans the entire width of the column (**Figure 2.13**). This would normally be a problem for flexible design, but when you decrease the width of your browser window, the images simply "crop" from the right side. You can use the same technique for cropping the height of an image.

■ NOTE: We'll go over this variable cropping technique in Chapter 9.

FIGURE 2.13 These images can always stay matched up with the width of the text below them because they are cropped dynamically from the right side as the column width changes with the viewport.

■ **NOTE:** The extended width of the images means that, in preparation for putting them on the web, you'll slice them from your comps in a different way than you normally would with images that will only be seen at a single, smaller, fixed width. We'll go over slicing techniques in the next chapter.

When you use this technique in your pages, you'll need to make the images much larger than you normally would, since there's no telling how far the design might get stretched and thus how much of the image could be revealed. Of course, you can limit this with a maximum width, but just keep the potentially large size in mind as you search for images that will suit your design. If you're worried about the width of your images not being quite long enough, you can also try stitching together multiple images like on the Dartmouth College home page (www.dartmouth.edu). At most viewport sizes, it appears that the banner image is just made up of one long image (**Figure 2.14**). But if you widen your window past about 1216 pixels, more images gradually appear on the right to fill up the new space (**Figure 2.15**).

FIGURE 2.14 At most viewport sizes, the banner on the Dartmouth College home page appears to be a single image.

FIGURE 2.15 The banner can extend to a very large width because of the additional images that appear to the right of the original one in larger viewports.

IMAGES THAT BLEND INTO BACKGROUND COLORS OR PATTERNS

All images have limits on how far you can go before you simply run out of image to show. When you reach the full extent of an image, you can often blend its edges into a background color, pattern, or even another image to stretch it even further.

These days, when I think *banner image faded into background color,* I can't help but think of late-'90s web design, and a little shudder goes through me. But the effect doesn't have to be heavy-handed or cheesy. The Air Adventure Australia site (www.airadventure.com.au) features three different banner images that you can choose among by pressing one of the colored buttons at the bottom right of the banner (**Figure 2.16**). Each one of the banner images blends in with a different color that is predominant in the image, to make the blend look more natural instead of contrived.

FIGURE 2.16 Each of the banner images you can choose on the Air Adventure Australia site blends in with whatever color is predominant in the image, to extend the width the banner can cover.

You can see another example of skillful blending of image with background color at www.defacto-cms.com. The feature image under the nav bar not only uses variable cropping on its left side to show more or less of itself, but is also blended into a matching background color on both its right side and bottom (**Figure 2.17**). This makes the image extremely amenable to window and text resizing; it's almost impossible to get the text to overflow.

FIGURE 2.17 This banner image uses variable cropping as well as background color blend to extend its range of both width and height, making it very accommodating to the text placed over it.

IMAGES THAT CAN SCALE WITHOUT LOOKING TOO PIXELATED

As you'll learn in Chapter 9, it's actually possible to make images scale with their container or the text size, instead of being stuck at a particular pixel width and height. The technique is not a great fit for a lot of designs, though, because relying on the browser to scale your images for you can result in much more jagged or blurry-looking images than if you did the scaling yourself in a graphics program. However, it can work reasonably well with certain imagery, where the distortion won't be as noticeable.

This is best seen on a live site, rather than through static images, so head to www.simplebits.com/work/sphere for an example. Try increasing or decreasing your browser's text size; the image shown under the heading

"Sphere" changes in size proportionally, so the text next to it always has the same number of characters per line (**Figure 2.18**). The same image file is used at all sizes, but the browser itself simply scales it to some percentage of its original size. In this particular example, the image is elastic, but you can also make liquid images that scale with the browser window. For instance, the images under the left-hand column labeled "turismo accessibile" on the home page of www.liberatutti.it change in size as you change the window size (**Figure 2.19**).

FIGURE 2.18 The main image within this page scales with the text around it, so the text never has to wrap differently.

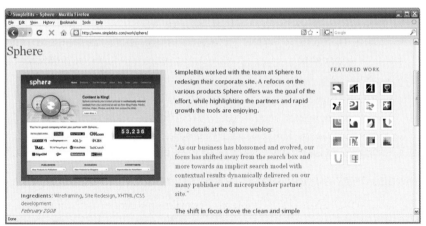

FIGURE 2.19 When this column changes in width—note that the text within hasn't changed in size—the images within it also change to match.

Pixelation or distortion is not very noticeable in these images for a couple of reasons:

- The images are larger than the sizes they appear on the page most of the time, so the browser is scaling them down, not up, in most cases. There is still some distortion when browsers scale images down, but this is not nearly as noticeable and ugly as the pixelation that occurs when images are scaled up. There are file-size implications to using larger images, of course, so you may want to let some up-scaling occur at the more extreme browser window sizes in order to balance quality with file size and load times.

- The subject matter of the images simply covers up a lot of the distortion. If there were people in the photos, especially faces, the distortion would be more noticeable. But reasonably complex images of illustrations, buildings, and landscapes don't need such smooth lines to look "correct."

NOTE: We'll go over the CSS techniques for creating scaling images—both elastic and liquid—in Chapter 9.

IMAGES THAT SIMPLY DON'T HAVE TO MATCH IN HEIGHT

The simplest solution to the problem of overflowing text next to images is just to choose not to have them match in height in the first place. The Simon Wiffen site that we saw in Figure 2.7 and the Sesame Communications site shown in Figure 2.12 both go this route with the images and text in their banners. Sometimes the text in each banner takes up fewer rows and is shorter than the photo beside it, and sometimes it takes up more rows and either matches or exceeds the height of the photo. This was planned for in the design, so it looks just fine.

ACHIEVING MATCHING HEIGHTS WITH ELASTIC DESIGN

If you absolutely must have the height of an image and a block of adjacent text match, your best bet is to use an elastic layout along with scaling, elastic images. You could set the height of both the box and the image within to a certain number of ems. This would allow the proportions of the image and text to remain matched, so that the text won't wrap onto additional lines. When you can ensure a fixed number of lines of text—only possible with elastic design—you can plan the height of the adjacent image accordingly and make them match in height.

If either of these designs had boxed in the photos more, the text would have looked more awkward when not matched up with the photo's height. For instance, on Simon Wiffen's site, he could have chosen to not make the photo tilted and overlapping the edges of the red banner. Instead, he could have made it straight and right up against the borders of the banner, touching its right edge and filling it from top to bottom. Though this might not have looked so bad if the text was shorter than the image, it would look quite awkward if the text was longer than the image—a gap would appear underneath the image but not on top of it or to its right.

Avoid: Fixed-Width, Full-Width Content

Images can be problematic for flexible design not just when they're used in conjunction with text, but also any time they fill up the entire width of a column. They essentially create a minimum width for the design, as it can't become any narrower than the large image without the image overflowing. They also can dictate a maximum width, as the design would look imbalanced and awkward if the image wasn't filling up the entire width of the column.

The MCR Foundation web site (www.mcrfoundation.com) uses images or Flash movies that fill the entire width of their columns as a design element throughout the site. On the About Us page, for instance, a large, horizontal photo of the site's namesake, Mary Cameron Robinson, spans the entire main content column (**Figure 2.20**). The subject matter of this photo doesn't lend itself to variable cropping (described in the previous section), as there's not much "dead space" that can be cropped out if the photo needed to get narrower, nor is it likely that there is a great deal more dead space beyond the current bounds of the photo that could be revealed if it needed to get wider. It also wouldn't look good for the main content column to be wider than the photo, as this would create an awkward empty space to the right of the photo. Its long, horizontal alignment lends itself to spanning the entire width, as does the overall design of the site, which uses solid blocks of color that fill their columns as a consistent design theme.

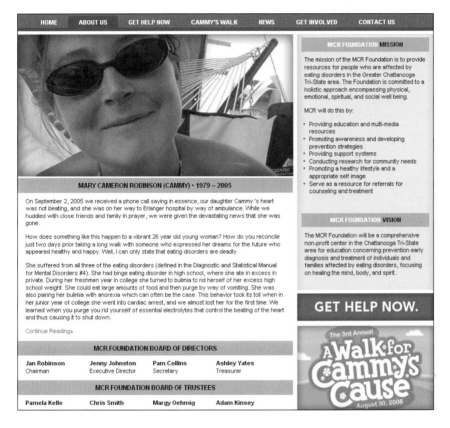

FIGURE 2.20 Both the main content column and the sidebar must be a fixed number of pixels wide to match the images within them that span the full widths of each column.

The full-width images in the sidebar, such as the "A Walk for Cammy's Cause" feature ad, also prevent that column from being able to resize. Since they are images of text, they can't be cropped dynamically. They could be scaled dynamically, but image-text scaled by the browser usually results in a lot of noticeable distortion. Since neither the main content column nor sidebar can resize, the design has to be fixed-width.

This inability to create flexible columns due to their fixed-width, full-width content is not caused simply by single images that span the entire width of a column; it also occurs because of multiple images that are placed side by side, as well as other types of fixed-width content like Flash movies and tables. The home page of the Borealis web site (www.borealisoffsets.com) has two rows of three images placed side by side that together span the full width of the layout (**Figure 2.21**). You can see a similar design at the Habitat for Humanity Youth Programs site (www.habitat.org/youthprograms). On Martha Stewart's web site (www.marthastewart.com), a large Flash banner helps dictate the fixed width of the design.

FIGURE 2.21 These images, placed side by side, together span the full width of the design and effectively set a fixed width for it to conform to.

To avoid this design problem, you can use the same techniques described in the previous section to create images that can expand and contract in some way. That way, you can still design with images that fill the entire width of their columns, but allow them to change in width as the columns do.

There are also additional techniques that you can use to avoid unwrappable full-width images.

DON'T DESIGN IMAGES TO SPAN THE FULL WIDTH

The most obvious approach, of course, is to not design with images or other content that fill the entire width of their columns in the first place. Place text or other resizable, wrappable content next to images and Flash movies instead of giving those less flexible elements a long, horizontal alignment.

We've already seen some examples of this in the Simon Wiffen, Sesame Communications, Air Adventure Australia, and Simple Bits sites. All of these use different techniques to work around the need for full-width images.

You can see another example of purposely choosing not to have images span the full width on the Todd Silver Design site at www.toddsilverdesign.net (**Figure 2.22**). This is the same concept we saw in Figure 2.13—a list of featured or recent work shown in a sidebar. Unlike in Figure 2.13, however, the images that go along with Todd Silver's listed projects do not span the full width of the column, but instead have text placed to their right. The images can remain a fixed width, with no need for variable cropping, since the text beside the images can wrap and allow the column to resize in this liquid design.

FIGURE 2.22 Because wrappable text content is placed next to fixed-width images, instead of having the images span the entire column width, this column can resize in width.

CREATE FULL-WIDTH IMAGES OUT OF MULTIPLE SLIDING PIECES

You can create images that appear to be a single image spanning the column, but are really made up of two or more pieces, each one anchored to opposite sides of the column, that slide closer to and farther from each other to adjust to the changing width of the column. The footer image on the Ronin Snowboards site (www.roninsnowboards.com) is a great example of this. **Figure 2.23** shows the footer when the window is at a width of 800 pixels; the imagery in the footer appears to be a single graphic—and an irregular one at that, with no piece that could be tiled to make it expand. **Figure 2.24** shows the footer at a width of 1024 pixels, and the two pieces of the footer image have spread apart so that they continue to fill the width of the overall design while still appearing cohesive.

■ NOTE: We'll go over the CSS for creating composite images in Chapter 9.

FIGURE 2.23 At 800 pixels, the footer graphic appears to be a single image.

FIGURE 2.24 At 1024 pixels, you can see that the footer graphic is actually made out of two separate pieces, yet the overall effect is still unified.

GENERATE SCROLLBARS FOR OVERLY LARGE CONTENT

Large, fixed-width content isn't just seen in banners and other decorative areas of the page, but can also be part of the actual content of the site. You may have charts mixed in with your text, for instance, that need to be large to be readable. If you don't want these large pieces of content to dictate the minimum width of your design, but also don't want them to overflow, you can generate scrollbars just on the large piece of content itself.

■ **NOTE:** We'll go over the CSS for giving individual pieces of content their own scrollbars in Chapter 6.

The blog Bokardo (http://bokardo.com) is liquid, but uses many large images in the text because they are comics and must be readable. On some of them, when the design is too narrow for the comic images to fit, they simply generate their own scrollbars (**Figure 2.25**). You are still able to narrow the text to a point that you find comfortable to read without the large images pushing things out wider than you prefer, and you can still access the cut-off portions of the images without too much trouble, simply by using their own scrollbars.

FIGURE 2.25 Scrollbars on an individual image keep the entire image accessible at any size.

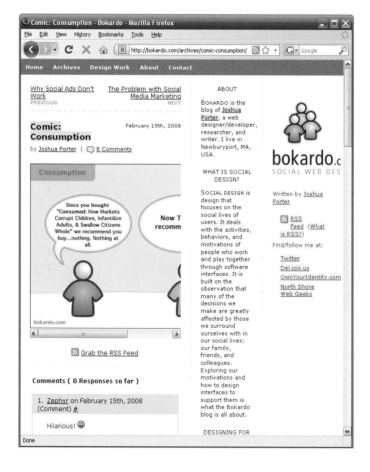

Avoid: Horizontal Alignment Across Columns

As we've already discussed, you can't rely on heights of text blocks being constant. This means that you can't be sure where the top of the boxes that come underneath text blocks are going to land. And this, in turn, means that you can't line up items across columns when they have separate text boxes above them. (If the items across columns have the same text block above them, it's going to push both columns down equally, of course, so in these cases it's fine to align horizontally.)

For instance, the Cafédirect web site at www.cafedirect.co.uk has multiple boxes containing text; the boxes are in separate columns but are aligned horizontally (**Figure 2.26**). If we use our text-resizing trick to emulate how this site would act if it were liquid, however, many of these boxes become misaligned (**Figure 2.27**). Because a single Flash movie sits above the first row of three boxes, they all get pushed down equally and stay aligned with each other along the top—but not along the bottom. This, in turn, causes the second row of boxes to become misaligned with each other on both the top and the bottom.

FIGURE 2.26 At the default text size, the boxes of this layout fit together in a neat grid.

FIGURE 2.27 When the text size is increased to simulate wrapping text in a liquid layout, many of the boxes become misaligned.

Fortunately for Cafédirect's design, it doesn't really look wrong for these boxes to be misaligned and unmatched in height; those browsing with a text size other than 16 pixels are never going to suspect that what they're seeing is not exactly what the designer had intended, and will still be able to use the site just fine. Other designs, however, make the alignment much more integral to the design, so that without it, the design appears "broken." For instance, the UX Magazine home page (www.uxmag.com) is set up as one big grid, with several rows of matching-height boxes (**Figure 2.28**). If any of these boxes were to no longer match in height with the others in its row, causing the boxes below to become misaligned horizontally, it would look quite chaotic. This type of design is best left fixed-width.

FIGURE 2.28 The UX Magazine home page depends heavily on horizontal and vertical alignment of boxes, so making those boxes flexible and thus moveable is not really an option.

There are really no fancy tricks when it comes to avoiding the problem of horizontal alignment—just don't design it into your flexible layouts. When you do need horizontal alignment for some number of blocks, make sure there is some way to group the preceding blocks into a single div so that the following blocks can all get pushed down equally and stay aligned.

AN EXAMPLE OF A RESOLUTION-DEPENDENT LAYOUT

You may remember a sidebar on resolution-dependent layouts back in Chapter 1. The UX Magazine site is a great example of this technique on a real site. If you narrow your window, the right sidebar you see in Figure 2.28 drops down below the grid of story boxes and becomes a long horizontal block instead. Implementing a resolution-dependent layout was a great choice for this site, since the boxy design doesn't allow it a lot of flexibility otherwise. It's a smart compromise to keep a horizontal scrollbar from appearing quite as often.

Even in these cases where you can keep the tops aligned, however, it may not be possible to also keep their bottoms aligned. In other words, don't count on the height of the aligned items matching. Unlike table cells, where cells in the same row all match each other in height, `div`s and other non-cell elements have no connection with each other, and thus no reason to match each other in height. The only way to get elements across columns to match each other in height is to group them together in some way and apply the proper CSS. However, grouping the blocks together doesn't always make the best sense for the order of the items in your (X)HTML.

For instance, the Continuing Professional Development section of The Open University web site at www.open.ac.uk/cpd has three liquid columns under the banner, each one made up of a heading with a background color, an image, and one or more paragraphs of description (**Figure 2.29**). The designer of this site has made no attempt to make the colored heading blocks match each other in height, so as you change the width of your window they vary between two to four lines of text each. At some viewport widths they match up, at others they don't.

FIGURE 2.29
The headings in colored blocks over the photos do not match each other in height, since they contain different amounts of text and can wrap in many different ways in this liquid layout.

EMULATING TABLE CELLS WITH THE display **PROPERTY**

One way to get unconnected divs to match each other in height is to set each of them to display: table-cell. This makes them act just like table cells: they will line up side by side as if in a row, and each will be as tall as the tallest div in the row. However, none of the table-related values of the display property are supported by IE 7 and earlier. Also, using display: table-cell often still requires a less than ideal grouping and order of the divs in the (X)HTML source of the page. It's still best to avoid creating matching heights across columns when possible.

The only way it would have been possible to make the headings always match in height would have required compromising the integrity of the source order. The three headings would need to be grouped together in a single div, each one following right after the other in the (X)HTML. Then you would have another div holding the three images, and finally a third holding the three descriptions. Each heading would now no longer immediately precede its description in the source or be grouped together with it. This would harm the accessibility of the site, as well as its usability for people using small-screen devices or other non-CSS-enabled browsers. It would also have made the design much more difficult to restyle, as it replicates table markup, simply using div elements instead of tr elements to group the items in a very rigid way. Choosing to allow the blocks to not have horizontally aligned bottoms was a much better design choice for this liquid layout.

Plan For: Images Extending Past Their Original Dimensions

Enough about what to avoid—let's talk more about what you should plan to put into your designs.

We've already talked about the importance of choosing and designing images that can scale or otherwise adjust to changing dimensions in some way. But this doesn't just apply to foreground images, like the banner- and feature-image examples you've seen thus far. It also applies to your background images, including tiling patterns, textures, and decorative borders.

We already saw an example of this in Figure 2.8—the curved top section of the page design needed to extend past a single fixed width, although the designer would have had to lay the graphic out at some fixed width when creating the design comp. The designer had to plan for what would happen to the image when the elastic design was narrower or wider than the original width shown in the comp, and then make sure this functionality was built into the design.

Another example of planning for variable-width background images can be seen in the flexible gradient blocks on the e-days web site (www.e-days. co.uk). On the home page, the two feature items labeled "download brochure" and "get in the know" both change in width to reveal more or less of the darkening gray on the left side of the gradient background image, while the button graphics layered over the gradients always stay pinned to the left side (**Figure 2.30**). The designer couldn't just create a single fixed-width graphic for the background on each feature item, but instead had to plan for the background image potentially being much larger.

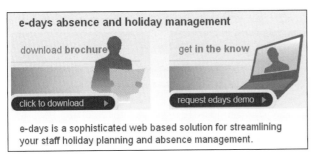

FIGURE 2.30 Each button graphic and gradient background on these feature items could not have been created as a single, small fixed-width graphic, but instead had to be created out of two pieces, sliced from a larger graphic in the comp.

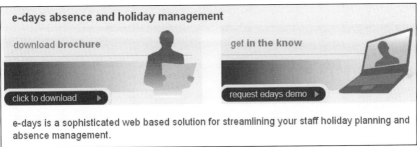

Another example of planning ahead with a very large background image can be seen on www.taptaptap.com. The cutting-board graphic on the site can't be tiled because it is diagonal, but the designers of the site didn't let that stop them from keeping the height of the site flexible to varying text sizes. Instead of making the cutting board only as tall as the height shown for most users' default text sizes, they instead created a much taller image of the cutting board that can be revealed as needed (**Figure 2.31**).

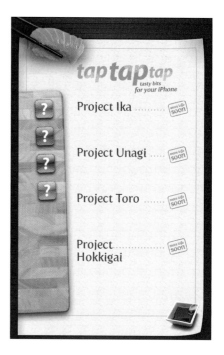

FIGURE 2.31 More or less of the very large cutting-board graphic is revealed as the changing text size alters the height of the design.

To put this principle into practice when designing your own comps, you often need incredibly large swaths of background image to slice from. You might be accustomed to creating a comp at a fixed size and then slicing that same comp to produce the background graphics for the site. With flexible design, you often need to create a comp at a fixed size in order to get an idea of how it will look for the majority of your audience, but then you have to create a second version of the comp that is stretched out to its maximum width in order to slice the large pieces of background images that are required for a flexible design. We'll work through an example of this adjustment in the next chapter.

Plan For: Designed White Space Beyond the Maximum Width

One of the complaints with fixed-width designs is that if a user has his viewport very large, the design looks puny—floating in the middle, or off to one side with piles of empty space around it. One way to downplay this problem is to create some decorative background elements to fill up the space beyond the main page design. Designing the white space is applicable to flexible layouts as well, since most of the time you will assign them a maximum width beyond which the design will no longer stretch.

An example of this technique on a fixed-width site is the wild floral graphic on Web Designer Wall (www.webdesignerwall.com) that appears behind the main content container (**Figure 2.32**). Even if you have your window set at a very large size, this imagery creates visual interest and lessens the feeling that space is being "wasted" by the fixed width (a complaint I've heard from users with large resolutions and who like to maximize).

FIGURE 2.32 The floral graphic in the background of Web Designer Wall fills up the space around the fixed-width content area in larger viewports.

The design of the white space doesn't need to be anything this intricate, though. The blog of Jason Santa Maria (www.jasonsantamaria.com) simply fills the space left after the liquid design has reached its maximum width with tiling bars of color at the top of the page and a subtle watercolor effect over a small portion of the main content background color (**Figure 2.33**). On www.stylizedweb.com, the contours of an illustration of mountains, water, and ocean floor gradually straightens out to form simple bands of color that can fill the rest of the viewport (**Figure 2.34**).

BUT MA, DO I HAVE TO?

It's certainly not a requirement that you design some sort of color or graphic to fill the remaining viewport space once the design has reached its maximum width. There are plenty of beautiful and effective sites that don't do so. But it is something you at least need to consider and plan for when creating your design comps. Know up front how you are going to handle the extra white space so you can build your solution—whatever it may be—into the design.

FIGURE 2.33 This subtle watercolor effect fills the space beyond the edges of the content area of the design.

FIGURE 2.34 To keep the background illustration from ending abruptly, the background instead blends into strips of solid color that fill the remaining horizontal space.

By designing the white space, you're acknowledging that people have all sorts of different viewport sizes, even if you can't design your layout for all of them.

Plan For: Side-by-Side Items Wrapping onto Multiple Lines

When widths change, inline elements wrap to fit. Wrapping is a fact of life with flexible layouts—avoidable to some degree with elastic layouts, but still possible—so it's best to build it into your designs.

NAVIGATION BARS

Navigation bars are one of the places that designers are least likely to want wrapping to occur, and thus they are rarely designed and built for such an eventuality. If you design your nav bar to not have very many items across it, you lessen the chances that a wrap will ever have to occur. But, when a nav bar contains several items across it, it's likely that the viewport will sometimes need to be narrower than the full width of the nav bar. In these cases, you have to choose how your design will adapt. You have three basic choices:

◆ The nav bar dictates the minimum width and a horizontal scrollbar is generated for the entire design.

◆ The nav bar overflows, necessitating a horizontal scrollbar to view all of it, but the rest of the design stays within the viewport.

◆ The items in the nav bar wrap to fit within the viewport.

None of these options are more "right" than any other, as each works with different types of designs and content.

The first option works well when there aren't too many items in the nav bar, your content doesn't need to be too narrow, or the nav bar would look particularly awkward wrapped or overflowing. On the liquid Django web site (www.djangoproject.com), the nav bar is aligned to the right side of the viewport. It moves closer to the logo on the left as you narrow the window, until it finally bumps against the logo and goes no further. When this happens, the entire design stops acting liquid and generates a horizontal scrollbar (**Figure 2.35**). If you increase your text size, the nav bar items still don't wrap, but instead the entire nav bar increases in width. The minimum width of the design also increases accordingly, requiring an even larger horizontal scrollbar.

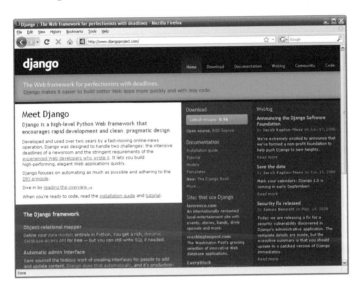 

FIGURE 2.35 The Django web site can be narrowed, but not any further than the combined width of the logo and the nav bar.

I wouldn't pick the first option if the minimum width it would require for the content is significantly greater than you would otherwise choose, if the nav bar weren't part of the equation. For instance, let's say the minimum width you would want for the content would be about 10 ems, to allow a pretty narrow width that would make the content more readable for people with small screens or certain disabilities. But the number of characters in your nav bar might require a minimum width of 20 ems. Forcing your content to a minimum width of 20 ems, when you really feel it might be better for the user to let it get much narrower than that, would probably not be a good choice. You'd be making your design much more rigid than necessary. For an example like this, if you're trying to design a flexible layout, I'd change the design of the nav bar to work with the second or third option.

With the second option, you allow the minimum widths of the nav bar and the rest of the content to be separate, with each section optimized separately. You can let the nav bar "overflow" without actually looking like it's overflowing—it simply appears to be a longer width than the content below it. You can see an example of this on the Webdesign UK site (www.wduk. co.uk) when your window is very narrow (**Figure 2.36**). At the default font size, the nav bar is 737 pixels wide and will not get any narrower or wrap when you make the window smaller than this width, but the rest of the content on the page will continue to scale to a narrower width.

FIGURE 2.36 At this window size, the content is still adapting to the window and does not require a horizontal scrollbar to view it. But the nav bar has stopped getting narrower and does require horizontal scrolling to view all of the items within it.

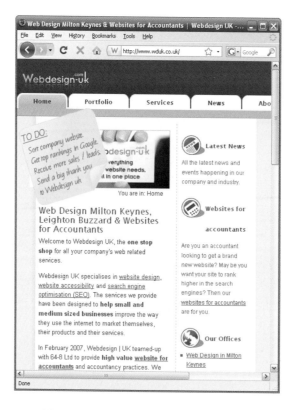

A problem with this approach, however, is the possibility that the user will not realize that the nav bar is overflowing off the right side of the screen and will never use the horizontal scrollbar to view the remainder of it. This is not as likely in a tabbed nav bar design such as that on Webdesign UK, since the user's window probably won't cut off the nav bar exactly between two tabs, and thus, the cut-off appearance of the last tab should be a clue that there's more off to the right. But the possibility of not looking cut off may be more problematic on nav bars that aren't so highly designed—such as the one we're going to see next.

That leaves us with the third option: wrapping the items in the nav bar. One of the main reasons for choosing to make a flexible design in the first place was to avoid horizontal scrollbars, after all, so this really is the most flexible option. It may sound unattractive, but it doesn't have to be, and it does have the advantage of always keeping all the nav items in view of and usable by your site visitors. For example, the items on the nav bar on SPARC (www. sparc.org.nz) remain on one line at larger window sizes, but when the window is narrower, they wrap onto multiple lines (**Figure 2.37**). The flexible height of the nav bar's gray background allows it to accommodate the wrapping without a problem.

How you design your nav bar has an impact on whether the items within it can wrap. For instance, an irregular shape for a nav bar may not allow a flexible height, as we've already discussed. In most cases, however, wrapping items in a nav bar is mostly a CSS issue, not a design one. Most nav bars can be made flexible in height to allow wrapping, regardless of whether the designer chooses to implement the proper CSS to make them so.

FIGURE 2.37
At smaller window sizes, the items in this nav bar simply wrap onto a second line and the background of the nav bar grows in height to match.

Still, there are certainly nav-bar designs that look better or worse when wrapped. One type of nav bar that I don't think looks very good wrapped is one with tabs. Tabs are supposed to stick up into empty space, not onto tabs above them, so the second row of tabs usually looks awkward. It may be best to avoid using tabs unless they take up only a small amount of the width of your design and thus are not very likely to wrap. A small number of visitors may still see a double row of tabs, but this is an acceptable compromise if you absolutely must have tabs in your design. Cody Lindley's personal site (www.codylindley.com) allows the tabs across the top of the site to wrap, but this only occurs when the window is extremely narrow or the text size is very large, because the tabs are so small to begin with (**Figure 2.38**).

FIGURE 2.38 Although these tabs are set up to wrap, it's going to take a very narrow window to make that happen; the window here is 500 pixels wide, but there's still a good amount of room between the last tab and the edge of the viewport.

PAGE CONTENT

Apart from navigation bars, there are many types of content within the main area of the page itself that need to be designed to wrap if you want a successful flexible layout.

One type of content frequently designed to sit side by side is what I call *feature boxes*. These are little graphics or boxes with small amounts of text that usually act as ads or gateways to some other piece of content on the site. If a row of feature boxes fills up the entire width of the area that houses it, those boxes either need to be able to scale with the width of the area or wrap onto multiple lines. Which they can and will do depends on the design of the boxes themselves, as well as their content.

The home page of Webdesign UK includes four feature boxes, stacked two on top of each other. Each one can expand and contract in width as needed because the straight sides of the boxes can be made out of tiling background images, and the illustration inside each box doesn't span its full width (**Figure 2.39**). Because the illustration inside each box is also pale and grayed out, the text can wrap on top of it without becoming unreadable. We saw another example of scalable feature boxes earlier in the chapter, on The Open University's Continuing Professional Development site in Figure 2.29. Other sites using scalable feature boxes are Igoo (http://igoo.co.uk) and Nomensa (on interior pages like www.nomensa.com/news.html).

FIGURE 2.39 The straight sides and non-full-width, grayed-out illustrations of these feature boxes allow them to expand and contract easily.

Almost all of the content you see on the portfolio page of Indelebile (www.indelebile.net/?cat=15) is designed in feature boxes, but instead of scaling, these boxes wrap to accommodate the size of the viewport (**Figure 2.40**). This makes the most sense for this design, as the images span the full width of each box. Although the images could technically be cropped dynamically from the side, as we've seen in examples earlier in the chapter, it probably wouldn't be a good choice for this type of content. Each of the images is already cropped from the featured piece of work, so the designer has carefully chosen what portion of each image to show in order to put his work in the best light. You can see a similar implementation of wrapping boxes at 6 Angry Men (http://blog.6angrymen.com).

A similar type of page content that needs to wrap is an image gallery made up of multiple thumbnail images. For the most part, whether or not thumbnails can wrap onto a variable number of lines depends on how you actually build the gallery and its parent container, not on the visual design of the gallery. Just make sure that you design the thumbnails to all be the same size, or at least the same height, if you can. It's tough to make a cross-browser-compatible flexible image gallery out of standards-compliant (X)HTML and CSS if the thumbnails vary from each other in height.

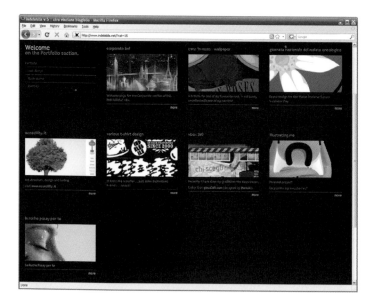
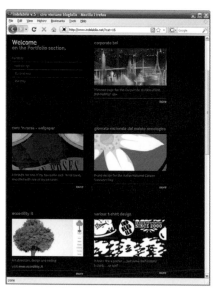

FIGURE 2.40 These boxes can wrap onto different numbers of lines as needed.

The photo gallery on Simon Wiffen's site (www.simonwiffen.co.uk/photos) lets the identically sized thumbnails wrap onto more or fewer lines depending on the size of the window (**Figure 2.41**). Another option is to let the thumbnails resize or crop dynamically, as we've seen in examples with banner images earlier in the chapter.

FIGURE 2.41 The photo thumbnails on this site can wrap onto different numbers of lines as needed.

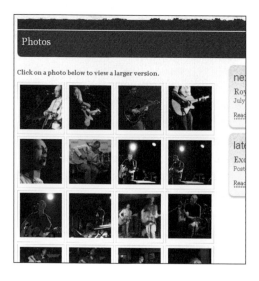

■ **NOTE:** We'll go over the markup and CSS techniques to build flexible image galleries—wrapping and scaling versions—in Chapter 9.

Basically, any time you design content sitting side by side in columns, ask yourself whether it would be possible for that content to resize, and if not, if it could instead wrap onto multiple lines. This content may be images, blocks of text, form fields, lists, or anything else.

"TOUGH" IS A RELATIVE TERM

The term "cross-browser-compatible" has no concrete definition in terms of what browsers you need to be compatible with. If, to you, it means you need to fully support IE 7, IE 6, and/or Firefox 2, that's where you're going to run into trouble creating a flexible image gallery when the thumbnails vary in height. (Nevertheless, you'll learn how to work around these problems in Chapter 9.) If you don't need to support these or earlier browsers, however, it's not tough at all. So the difficulty doesn't lie in a shortcoming of CSS, but rather in the shortcomings of browsers.

Before and After: Our Non-compatible Design, Fixed

We've looked at lots of examples of real web-site designs that do and don't work with flexible layout techniques. But knowing how to change a non-flexible design element into a flexible one is a step beyond merely recognizing what design elements are problematic for a liquid or elastic site. That's where our example site comes in. Throughout this book, we'll be working on creating a web site for the fictional Beechwood Animal Shelter, from designing the comp to putting the finishing touches on the CSS.

Our first step in creating the Beechwood Animal Shelter site will be transforming the first-draft comp (**Figure 2.42**) of its design into a more flexible-friendly final design. The first-draft comp has a number of design elements that won't work in a flexible design (you'll see the relevant areas marked in Figure 2.42):

1. Since the tabs take up so much of the width of the layout, it's very likely they would need to wrap (for a liquid layout—an elastic layout prevents much wrapping). The tab design of the main navigation bar could be built to wrap, but it won't look very good when it does so.

2. The width of the nav bar ought to be dependent on the width of the text within it, but it's been designed to exactly match the width of the banner image below it. This won't be possible to achieve unless the tabs are made into images, which is never ideal for a whole host of reasons including usability, accessibility, ease of maintenance, and search-engine optimization. Even with the tabs as images, to get them to match up with the image below you'll have to prevent them from wrapping, thereby sticking yourself with an unreasonably large minimum width for the layout.

FIGURE 2.42 The first version of the home page contains a number of design features that can't be incorporated into a liquid or elastic layout.

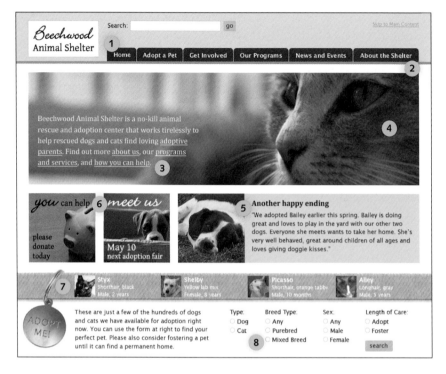

3. The text overlaid on the banner image fits in only a small area of the image, so it can't resize or wrap without becoming unreadable. It's been stuck in a fixed-width and fixed-height area.

4. The subject matter of the banner image can't be cropped off from the right as the layout is narrowed in the browser, forcing the design to be as wide as this very large image at a minimum. It's also not clear if the image can grow any larger, either vertically or horizontally, to fill up space as either the text on top of it grows or the entire layout is expanded. The image isn't blended into any background color or masked out to allow expansion.

5. The "happy ending" story below the banner is boxed into a block of color that must exactly match the fixed height of the image beside it. If the text within the box wraps, it either overflows or expands the height of the box. If the photo was sitting inside the box, with the box's colored background showing on all sides of it, it wouldn't look so awkward for the block of text to extend past its height. But since the photo doesn't sit inside the box but rather beside it—and even touching it—it would look quite awkward for the two elements to not be matched in height.

6. The feature boxes are designed to be a static height and width, as each would have to be simply an image, and to match up with the story box to their right. It's fine for all of these boxes to be a set width and height if the layout is going to be elastic and the images will be built to expand

with the text—although the two feature boxes will probably have noticeable pixelation or distortion because of the graphic text shown on them. Even if the layout is going to be liquid instead of elastic, it's fine for the two feature boxes to be a static size as long as the story box can resize, creating a hybrid layout. But, as was just mentioned, expanding the height of the story box isn't really an option, nor would it look very good for it to no longer match the feature boxes in height.

7. The listing of featured pets is in a fixed-height area. The background graphic, though straight, is essentially an irregular shape because of the collar-tag part of the graphic that keeps it from being able to be tiled vertically. Even if the text of each featured pet listing could wrap without overflowing off the collar graphic, the listings would look crowded and awkward when moved closer together with their text wrapped onto more lines.

8. The search form is designed in four columns, but it would not be very readable (and thus not very easy to fill out) if one or more of the columns were allowed to wrap. The form can be kept from wrapping if the entire row is elastic, but if the design is liquid, the paragraph of text to the left of the form would need to be able to resize to accommodate the fixed size of the form. This behavior could easily be built in, but at smaller window sizes or larger font sizes the paragraph of text would quickly become only two or three words wide and very tall, no longer matching the height of the form, and looking quite awkward.

Luckily, all of these problems can be fixed, to some degree, to increase the potential flexibility of the layout. Many of them could be addressed in multiple ways, as there are no set formulas for creating flexible designs, but I've created one variation that doesn't stray too far from the initial design's look and feel (**Figure 2.43**):

1. The tabs have been replaced with a simpler bar that can expand in width and height if the text size is increased or the links wrap onto multiple lines. The nav bar spans the entire width of the viewport, instead of matching the width of the banner below it.

2. The banner photo has been changed to allow a less constrained area for the text to sit in. There is plenty of solid colored space above the visible area of the photo that can be revealed and used to hold text if it needs to wrap onto more lines. This photo can also be cropped a good deal from the right side on narrower windows without making the subject matter of the photo indistinguishable.

3. The solid color box has been removed from around the happy-ending story, so it won't look so awkward now if the text needs to wrap onto more lines and becomes misaligned in height with the photo. The text can simply wrap around the photo or wrap down in a straight column to its right.

FIGURE 2.43 The revised version of the home page has the same content and a similar look and feel, but doesn't present problems for turning it into a liquid or elastic layout.

4. The feature boxes are still images and thus still a fixed width, but this is fine; the column they sit in can easily be made fixed-width, since the content in the adjacent column can shoulder the burden of being the flexible one. The feature boxes are no longer designed to match any pieces of text in height.

5. The featured pet listings are no longer in a fixed-height area. They're also stacked vertically instead of horizontally, so they won't crowd up on each other and get too narrow at narrower viewport sizes.

6. The featured pet form has also been switched from four columns to a vertical stack in order to avoid crowding and wrapping problems. While the individual radio button items may wrap at narrower viewport sizes or larger font sizes, they'll still be aligned underneath their headings. The groups of radio buttons can't wrap—they're already stacked vertically—keeping the form more readable and usable at variable viewport and text sizes.

3

Preparing Your Design for Construction

When building the graphic comp of your flexible layout (likely in a program like Adobe Fireworks or Adobe Photoshop), you'll need to keep in mind all the design elements you learned about in Chapter 2. You'll use the comp to give you an idea of what the finished page will look like, as well as to create graphic slices from it to use as foreground or background images in the page. How you set up and work with this comp—the canvas size you choose, your use of layers, how you slice it, and so on—affect how easily you can turn it into flexible (X)HTML and CSS.

Setting up Your Graphic Comp

■ **NOTE:** Throughout this chapter, I'll be using Fireworks as the graphics creation and editing program in my examples. However, you can use whatever program you like to create flexible web design comps.

Graphic comps are static images, not moving, user-controlled, flexible web pages. They can only go so far in approximating the appearance of the page you'll ultimately build. Nevertheless, there are steps you can take during the creation of the comp to make it more representative of your final page as well as easier to turn into that page when it comes time to slice it.

Choosing a Canvas Size

When you're creating a comp for a fixed-width design, it's easy to choose the size of the canvas you'll design on. You just decide what you want the fixed width of the page to be, and pick that same size for the canvas (or perhaps something a little bigger, if you'll be designing the excess white space that's left once the user goes past the fixed width).

When creating flexible designs, the width of the page in pixels is going to vary from user to user, so what width do you choose for your canvas? I think you have three options:

- Choose what you think will be the minimum width of the design.

- Choose what you think will be the maximum width of the design.

- Choose a width in the middle that you think the majority of your visitors will be viewing at.

Each option has its pros and cons.

MATCH THE MINIMUM WIDTH

Before creating your comp, you may want to decide the approximate smallest width that you'll let the design reach (or the smallest width that you think a significant portion of your audience will see). You can then use this minimum width, or something close to it, as the width of the canvas. This allows you to make sure that everything will really fit at such a small size. It also keeps you from inadvertently making images larger than they should be to fit within the eventual minimum width you'll set on the design.

However, designing to the minimum width can be problematic, primarily because you may end up with a design that looks far too sparse and awkward when it gets stretched out. Try to imagine what the design will look like when it's much wider, so you can change it if needed to accommodate a wider range of widths.

MATCH THE MAXIMUM WIDTH

In addition to a minimum width, you may also have a maximum width in mind for your design—either one that you plan on imposing or one that you can't imagine any of your users exceeding. If you choose this maximum width as the canvas size for your comp, you can avoid the problem of the design looking sparse and awkward at those larger sizes and can ensure that the line lengths won't become too long and hard to read. You also have the advantage of probably not having to modify the comp before slicing it—as you'll learn later in the chapter, creating comps that are smaller than the eventual page usually means you have to stretch out your comp before you can slice it, so that the slices will be as large as the page requires.

However, designing at such a large width could inadvertently lead you to make the design much harder to fit in a small space. You may make the images too large or put too much "stuff" in the design—feature boxes, images, sidebars—that will look crowded and hard to read at smaller widths. A column that looked great at a wide canvas size may look silly when it's so narrow that only a couple words can fit on each line of text before wrapping. Again, try to imagine what the design will look like when narrower to avoid these problems as much as possible.

CHOOSE A HAPPY MEDIUM

Instead of picking either the minimum or maximum widths, you could choose some width in between the two as your canvas size. Determine what size is likely to be used by the majority of your audience and pick this as the width to design to. You'll be optimizing the design for what the majority will see.

Using a middle-of-the-road canvas size can help you avoid the cons of the other two approaches, but it can also make your design more susceptible to the cons of *both* if you're not careful. For instance, you may want to make your design span from 600 pixels to 1200 pixels, and you create a comp with a width of 900 pixels. It's quite possible that you'll create a design where not only are the images too big to fit in the 600-pixel minimum width, but also where the page elements and text look too sparse and hard to read at 1200 pixels. Although the design will look great for the majority, you've created problems at both ends of the width range, instead of just one. However, the degree of severity of these problems is probably going to be less when you start off in the middle. An in-between width is probably the best bet for most designs—just be careful and continue to think about the other possible widths throughout the design process. Never forget that the web page you eventually create is not going to be a static image—it's going to be flexible.

Using Layers and Pages to Organize Your Comp

The intelligent use of layers (a feature available in all major graphics programs) and pages (a Fireworks-only feature) to organize the design elements in your comp is certainly a boon to fixed-width designs, but can be especially helpful in visualizing and planning for the range of sizes your flexible design will need to accommodate.

USING LAYERS TO VISUALIZE DIFFERENT WIDTHS

You can make multiple copies of the same page section or design element on different layers, each with a different width, to see how the section or element will look at different sizes.

For instance, you could create three different versions of the sidebar shown in the web comp in **Figure 3.1**—one narrow, one wide, and one medium in width. To make it easy to switch between viewing each of the three versions, all of the objects that make up each version should be placed on their own layer. Both Fireworks and Photoshop offer the ability to create sublayers, so you could first create a layer named sidebar, and then nest within it three sublayers named mid, narrow, and wide (**Figure 3.2**).

FIGURE 3.1 Like all comps, this one is fixed-width, but you may be curious what the sidebar looks like at other widths.

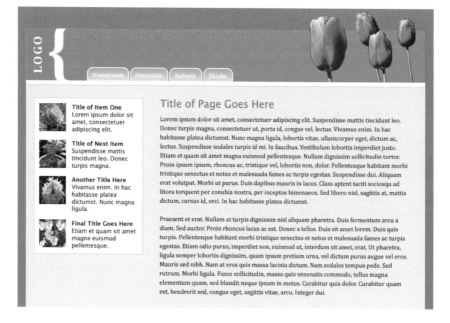

FIGURE 3.2 The mid, narrow, and wide sublayers of the sidebar layer.

To change the visibility of any of these layers in Fireworks, simply click the eye icon (the square farthest to the left) for that layer. The eye icon beside the layer named mid in Figure 3.2 indicates that that layer is visible, but you could make the layer named narrow visible by clicking the eye icon next to mid and then clicking the empty box next to narrow (**Figure 3.3**). You could follow the same steps to check out the appearance of the layer named wide (**Figure 3.4**).

■ **TIP:** You could use a similar technique to simulate the appearance of design elements in your page at different text sizes, not just for testing elastic web sites—where the text controls the widths of blocks on the page—but for all web sites, since the text size is always user-controlled.

FIGURE 3.3 The narrower version of the sidebar, stored on the layer named narrow in the comp, shows what the sidebar might look like on narrower screens.

FIGURE 3.4 The wider version of the sidebar, stored on the layer named wide in the comp, shows what the sidebar might look like on wider screens.

USING PAGES TO VISUALIZE DIFFERENT WIDTHS

Using pages in Fireworks is another way to make multiple copies to check how each will look at different widths, but pages allow you to more easily check the entire design at once.

Instead of creating a separate version of each design element on its own sublayer, create each version on its own page. For instance, create wider versions not only of the sidebar but also the header, nav bar, main body content, footer, and page background on a page named wide. You can give this page a wider canvas size without affecting any of the other pages in your document. You can then switch to this page to view all the design elements at a wider size at once rather than having to find every sublayer named wide

FIGURE 3.5 Use the Pages panel in Fireworks to create multiple versions of the same design but showing different widths.

within a single page and turn them all on—and turn all the non-wide layers off—one after the other.

Each page has its own set of layers. To create a new page using the layers from an existing page, first select that page in the Pages panel. Open the Pages panel menu by clicking the icon in the top right corner of the panel group, and then choose Duplicate Page (**Figure 3.6**). This creates a new page that contains all the same layers and objects as the selected page. You can then easily change the width or text size of each of those objects on the new page. This is a lot faster than having to create a new empty page and pasting each of the layers from the first page into the second.

If you have certain elements of the design that are going to look the same at each of the different widths or font sizes that you're testing using pages, such as the background or footer pieces of the design, you don't have to duplicate these layers on each of the pages. Instead, you can share a layer across pages so that it will show in them all or in whichever layers you choose.

To share a layer, select it in the Layers panel, and then choose Share Layer To Pages from the Layers panel menu. In the dialog box, you will see on the left a list of all the pages the layer is currently not shared with. Choose the pages that you *do* want the layer shared with, and then click Add (**Figure 3.7**). This will move all the selected pages into the right column of the dialog box, indicating that the selected layer will be included in all of these. Click OK to complete the sharing.

FIGURE 3.6 Choose Duplicate Page in the Pages panel menu to create a copy of the selected page with all layers intact.

FIGURE 3.7 Select the pages on the left that you want the selected layer to appear on, and then click the Add button.

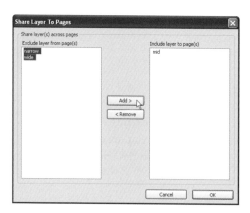

Once you've shared a page, the background of the layer name and all the names of its objects in the Layers panel turn yellow. If you edit the objects on the shared layer from within any of the pages on which it appears, those changes will be reflected on all of the other pages on which that shared layer appears.

THIS IS ALL OPTIONAL!

All this talk of creating multiple versions of the same design element or even the entire page probably sounds like a lot of extra work—and it can be. I'm certainly not suggesting that you must do all this to create comps that will eventually become flexible web pages. It's entirely optional. Most of the time, it's more efficient to create a single version of the page at a single width and simply think about how it will display at different widths or text sizes. Once you've gotten the hang of creating flexible-friendly designs, you will often be able to anticipate problems that might occur at different widths without having to ever duplicate the design at each of those widths.

But sometimes, creating multiple versions with layers or pages can actually save you time in the long run, or at least help you build a page you're happier with in the end. The point of creating multiple versions is to help you catch problems with the design that you can then fix before you've actually gotten your client to approve the design or spent time building it in (X)HTML and CSS—when it's much more difficult and time-consuming to make changes.

The bottom line is this: if you think creating multiple versions of each individual design element or the entire page will be helpful to you, do it. If you think it will just impede you, skip it!

Nondestructive Editing Techniques

In flexible designs, background and content images within your design could be displayed at a larger size on the real page than on the comp. To keep from running into trouble when it comes time to produce the web-ready versions of those images, you need to make sure you don't get rid of more of each image than you absolutely have to. Nondestructive editing techniques allow you to "roll back" to an original or earlier version if you make a mistake or simply need to save a larger version of an image than the one shown within your comp.

MASKING IMAGES

One of the most important ways to nondestructively edit images within your comp is to use *masking*. Masking is the process of selectively concealing certain parts of an image, rather than deleting those parts, to let only a desired portion of the image show. A black-and-white mask shape is placed over the image that you want to hide certain parts of (once the image is masked, you don't see the actual mask shape anymore). Pure white areas of the mask allow the image below to show through completely, pure black areas conceal the image below completely, and gray areas allow some degree of the image to show through at that spot.

Masks are easiest to understand through a visual example. **Figure 3.8** shows an image that hasn't been edited yet. Let's say you intend this image to use a variable cropping technique like that described in Chapter 2 and shown in Figure 2.13. You'd like more or less of the right side of the image to be revealed as the column the image is in changes in size, but you also want to crop out a little of the left side and bottom of the image to never show.

FIGURE 3.8 An unmasked image may have some portions you never want to show, and other portions you want to show only at certain times.

You could simply crop the image on the left, bottom, and right to make it fit within the comp. That would give you a good visual representation of what the image would look like when the page is at one particular size. But what happens when it comes time to export that image to be used in the actual page? You've deleted the extra portion of the image that ought to show when the page is wider than the size shown in the comp. If you've saved the original image, you could go back to that image and repeat your work of cropping out the unwanted portion of the left and bottom, sizing the image down overall, color-correcting it, and so forth. You *could* do all that, but you could also save yourself all this extra work if you had just used a mask to conceal the extra portion of the image, instead of deleting the extra portion.

To create a mask for this image, you'd first perform all the editing work that you definitely want done on the image, such as cropping out the left and bottom portions that you never want shown, color-correcting it, and sizing it down to the correct height. (Still be sure to save an original, untouched version of the image in case you ever want to undo these changes!) Then, create a white rectangle that matches the width of the area reserved for this image within the comp. Place this white rectangle over the image (**Figure 3.9**). Select both the image and the white rectangle, and then choose Modify > Mask > Group As Mask to turn the rectangle into a mask for the image below it. You can now place the resulting image into the comp; it looks the same as it did before, but the now-hidden portion of the image on the right side is still preserved.

FIGURE 3.9 The area obscured by the white rectangle will be shown once the mask is created; the rest of the image outside the white rectangle will be hidden, but not deleted.

When it comes time to export the image for use in the real page, temporarily disable the mask by choosing Modify > Mask > Disable Mask; this reveals the entire image and simultaneously hides the masking shape. You can then save the larger version of the image that is revealed. To bring the mask back, select the image that was previously masked, and choose Modify > Mask > Enable Mask.

This is just one example of a simple mask being put to good use in the comp of a flexible design. Masks are great to use in flexible design comps any time you have an image that you might want to reveal more or less of.

SAVING LARGE ORIGINALS OF IMAGES

Perhaps you don't intend to use variable cropping in your page, but would like the browser to dynamically scale some of the images for you. This would be a good time to make sure you save larger copies of images before placing the small ones in the design comp. As I mentioned in Chapter 2, one of the keys to getting nondistorted, browser-scaled images is to make the images very large and make sure the browser is primarily scaling them down, not up.

During your initial edits to the image to prepare to place it in the comp, such as cropping and color-correcting, perform the step of resizing the image at the very end. Save a copy of the image right before you do the resizing, so all your other edits are preserved. When it comes time to create the web-ready version of the image, you can return to this larger but edited version of the image and export that for use on the web, rather than slicing the smaller version out of the comp or repeating all your editing steps on the completely untouched original version of the image.

Slicing Graphics for Flexible Design

Once your comp is completed and approved, it's time to slice it into the web-ready graphics that you'll export for use in the actual page, either as img elements or CSS backgrounds. Slicing a fixed-width design is usually pretty straightforward, but slicing a flexible design can take a little more prep work, and you'll end up slicing different pieces than you would need if the same design were to be made fixed-width.

Creating Separate Files for Slicing

NOTE: If the images in your design will either be fixed-width or created out of small, tiling background image pieces, you can probably do all your slicing from the original comp, without having to edit it or create any additional files.

Unless you created your comp to match the maximum width of your eventual page, you'll probably need to create at least one extra source graphic to slice from, instead of slicing from the comp itself. This is because if your comp is smaller than the eventual page, you'll probably be forced to make the slices smaller than those the page will need. Extending the width of your comp or creating separate files (or pages, within a Fireworks document) for individual areas of your layout helps you create the much-larger slices that flexible designs often require.

INCREASING THE COMP SIZE

TIP: Use one of the Anchor buttons in the Canvas Size dialog box to choose to have the extra width on one side only, so you won't have to pull out your shapes in both directions.

Don't get worried that you'll have to create a whole new comp to slice from—you most likely will just have to extend the width of your existing comp to the maximum width the page might extend to.

The first step in increasing the size of your comp is to increase the canvas size, of course. In Fireworks, you can do this by clicking the Canvas Size button in the Property inspector or by choosing Modify > Canvas > Canvas Size. Both methods open the Canvas Size dialog box, where you can enter a new width.

INCREASING THE SIZE OF OBJECTS IN THE COMP

Once the canvas width is increased, you'll need to move and resize the elements on the canvas. Solid colored, straight-cornered rectangles are quite easy to resize, of course, but other shapes or rectangles with certain effects can become distorted if you're not careful while resizing.

Rounded rectangles are probably the most notorious culprit of distortion due to resizing. In Fireworks 8, resizing a rounded rectangle would flatten out the curved corners instead of resizing just the straight portion of the rectangle between the curves, as you might hope it would do (**Figure 3.10**). There were workarounds for this problem, but they usually fixed only rounded rectangles, not other shapes that might also suffer from distortion if the entire shape—rather than just a portion of it—were to be stretched out.

FIGURE 3.10 A rounded rectangle before (left) and after (right) scaling in Fireworks 8.

Fireworks CS3 provided a solution to this problem with the addition of a feature called *9-slice scaling*. 9-slice scaling allows you to define what portion of the shape you want to scale and what portions should retain their original sizes. When you select the 9-slice s scaling tool, a grid of dotted blue lines appears over your selected object. Drag the guides so that the center of the grid covers only the portion of the shape that you want scaled. For a rounded rectangle, this portion is the straight area between the curved corners (**Figure 3.12**).

When the guides are set where you want them, use the transform handles on the sides of the object's selection box (the little black squares) as you normally would to scale the shape. If you stretch the shape horizontally, only the center column of the grid is scaled, while the portions to its left and right are left untouched (**Figure 3.13**). If you stretch the shape vertically, only the center row of the grid is scaled, leaving the portions above and below it untouched. If you stretch it diagonally, only the center square in the grid is scaled.

> **NOTE:** In Fireworks CS3, this feature worked only on symbols, but Fireworks CS4 allows you to use 9-slice scaling on any object—even bitmap images. There is now a 9-slice scaling tool in the transformation tool group in the Select subsection of the Tools panel (**Figure 3.11**).

FIGURE 3.11
The 9-slice scaling tool is located in the transformation tool group in the Tools panel.

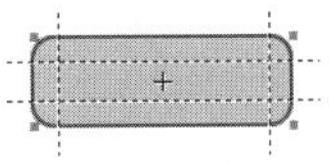

FIGURE 3.12
The center of the 9-slice scaling grid should cover the straight portion only.

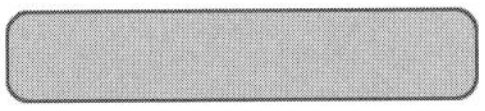

FIGURE 3.13 Dragging the transform handle on the right side of the rounded rectangle scales only the middle portion of the shape, leaving the corners the same size. Compare this scaled rectangle to the scaled and distorted rectangle shown in Figure 3.10.

> **NOTE:** The placement of the 9-slice scaling guides is not "remembered" by the object (unless it's a symbol and you placed the guides in the Symbol or Button editor). After you deselect the object, the guides will be discarded, and you'll need to reset them the next time you select that object.

The 9-slice scaling tool also comes in handy when you want to scale a shape with a gradient fill without scaling the gradient itself. If you use the regular Scale tool, the gradient stretches out to the same proportion as the shape itself (**Figure 3.14**). Sometimes this is what you want, but more often—especially in flexible designs—you just want the gradient to stay put and its ending, solid color to fill in the new extra space in the shape.

To keep the gradient from resizing, use the 9-slice scaling tool to select the portion of the shape that is filled with solid color, beyond the edges of the gradient (**Figure 3.15**). You can then stretch the shape and only that solid-colored area will scale.

■ **TIP:** Avoid scaling a gradient altogether by just creating a new shape with a solid color fill that matches the ending color of the gradient, and positioning this shape right up against the gradient-filled shape. You can group them together to act as one object. It's quick and dirty, but it works.

FIGURE 3.14 When you resize a shape containing a gradient fill, the gradient itself is also stretched out.

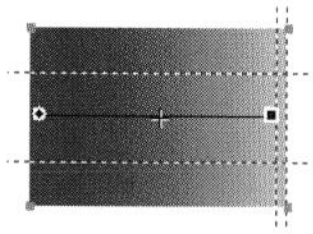

FIGURE 3.15 With the 9-slice scaling guides centered around the solid blue portion of the gradient, only that area will scale.

Increasing the size of a mask without increasing the size of the entire masked image can also be tricky if you're not careful. By default, when you select a masked image and use the Scale tool, the sizes of both the masking shape and the image that is being masked are altered. Again, sometimes this is what you want. But if you are increasing the width of a comp to prepare it for slicing for a flexible web page, you probably want to increase the width of the mask only, revealing more of the image inside it, rather than also increasing the size of that image.

To resize the mask only, you must first select the mask only. To do this, click on the mask shape in the Layers panel. Note that it's not good enough to select the entire mask object within the layer, but only the mask shape *within* that object. When you have only the mask selected, it will get a green outline around it, as opposed to the blue outline that shows up when you select the entire masked object (**Figure 3.16**).

FIGURE 3.16 Select the mask by clicking its icon within the masked object in the Layers panel. You know you have only the mask selected when it has this green outline.

Once the mask is selected independently of the image within it, you can position your pointer over one of the corner points, select it, and drag the mask to the new size that you want (**Figure 3.17**).

This method of resizing the mask works well when you don't need to be too exact, or when you want to change both the width and height at once, but it doesn't offer you as much control as the full Scale tool does. For instance, you may want to change the width only by dragging the transform handle on the side of the shape instead of its corner. To be able to use the Scale tool on the mask without scaling the image inside the mask, you must first unlink the mask by clicking the chain icon between the image and its mask in the Layers panel (**Figure 3.18**). Then, click the mask shape to again bring up the green outlines around the mask. This time, though, you can select the Scale tool from the Tools panel (or choose Modify > Transform > Scale) and it will apply to the mask alone, so you can use the transform handles on any side of the object, as you normally would. When you're finished scaling the mask, click the empty space where the chain icon used to be in the Layers panel, to bring the chain icon back and relink the image to its mask.

FIGURE 3.17 Drag one of the green corner points to resize the mask shape and not the image within it.

USING SEPARATE FILES FOR INDIVIDUAL AREAS OF THE LAYOUT

Depending on your design, it may be more effective to create separate source graphics for individual areas or elements of the layout instead of resizing and rearranging the entire comp. You could save these individual source graphics as separate files entirely or use Fireworks' pages feature to keep everything together but on independent canvases.

For instance, we already discussed the importance of saving original versions of masked or resized images. Instead of increasing the comp size, pasting in the original, larger versions of the images, and then slicing from the larger comp, you could simply export web versions from the individual image files you saved.

Another time when you might want to create individual files to slice from, rather than changing the entire comp size, is when there are only one or two areas on the page that will need very large background image slices. For instance, nearly all of the images shown in the comp in Figure 3.1 can be sliced directly from this comp, even if it doesn't match the maximum size of

FIGURE 3.18 Click the chain icon to unlink the mask shape from its image (top); when you do so, the icon disappears (bottom).

the page. This is because the repeating pattern in the header can be created out of a very small slice that tiles, and the other images in the header plus the content images will be fixed-width. The only images that can't be sliced from the comp are the tabs with a gradient background.

A popular way to create resizable tabs like these is to use a "sliding doors" technique, coined by Douglas Bowman in his article "The Sliding Doors of CSS" on A List Apart (www.alistapart.com/articles/slidingdoors). Each tab is composed of two images: one very thin but tall and the other very large in both dimensions, matching the maximum size you expect any one tab to grow to. You could expand the size of one of the tabs within the comp itself, but it would probably be easiest to just create a whole new file or page for the tab graphic alone. You could then slice it into the two needed pieces without any other objects getting in the way (**Figure 3.19**).

FIGURE 3.19 Creating a separate file or Fireworks page for just the enlarged tab makes slicing it into the two required pieces much easier.

Slicing Pieces of Flexible Boxes

Once you have source graphics ready for slicing, you need to know how to actually create the slices.

Deciding where to slice a graphic is hard to describe in the abstract—it's different for each design. But the general idea is that any shape that needs to expand cannot be made out of one slice, unless that one slice is going to blend in with a background color to form the expanding portion of the shape. For instance, the header of the comp shown in Figure 3.1 could be created out of a single slice if the design were to be built fixed-width. But if you want the eventual page to be liquid or elastic, you'll need to set up your slices differently.

You'll first need to determine what portion of the shape needs to expand to fill in the variable width or height. With this header image, it's the patterned portion in the middle, between the logo on the left and the flowers on the right, that needs to expand in width; the height can stay fixed, since there's no text within it. Other shapes may need to expand on one end, and they may need to do so vertically as well as horizontally to accommodate text-size differences. Take a look at each of the elements on your page and ask yourself which areas you want to see expand and which should stay the same size.

■ **TIP:** Sometimes you won't need any slice for the expandable area at all—if you can create it out of a background color instead of an image, do so.

Next, you need to decide how the expanded area will be "filled in"—do you want a small piece of image to be tiled, or do you want a very large image to have more of itself revealed? Often, the content or design itself will dictate which option you should use, but sometimes you have a choice of either. For instance, to make the middle portion of the tab shown in Figure 3.19 expandable, a very large image—the right slice—is going to have more or less of itself revealed as the tab changes in size. This tab could just as easily have been made expandable by instead creating three slices: one for each of the corners plus a thin slice in the middle that could tile to fill the expanded space. Either option is fine. Using the three images simply means you'll need three separate elements in the (X)HTML to place the images on, instead of just two. Think about the (X)HTML implications when deciding how you want the expanded area to be filled in.

Site-Building Exercise: Preparing the Beechwood Animal Shelter Comp for Construction

In the last chapter, you saw how the comp for the fictional Beechwood Animal Shelter site was transformed from a design that couldn't be made liquid or elastic to a flexible-friendly design. It's now time to make the slices from the revised comp that you'll use in later chapters as images in the pages.

You'll work with the exercise files from this book's companion web site at www.flexiblewebbook.com. Download and unzip the file ch3_exercise.zip. The comp file inside the zip is named comp.png and is an Adobe Fireworks file, compatible with versions CS3 and later. If you don't have one of these versions of Fireworks, you won't be able to work directly with the file. However, the choices we'll make—concerning what should be resized and how to slice—apply to the comp regardless of what program it was made or edited in, so follow along with the steps to learn how to prepare a real-world comp for construction.

■ NOTE: When you open comp.png in Fireworks, you'll probably get a warning about not having all the fonts used in the design. Just choose Maintain Appearance and don't worry about it. You won't be editing any text here.

Navigating Around the Comp

Before you get into creating the slices, you need to familiarize yourself with how the comp PNG file is set up.

The PNG contains designs for two separate web pages—the home page and an inner page—with the layers for each stored separately using Fireworks' pages feature. By default, you should see the page named home. To switch to viewing the page named inner, first open the Pages panel by choosing Window > Pages (it's also under the very descriptively named Pages and Layers and Frames and History panel group). You'll see both pages listed, with a thumbnail view of each. Click on the page named inner to view it. You can also quickly switch to viewing any other page by choosing the page name

FIGURE 3.20 The Slice tool in the Tools panel.

from the drop-down menu listing all the pages at the bottom of the document window.

Some of the layers are shared between the pages because the objects on those layers appear on both the home and inner pages in the same spots; these layers are highlighted in yellow in the Layers panel. Each page has its own Web Layer where the slices that you'll create will be stored.

Both pages have a canvas size of 1000 pixels by 1000 pixels—a size that falls between the minimum and maximum widths of the layout.

Creating the Slices for the Header

The only graphics in the header are the logo, the background color bands, and the gradients on the nav items.

THE LOGO SLICE

1. Select the Slice tool in the Web section of the Tools panel (**Figure 3.20**).

2. Position the cursor of the Slice tool over one corner of the logo, click and drag over the entire logo, and then release. A green, partially transparent rectangle appears over the logo, indicating the bounds of your slice. The size of this slice should be 170 pixels by 85 pixels.

3. Change the name of the slice to logo in the object name field on the left side of the Property inspector (**Figure 3.21**).

4. Open the Optimize panel under the Optimize and Align panel group. Choose GIF from the Export file format drop-down menu (**Figure 3.22**).

■ **NOTE:** You can make the slices for the header in either of the pages. They'll show up only on the Web Layer of the page that you're in when you create them, but that's OK—you don't need them repeated on both pages.

FIGURE 3.21 Name the slice logo in the object name field in the Property inspector.

FIGURE 3.22 Choose GIF from the list of preset export settings in the Optimize panel.

THE BACKGROUND COLOR BANDS SLICE

The background for the header needs to be able to expand in width horizontally to always fill the entire width of the viewport. Because the background is made up of straight, solid bands of color, it can easily be created out of a thin tiling image instead of a very large image that has more or less of itself revealed as the viewport changes in width. Thus, there's no need to increase the width of the header or the canvas as a whole to create the slice.

If none of the three bands of color needed to change in height, you could create a single slice encompassing all three. But this won't allow the brown band, containing the text of the nav bar, to grown in height. Luckily, you can create the three bands without needing three slices: the light blue band can be an image, the brown band can be a background color, and the medium blue band can be a border.

1. Select the Slice tool, and use it to drag out a thin rectangle from the top left corner of the header down to the bottom of the light blue portion of the header background. The height of this slice should be 79 pixels. The width is not as important; it only needs to be one pixel wide, but you might want to make it a little wider so it's easier to see and select later.

2. Change the name of the slice to bg-header in the object name field in the Property inspector.

3. Choose GIF from the Export file format menu in the Optimize panel.

THE NAV BAR GRADIENT SLICES

Each item in the nav bar has a gradient on both its left and right sides. The area in between the two gradients has to vary in width with the width of the text, so there's no way to make the gradient background out of a single slice. You'll need two slices, one for the left side and one for the right. Each can tile vertically to accommodate the height of the text, so you don't need to increase the size of the nav bar before making these slices.

1. Zoom in on the document using the Zoom tool or the Set Magnification drop-down menu at the bottom of the document window until you can see the gradients on the nav bar clearly enough to slice them.

2. Select the Slice tool, and use it to drag out a rectangle from the left border on one nav item gradient to the end of that left gradient (**Figure 3.23**). The height of this slice doesn't matter since it will be tiled vertically; just make sure your slice doesn't contain any of the nav bar text within it.

3. Change the name of the slice to nav-main-left.

4. Choose JPEG as the export format in the Optimize panel.

■ **NOTE:** There's no need to create a third slice for the area between the two gradients, because this can be created with a background color.

FIGURE 3.23 The slice for the left background on the nav bar items needs to include its left border as well as the left gradient.

■ **NOTE:** You've created slices, but you haven't actually exported them yet. You'll do that later, after you've created all the slices for the entire document.

FIGURE 3.24 The four slices for the header area.

5. Set the Quality value in the Optimize panel to 90.

6. With the Slice tool, drag out a rectangle from the right border on one nav item gradient to the end of that right gradient.

7. Change the name of the slice to `nav-main-right`.

8. Choose JPEG and set the Quality to 90 in the Optimize panel.

This completes all the slices needed for the header area of the home and inner pages of the site (**Figure 3.24**).

Creating the Slices for the Home Page

The home page includes a number of images for which we need to create web versions. Some of these are best handled as slices from the main comp; others will be better to export from new, separate Fireworks pages. We'll deal with the slices from the existing page first.

SLICING FROM THE MAIN COMP PAGE

The two ad-type images on the left side of the home page, as well as the image of the dog that goes along with the happy-ending story, will be fixed-width images—no scaling, tiling, variable cropping, or other flexible image effects— so each one will simply be made up of one fixed-width-and-height slice.

1. If you are not already in the home page, select the home page from the Pages panel or the drop-down menu of pages at the bottom of the document window.

2. To quickly make a slice that exactly matches the size of the first feature image (with the text about the adoption fair), right-click (or Control-click on a Mac) on the image, and then choose Insert Rectangular Slice from the contextual menu.

3. Change the name of the slice to `feature-fair`.

4. Choose PNG32 in the Optimize panel.

5. Repeat steps 2–4 with the second feature image, naming it `feature-donate`.

6. Right-click on the photo of the dog next to the happy-ending story, and choose Insert Rectangular Slice.

7. Change the name of the slice to `story`.

8. Choose JPEG and set the Quality to 90 in the Optimize panel.

The four featured pets are going to be scalable images, so they need to be large enough that the browser will usually be scaling them down, not up. This usu-ally means you do not want to slice from the comp, but instead will export the non-resized images from the original source files. In this case, however, these four images actually appear at a larger size than they will on the page at most reasonable text sizes, so it's fine to slice them from the comp.

1. Right-click on the first featured pet photo, and then choose Insert Rectangular Slice.

2. Change the name of the slice to *adopt1*.

3. Choose JPEG and set the Quality to 90 in the Optimize panel.

4. Repeat these three steps with the remaining three featured pet photos, naming the slices *adopt2*, *adopt3*, and *adopt4*.

   The final image on the home page that you'll create from a slice in the main comp page is the gradient background for the featured pets area. This gradient can be tiled horizontally to fill in the variable width, and a background color matching the bottom color of the gradient can be used to fill in any height beyond the height of the gradient. Thus, neither the gradient nor the canvas needs to be resized in order to create the slice.

5. With the Slice tool, drag out a rectangle from the very top of the gradient to the very bottom. The width of the slice doesn't matter; the height should be 411 pixels.

6. Change the name of the slice to `bg-adopt-pets`.

7. Choose JPEG in the Optimize panel, and leave the Quality set at 80.

This completes all the slices for the home page that we can make from the main comp page itself (**Figure 3.25**). The remaining images in the layout will be handled using separate Fireworks pages.

FIGURE 3.25 The eight slices for the content area of the home page.

CREATING SEPARATE PAGES FOR INDIVIDUAL IMAGES

The large photo of the dog that makes up the banner of the home page needs to be able to grow in width and height to reveal more or less of itself as the text laid on top of it changes in size. Because this image is masked, it will be easy to reveal the hidden portions of the photo and export the entire thing as one big image. But because the image *is* so big, it will be best to disable the mask in a separate page, where it won't obscure other elements on the home page and have their slices overlapping it.

1. Select the masked image, and choose Edit > Copy.

2. Open the Pages panel and use the New/Duplicate Page button at the bottom to create a new, blank page. Double-click on it to bring up the Page name field, and enter home banner as the page's name.

3. Click the Canvas Size button in the Property inspector. Enter 977 and 597 for the width and height, respectively. Click OK.

4. Choose Edit > Paste. The masked image will not appear to fill up the entire canvas, since the mask is still enabled, but the blue selection outline around it should line up exactly with the edges of the canvas, and the X and Y values in the Property inspector should both be zero.

5. With the masked image still selected, choose Modify > Mask > Disable Mask. This reveals the entire image, which fills the entire canvas (**Figure 3.26**).

FIGURE 3.26
The home page banner image is no longer partially obscured by its mask.

6. Right-click the image, and choose Insert Rectangular Slice.

7. Change the name of the slice to banner.

8. Choose JPEG in the Optimize panel, and leave the Quality set at 80.

This takes care of the banner image, so the only image left on the home page is the pet tag that says "Adopt Me!" You could slice this from the main comp if you wanted to, but it would involve either resizing the comp's canvas so the entire tag shows—right now it's cut off on the right side—or moving it to another spot where the entire tag can show. You'd also need to turn off the background underneath the tag before exporting it, because it needs to be an alpha-transparent PNG in order to lay over both the white and gradient backgrounds of the home page. It's easier to avoid this hassle by just moving it into its own page and exporting from there.

1. Select the pet tag image, and choose Edit > Copy.

2. In the Pages panel, click the New/Duplicate Page button at the bottom to create a new, blank page. Name it home pet tag.

3. Click the Canvas Size button in the Property inspector. Enter 105 and 116 for the width and height, respectively. Click OK.

4. In the Property inspector, click the Canvas color box, and then click the None button in the Swatches pop-up window.

5. Choose Edit > Paste.

6. Reposition the image so it fits exactly within the bounds of the canvas. This will mean the X value is -25 and the Y value is -17.

7. Right-click the image, and choose Insert Rectangular Slice.

8. Change the name of the slice to adopt-header.

9. Choose PNG32 in the Optimize panel.

Creating the Slices for the Programs Page

The Programs page, mocked up on the inner page in the comp, is a lot less complicated graphically than the home page (**Figure 3.27**). There are only two slices we need to make for it: the banner image and the background on the secondary navigation menu.

FIGURE 3.27 The comp of one of the inner pages, the Programs page.

■ **NOTE:** Even though this banner contains text, the text takes up a very small portion of the banner. It would need to grow to an extremely large size to overflow off the banner, so I feel comfortable leaving the height of this banner fixed.

The banner will need to resize in width, but the solid green color that makes up most of the banner can handle this. Only the image of the dog on the right side of the banner needs to be included in the slice.

1. Select the inner page from the Pages panel or the drop-down menu of pages at the bottom of the document window.

2. With the Slice tool, drag out a rectangle from the top right corner of the banner to the end of the faded left edge of the photo in the banner. The height of the slice should be exactly 129 pixels; the width should be at least 278 pixels. (There's no need to make it wider than this, but if it is a bit wider, there's no harm—it's just a little more of the solid green color in the image.)

3. Change the name of the slice to header-programs.

4. Choose JPEG and set the Quality to 90 in the Optimize panel.

This takes care of the banner—now, on to the sidebar.

In this exercise, we're only going to worry about the background on the navigation menu portion of the sidebar, not the sidebar as a whole. That's because creating the background slice for the sidebar as a whole involves knowing how liquid faux columns work. You'll learn about this technique, and create the source graphic for the sidebar's background, in Chapter 8.

The subtle gradient background of the menu within the sidebar can be tiled vertically to take care of the necessary height expansion. The width expansion can be handled by blending the gradient into a background color that matches the end color of one side of the gradient. Thus, there's no need to resize the sidebar or the canvas before making the slice.

1. With the Slice tool, drag out a rectangle from the left edge of the gradient to the right edge. The height of the slice doesn't matter; the width should be 200 pixels. Make sure that you didn't include any of the text of the links in the bounds of your slice.

2. Change the name of the slice to bg-section-links.

3. Choose JPEG and set the Quality to 90 in the Optimize panel.

This completes all the slices for the Programs page that we can make from the main comp itself (**Figure 3.28**).

FIGURE 3.28 The two slices for the content area of the Programs page; the slices for its header are on the Web Layer for the home page.

Export the Images

Once you have all the slices drawn out, it's time to export them into their web-optimized versions. In each of the subsequent chapters' exercises, I'll provide you with the particular images you need, so you don't actually have to export these slices and save them on your computer. Nevertheless, it's good to practice using Fireworks' export feature so you can easily use it to create slices in your own designs later.

■ **NOTE:** Don't worry about the File name field. Each of the slices will export with the name you've set for it individually.

1. Choose File > Export to open the Export dialog box.

2. Choose a location on your computer to save all the images to.

3. In the Export drop-down menu, choose Images Only instead of HTML and Images.

4. In the Slices drop-down menu, choose Export Slices. (This should be the default value.)

5. Deselect both "Include areas without slices" and "Current page only" at the bottom of the dialog box. Deselecting these options ensures that only the slices you created are exported and that the slices on both the home and inner pages are exported, instead of just whichever page you are currently on.

6. Click Save to export all the slices into the folder you chose.

FIGURE 3.29 Make sure all the settings in your Export dialog box match the ones shown here.

4

Building Liquid Layout Structures

Throughout this chapter, I'll demonstrate a variety of liquid layout methods using simple web page examples. Each one will rely on CSS floats to create multiple columns. The methods differ in how easy the CSS is to remember and apply, how many extra divs or hacks are required, what order the divs need to appear in the (X)HTML, and other relative advantages and disadvantages, so you have the option of picking the one that best fits with your comfort level and your site requirements. At the end of the chapter, we'll apply what we've learned from some of these methods to a hands-on exercise: building a page of our Beechwood Animal Shelter site.

Preparing the Page for CSS Layout

The steps involved in preparing your page for CSS flexible layout are no different than those for CSS fixed-width layouts. Since this isn't an introductory book on CSS, I'm assuming you already know the basic steps of page setup. For a quick review, however, here's what you need to do in between slicing the graphics (as we did in the last chapter) and writing the CSS for layout (as we'll do in this chapter).

Universal Page Setup Steps

■ **NOTE:** You can read up on the XHTML rules at http://xhtml.com/en/xhtml/serving-xhtml-as-html and http://en.wikibooks.org/wiki/XHTML_(XML)#Converting_HTML_to_XHTML. Most of these rules can be complied with even when writing HTML, in order to make conversion to XHTML or XML easier if you decide to go that route in the future.

To set up your (X)HTML pages properly to the point where CSS can be applied to them, do the following:

1. Choose a DOCTYPE.

The latest version of either HTML or XHTML is fine to use for both fixed-width and flexible layouts. Just make sure you choose a DOCTYPE whose requirements you can successfully meet to create valid markup, which will have a much better chance of rendering correctly across browsers. We'll be using HTML 4.01 for the examples in this book, but you can convert any example to XHTML following the simple rules for XHTML syntax that distinguish it from HTML.

WHICH DOCTYPE TO CHOOSE?

My general advice is, if you don't have a reason for using XHTML over HTML, don't use it. Because no version of IE (including IE 8, which is in beta at the time of this writing) supports XHTML, you'll probably just end up serving XHTML as HTML anyway, which doesn't offer you any advantages over HTML, since it *is* HTML at that point. This can be dangerous in that XHTML served as HTML shares HTML's more lax error-handling, and you don't want to get used to that, in case you do decide to start serving it as XHTML in the future. For more about all the considerations that should go into choosing XHTML as your markup language, see "XHTML is not for Beginners" at http://lachy.id.au/log/2005/12/xhtml-beginners.

You can see a list of your most likely DOCTYPE choices—for HTML 4.01 and XHTML 1.0—at http://css-discuss.incutio.com/?page=DocType. A more comprehensive list is available from the W3C at www.w3.org/QA/2002/04/valid-dtd-list.html.

2. Place the content in the page, and apply semantic markup.

   Each piece of content needs to be marked up with the proper (X)HTML element to indicate what it is, such as a paragraph, first-level heading, or block quotation. Don't add any presentational markup, such as font, b, or center elements, as this will all be controlled with CSS. One of the many benefits of semantic markup is that it provides more "hooks" to attach our CSS to, which we will definitely be taking advantage of later, when we style our layouts. For more on semantic markup, read "Integrated Web Design: The Meaning of Semantics (Take I)" by Molly Holzschlag (www.peachpit.com/articles/article.aspx?p=369225).

3. Group the content with divs.

   Although divs are semantic-neutral elements, they're fine to add to your page—in moderation. Use the minimum number needed to group large chunks of content into organizational or thematic groups, such as navigation, main content, and footer. Ideally, you would never have to add any extra divs to accomplish visual effects, and your divs could be put in the most logical order in the source without regard for where they will appear visually on the page, but this is rarely how it works out in reality. Browser and CSS limitations make it necessary to adjust divs somewhat to accommodate visual formatting, so we'll go over the proper div structure for each of the layouts we'll be building as we come to them.

4. Attach one or more style sheets.

   Use the link element or @import directive in the head of the page to attach your style sheets. You may want to simply embed the styles in the individual page during initial development, by placing them in the style element in the head. You can then move the styles to an external style sheet once you're satisfied with them and ready to apply them to multiple pages, before you make your pages live. Most of this book's example files are set up with embedded styles so that you have everything in a single file to work with and refer to.

Once you've completed these initial steps, you're ready to start filling in those style sheets to create your layout.

Preparing the Pages for This Chapter's Examples

In addition to the universal page setup steps that you'd follow for every page, there are a few things you can expect to see in all of the examples in this chapter.

First, all of the examples shown in this chapter will use the following basic div structure (so get familiar with it!):

```
<div id="header"></div>
<div id="content-main"></div>
<div id="sidebar"></div>
<div id="footer"></div>
```

Second, for each method we go over, we'll start out with two-column structures to demonstrate the basic techniques, and then move on to adding more columns.

NAMING CONVENTIONS

Feel free to use whatever naming convention you like for your id values. I'm partial to using dashes to separate words, so that's what you'll see throughout this book, but it's no more "correct" than using underscores or camelCase or just smooshing all the words together. Just be consistent with whatever you choose.

However, in terms of the actual words that you choose, I do have some universal advice. It really is best to avoid vague and presentational names like "sidebar" for your divs whenever you can help it. Use id values that are more descriptive of the content within the div, such as "secondary-nav" or "featuredProducts" or "latest_news." But since this chapter contains simple examples in which we don't know or care what the content within the sidebar will be, we'll stick with a generic name of "sidebar" here, which you can later replace with an id more appropriate to your page.

If you're interested in using the same names as other CSS developers use, see Andy Clarke's suggestions in his article "What's in a name (pt2)" at www.stuffandnonsense.co.uk/archives/whats_in_a_name_pt2.html. Andy advocates for names that are not only meaningful but standardized across sites, which can help you reap the following benefits:

- You'll be able to set up divs on new pages more quickly and reuse snippets of CSS for them from previous sites.

- You'll have an easier time remembering what div does what while maintaining your sites.

- Designers who come after you will be able to find their way around more quickly.

- Site users will be able to create their own style sheets that can restyle multiple sites in ways that make those sites easier for them to read and use.

Third, I've applied some basic CSS for visual formatting to the page; mostly background colors on the `divs` so that you can see where each one lies in the example pages you'll see throughout the book.

```
body {
    margin: 0;
    padding: 0;
    font-family: "Lucida Sans Unicode", "Lucida Grande",
sans-serif;
}
div {
    padding: 1px 0;
}
#header {
    background: #DDDDDD;
}
#sidebar {
    background: #FFA480;
}
#content-main {
    background: #F0EE90;
}
#footer {
    background: #DDDDDD;
}
```

With these `divs` in place and no styling apart from changing the font and background colors, we already have a liquid layout (**Figure 4.1**). Divs, and all other block elements, automatically expand to fill all available horizontal space in their parent elements. That means, for instance, that our sidebar `div` is always as wide as the viewport, because it expands to fill the full width of the body element (its parent in this case), which is equal to the viewport size.

■ **TIP:** When you want to see where `divs` or other block elements lie, background colors can be much more effective than borders. Borders affect both the box model and margin collapsing; therefore, they influence how elements are spaced out from each other and can change where `divs` lie once they are removed. Background colors don't interfere in the layout this way, so they're a safer option for developing and debugging CSS.

■ **NOTE:** Each of the completed example files is available for download from this book's companion web site at www.flexiblewebbook. com. Download the file ch4_examples.zip to get the complete set. I'll let you know which file goes with which technique as we go along.

FIGURE 4.1 Each div by default expands to fill the width of its parent and stacks on top of the next to form a single-column liquid layout, even without applying any layout-related CSS.

WHAT'S THE POINT OF ONE PIXEL OF PADDING?

You may notice that the formatting CSS shown on the previous page contains a rule setting one pixel of top and bottom padding on every div. That padding is there to stop margin collapsing. Margin collapsing is when two vertical margins that touch each other combine together into whichever margin value is larger. This happens all the time without you knowing it: paragraphs have both top and bottom margins on them by default, but instead of the two margins between successive paragraphs stacking on top of each to leave a doubly large margin, the two touching margins collapse together into one.

The divs in our example pages each contain paragraphs whose default top margins touch the margins of their containing divs. Because those containing divs have margins of zero by default, the paragraph margins are larger and therefore "win," collapsing together with the div margins and leaving a gap on top of every div. A quick and easy way to stop this gap from appearing is to put something in between the edge of the div and the edge of the paragraph to stop the margins from touching. Padding and border can both be used, but since one pixel of padding is less noticeable than a border, that's the solution I've gone with here.

If this were a real page, you'd probably want to remove the top margins from the paragraphs to keep them from collapsing outside the div. But for the purposes of these simple examples, the padding trick works just fine.

You can read more about how margin collapsing works in the article "Uncollapsing Margins" by Eric Meyer (http://complexspiral.com/publications/uncollapsing-margins).

Creating Liquid Columns Using Floats

At this point, since our divs are already liquid, all we need to do is stop the default top-to-bottom stacking on some of the divs and create some columns instead. There are a few ways to do so.

ABSOLUTE POSITIONING VERSUS FLOATING

You'll notice that none of the column-creating methods discussed in this chapter use absolute positioning—only floats. This is intentional. While absolute positioning can be used to create columns, most professional CSS developers don't find it a robust way to create an entire layout. It's much too rigid—even for fixed-width designs—because it pins a piece of content to an exact spot on the page. It can't adjust to the content around it, and, unless you have a very simple layout, you almost always end up with content overlapping and other nasty surprises. Absolute positioning is best reserved for positioning small design elements, such as a search bar in a header, not for creating the overall structure of layouts.

Creating Columns with Floats and Matching Side Margins

A quick and easy way to create columns out of divs is to float the div or divs that you want to be on the edges of the page either to the right or the left, and then give the remaining div a matching margin facing the float to make room for it. In order for this to work, the floated div has to come before the non-floated div in the (X)HTML source for the page. This is because floating does not move content up—only over to either side. The content that *follows* the float is what moves up to sit beside the float.

With our basic div structure, all we need to do to see this in action is apply the following CSS:

```
#content-main {
    float: right;
    width: 75%;
    background: #FFFFDD;
}
```

This restricts the width of the main content div so it no longer spans the entire width of the window, leaving room for the sidebar div to move up to the main content div's left side (**Figure 4.2**).

■ **NOTE:** If you need a refresher course on float theory, see the extensive list of tips and links to articles and tutorials on floats at the Smashing Magazine article "CSS Float Theory: Things You Should Know" (www.smashingmagazine. com/2007/05/01/ css-float-theory-things-you-should-know). Another excellent source is www. communitymx.com/ abstract.cfm?cid=AC008, although it is not a free article.

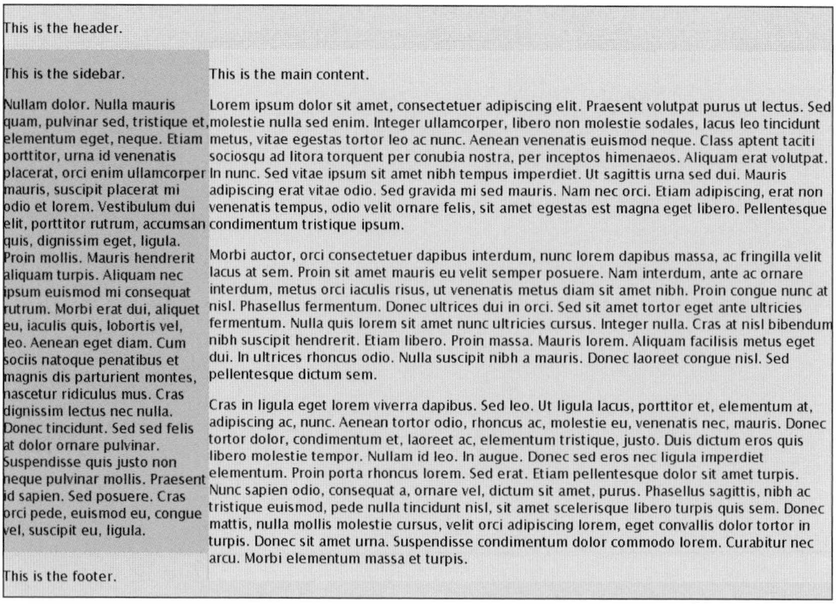

FIGURE 4.2 The main
content div now takes up
the rightmost 75 percent
of the viewport, with the
sidebar div taking up the
remaining space to its left.

This is the header.

This is the sidebar.

This is the main content.

Nullam dolor. Nulla mauris quam, pulvinar sed, tristique et, elementum eget, neque. Etiam porttitor, urna id venenatis placerat, orci enim ullamcorper mauris, suscipit placerat mi odio et lorem. Vestibulum dui elit, porttitor rutrum, accumsan quis, dignissim eget, ligula. Proin mollis. Mauris hendrerit aliquam turpis. Aliquam nec ipsum euismod mi consequat rutrum. Morbi erat dui, aliquet eu, iaculis quis, lobortis vel, leo. Aenean eget diam. Cum sociis natoque penatibus et magnis dis parturient montes, nascetur ridiculus mus. Cras dignissim lectus nec nulla. Donec tincidunt. Sed sed felis at dolor ornare pulvinar. Suspendisse quis justo non neque pulvinar mollis. Praesent id sapien. Sed posuere. Cras orci pede, euismod eu, congue vel, suscipit eu, ligula.

Lorem ipsum dolor sit amet, consectetuer adipiscing elit. Praesent volutpat purus ut lectus. Sed metus, vitae egestas tortor leo ac nunc. Aenean venenatis euismod neque. Class aptent taciti sociosqu ad litora torquent per conubia nostra, per inceptos himenaeos. Aliquam erat volutpat. In nunc. Sed vitae ipsum sit amet nibh tempus imperdiet. Ut sagittis urna sed dui. Mauris adipiscing erat vitae odio. Sed gravida mi sed mauris. Nam nec orci. Etiam adipiscing, erat non venenatis tempus, odio velit ornare felis, sit amet egestas est magna eget libero. Pellentesque condimentum tristique ipsum.

Morbi auctor, orci consectetuer dapibus interdum, nunc lorem dapibus massa, ac fringilla velit lacus at sem. Proin sit amet mauris eu velit semper posuere. Nam interdum, ante ac ornare interdum, metus orci iaculis risus, ut venenatis metus dictum sit amet nibh. Proin congue nunc at nisl. Phasellus fermentum. Donec ultrices dui in orci. Sed sit amet tortor eget ante ultricies fermentum. Nulla quis lorem sit amet nunc ultricies cursus. Integer nulla. Cras at nisl bibendum nibh suscipit hendrerit. Etiam libero. Proin massa. Mauris lorem. Aliquam facilisis metus eget dui. In ultrices rhoncus odio. Nulla suscipit nibh a mauris. Donec laoreet congue nisl. Sed pellentesque dictum sem.

Cras in ligula eget lorem viverra dapibus. Sed leo. Ut ligula lacus, porttitor et, elementum at, adipiscing ac, nunc. Aenean tortor odio, rhoncus ac, molestie eu, venenatis nec, mauris. Donec tortor dolor, condimentum et, laoreet ac, elementum tristique, justo. Duis dictum eros quis libero molestie tempor. Nullam id leo. In augue. Donec sed eros nec ligula imperdiet elementum. Proin porta rhoncus lorem. Sed erat. Etiam pellentesque dolor sit amet turpis. Nunc sapien odio, consequat a, ornare vel, dictum sit amet, purus. Phasellus sagittis, nibh ac tristique euismod, pede nulla tincidunt nisl, sit amet scelerisque libero turpis quis sem. Donec mattis, nulla mollis molestie cursus, velit orci adipiscing lorem, eget convallis dolor tortor in turpis. Donec sit amet urna. Suspendisse condimentum dolor commodo lorem. Curabitur nec arcu. Morbi elementum massa et turpis.

This is the footer.

If, instead, you want the sidebar to be on the right side with the main content on the left, simply change the float: right to float: left. There's no need to change the order of the divs in the source. The main content div will simply move to the left instead of the right, and the sidebar will just move up to its right to take over the remaining space.

The 75-percent width means that the main content div will always be 75 percent as wide as the width of its parent element—in this case, the body element. Since in this example the body doesn't have any width assigned and just matches the viewport width, the main content div bases its width off the viewport as well. As you change the window size, the width of the main content div changes in proportion. The sidebar just takes whatever is left—in this case, 25 percent.

■ **NOTE:** Later in the
chapter, we'll look at
what happens when the
parent element does
have a width assigned.

We now have two divs sitting side by side, but some funky things happen at the bottom of the page. If the main content div is longer than the sidebar, it overlaps the footer (as we saw in Figure 4.2). If the sidebar is longer, it wraps underneath the main content div (**Figure 4.3**).

FIGURE 4.3 If the sidebar is longer than the main content div, it wraps underneath.

In both cases, this is correct behavior based on the mechanics of floating. This book assumes you already know basic float theory, so we won't get into the nitty-gritty of what's going on with these divs, but the basic reason both of these oddities are happening is because floats only displace inline content, like text, not block-level elements, like the entire footer or sidebar divs. Floats are removed from the flow of the page, so other blocks act like they don't exist and can get covered up by them.

Although both of these display issues are correct, they're usually not the look we want. Luckily, they're quite easy to change by adding just a bit more CSS.

To fix the footer overlap, simply add the clear property to the footer to force it to sit below any previous floats (**Figure 4.4**):

```
#footer {
    clear: both;
    background: #DDDDDD;
}
```

■ TIP: Although we could have used clear: right instead of clear: both since the float we need to clear is on the right side, using a value of both makes our layout more "accepting" of changes in the CSS that might come later.

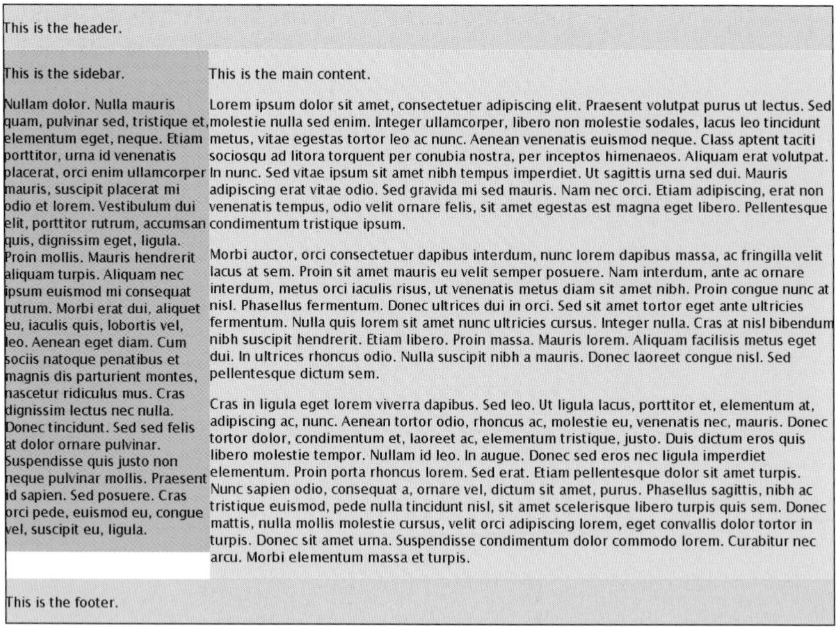

FIGURE 4.4 The `clear` property on the footer moves it fully below the floated main content `div`.

This is the header.

This is the sidebar.

Nullam dolor. Nulla mauris quam, pulvinar sed, tristique et, elementum eget, neque. Etiam porttitor, urna id venenatis placerat, orci enim ullamcorper mauris, suscipit placerat mi odio et lorem. Vestibulum dui elit, porttitor rutrum, accumsan quis, dignissim eget, ligula. Proin mollis. Mauris hendrerit aliquam turpis. Aliquam nec ipsum euismod mi consequat rutrum. Morbi erat dui, aliquet eu, iaculis quis, lobortis vel, leo. Aenean eget diam. Cum sociis natoque penatibus et magnis dis parturient montes, nascetur ridiculus mus. Cras dignissim lectus nec nulla. Donec tincidunt. Sed sed felis at dolor ornare pulvinar. Suspendisse quis justo non neque pulvinar mollis. Praesent id sapien. Sed posuere. Cras orci pede, euismod eu, congue vel, suscipit eu, ligula.

This is the main content.

Lorem ipsum dolor sit amet, consectetuer adipiscing elit. Praesent volutpat purus ut lectus. Sed molestie nulla sed enim. Integer ullamcorper, libero non molestie sodales, lacus leo tincidunt metus, vitae egestas tortor leo ac nunc. Aenean venenatis euismod neque. Class aptent taciti sociosqu ad litora torquent per conubia nostra, per inceptos himenaeos. Aliquam erat volutpat. In nunc. Sed vitae ipsum sit amet nibh tempus imperdiet. Ut sagittis urna sed dui. Mauris adipiscing erat vitae odio. Sed gravida mi sed mauris. Nam nec orci. Etiam adipiscing, erat non venenatis tempus, odio velit ornare felis, sit amet egestas est magna eget libero. Pellentesque condimentum tristique ipsum.

Morbi auctor, orci consectetuer dapibus interdum, nunc lorem dapibus massa, ac fringilla velit lacus at sem. Proin sit amet mauris eu velit semper posuere. Nam interdum, ante ac ornare interdum, metus orci iaculis risus, ut venenatis metus diam sit amet nibh. Proin congue nunc at nisl. Phasellus fermentum. Donec ultrices dui in orci. Sed sit amet tortor eget ante ultricies fermentum. Nulla quis lorem sit amet nunc ultricies cursus. Integer nulla. Cras at nisl bibendum nibh suscipit hendrerit. Etiam libero. Proin massa. Mauris lorem. Aliquam facilisis metus eget dui. In ultrices rhoncus odio. Nulla suscipit nibh a mauris. Donec laoreet congue nisl. Sed pellentesque dictum sem.

Cras in ligula eget lorem viverra dapibus. Sed leo. Ut ligula lacus, porttitor et, elementum at, adipiscing ac, nunc. Aenean tortor odio, rhoncus ac, molestie eu, venenatis nec, mauris. Donec tortor dolor, condimentum et, laoreet ac, elementum tristique, justo. Duis dictum eros quis libero molestie tempor. Nullam id leo. In augue. Donec sed eros nec ligula imperdiet elementum. Proin porta rhoncus lorem. Sed erat. Etiam pellentesque dolor sit amet turpis. Nunc sapien odio, consequat a, ornare vel, dictum sit amet, purus. Phasellus sagittis, nibh ac tristique euismod, pede nulla tincidunt nisl, sit amet scelerisque libero turpis quis sem. Donec mattis, nulla mollis molestie cursus, velit orci adipiscing lorem, eget convallis dolor tortor in turpis. Donec sit amet urna. Suspendisse condimentum dolor commodo lorem. Curabitur nec arcu. Morbi elementum massa et turpis.

This is the footer.

FLOATING THE SIDEBAR IN HYBRID LAYOUTS

You can float the sidebar instead of the main content `div`, but you'd have to put the sidebar first in the (X)HTML source, so there's not much point to doing so—unless you're creating a hybrid layout. If you want the sidebar to be a fixed number of pixels or ems wide, and you want the main content `div` to just take up the remaining space, the only way you can do this is to leave a width off the main content `div` entirely. There's no way to know the value of 100 percent minus, say, 200 pixels. Without knowing this value, you have to leave a width off the main content `div`. And without a width, you can't float the main content `div` and have to use margins to move it out of the way of the sidebar, which must be floating first in the source.

It actually is possible to create a hybrid layout where the main content comes first, using one of the negative margin techniques described later in this chapter. However, it's a much more complicated layout method and not suitable for everyone. You may want to keep this simple sidebar-only floating method in your pocket for everyday use.

We'll go over techniques for creating hybrid layouts in Chapter 6.

To stop the wrapping of the sidebar under the floated main content `div` and create a truly columnar look, add a margin to the side of the sidebar facing the float that is equal to or greater than the size of the float. In our case, that means we need a margin on the right that's at least 75 percent (**Figure 4.5**):

```
#sidebar {
    margin-right: 75%;
    background: #FFA480;
}
```

■ **NOTE:** The page showing this completed technique is liquid_margins_twocol.html in the ch4_examples.zip file.

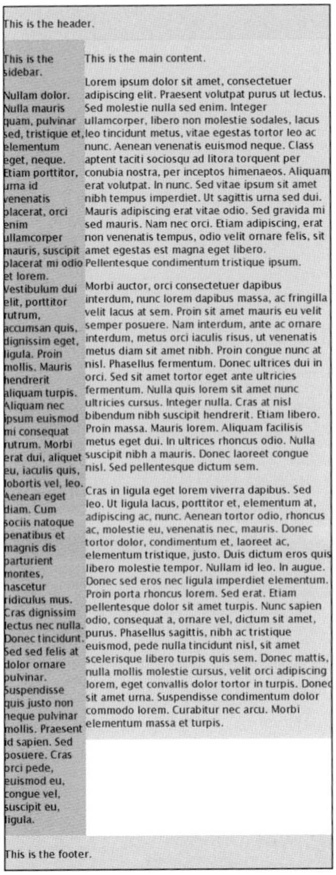

FIGURE 4.5 The right margin on the sidebar moves it out from underneath the floated main content `div` to create two distinct, straight columns.

If you want a gap between the columns, you can increase the margin. For instance, a margin of 80 percent would create an implicit gap of 5 percent between the columns as well as decrease the implicit width of the sidebar to 20 percent (**Figure 4.6**):

```
#sidebar {
    margin-right: 80%;
    background: #E0D482;
}
```

■ **NOTE:** Don't worry about the lack of spacing inside the columns right now—we're just focusing on getting the columns in their proper places, not making them or their text look pretty. We'll cover these typographical niceties in Chapter 7.

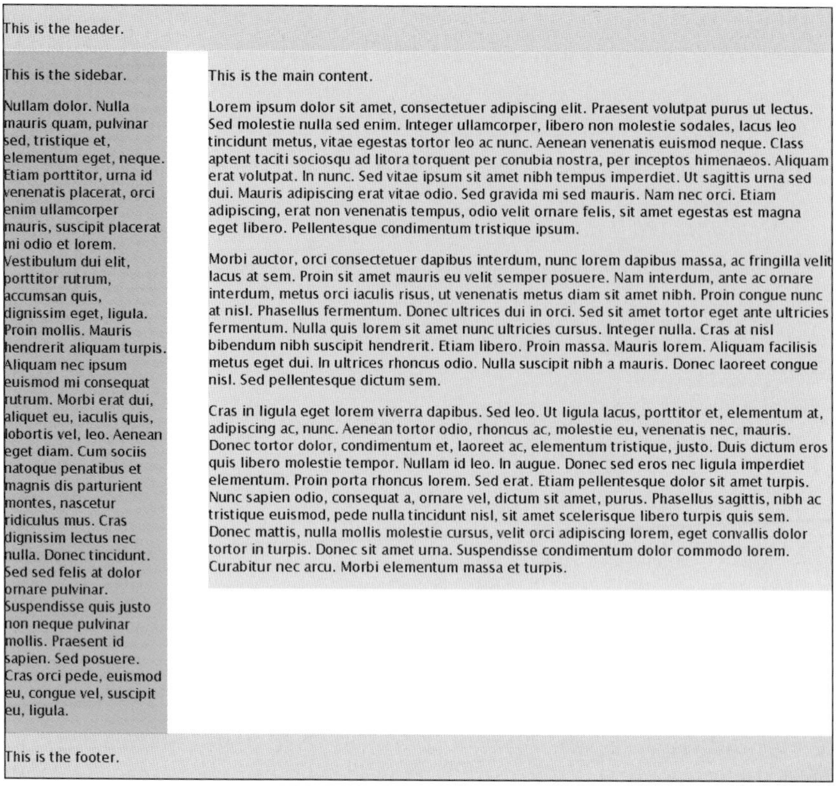

FIGURE 4.6 A margin value that exceeds the width of the float creates a gap between the columns.

ADDING A THIRD COLUMN

You can use this same floats-and-matching-side-margins technique for creating three-column layouts, with a sidebar on either side of the main content div, but you'll need to make one of the following two compromises to the purity of your (X)HTML:

* Compromise the semantic purity by adding a wrapper div around the main content and secondary content (third column) divs.

    The div structure for this option would look like this:

    ```
    <div id="header"></div>
    <div id="content-wrapper">
      <div id="content-main"></div>
      <div id="content-secondary"></div>
    </div>
    <div id="sidebar"></div>
    <div id="footer"></div>
    ```

RETHINKING THE TWO FLANKING SIDEBARS

If you need to have three columns, consider placing both of the sidebars on the same side instead of one on each side of the main content column, as you see most commonly done. Andy Rutledge argues against the usability shortcomings of the typical three-column layout in "Killing Some Bad Layout Conventions" at www.andyrutledge.com/bad-layout-conventions.php. Among the shortcomings that he lists are the tendency to overload the page with too much ancillary information as well as force the site visitors to learn where to look on the page for a particular sort of ancillary information, instead of grouping it all together in one place on the page.

I'll add poor source order to his arguments against the typical three-column layout. If you can put both sidebars on the same side, you should be able to keep the ideal source order of main content first, secondary content second—without any need for an extra wrapper div.

* Compromise the ideal source order by placing both of the sidebar divs before the main content div in the source.

  The div structure for this option would look like this:

  ```
  <div id="header"></div>
  <div id="sidebar"></div>
  <div id="content-secondary"></div>
  <div id="content-main"></div>
  <div id="footer"></div>
  ```

I see the first option—the extra wrapper div—as less of a compromise. Although the extra div adds bulk to the (X)HTML for purely presentational purposes, it's a very small addition, and in reality few pages get away with absolutely no presentational divs. That one extra div is not going to hurt anyone; keeping the main content first in the source, on the other hand, can have definite benefits.

Whenever possible, try to order the content in the (X)HTML source of the page in the most logical sequence. Pretend that you were reading the page out loud—what pieces of content would you read first? In general, you want to put your main content as close to the top of the page as possible. This is an immense benefit to users of screen readers, text browsers, and many hand-held devices, as they will get to the most important content more quickly, without having to wade through repetitive navigation menus and sidebars on every page. It can also help you and your client, since content that comes earlier in the source is often weighted more heavily by search engines, and your main content is most likely to contain the keywords for which you're optimizing each page.

Although good source order is important, it often comes at a cost of more complex CSS, and, as you can see in this case, can require extra divs. Let's go over the simpler method first, which doesn't involve the extra wrapper div but compromises the ideal source order.

Without the Extra Wrapper Div Once again, without the extra wrapper div you'll need to put both sidebars before the main content in the (X)HTML:

```
<div id="header"></div>
<div id="sidebar"></div>
<div id="content-secondary"></div>
<div id="content-main"></div>
<div id="footer"></div>
```

You'll then apply float: left to one sidebar and float: right to the other, along with their percentage widths:

```
#sidebar {
    float: left;
    width: 25%;
    background: #FFA480;
}
#content-secondary {
    float: right;
    width: 25%;
    background: #9BF598;
}
```

■ **NOTE:** It doesn't matter which sidebar div comes first in the source, nor whether the left float comes before the right float or vice versa.

Next, get rid of the float and width we used earlier on the main content div. Instead, apply left and right margins to the div that match or exceed the widths of the sidebars (**Figure 4.7**):

```
#content-main {
    margin: 0 25%;
    background: #F0EE90;
}
```

This is the header.

This is the sidebar.

Nullam dolor. Nulla mauris quam, pulvinar sed, tristique et, elementum eget, neque. Etiam porttitor, urna id venenatis placerat, orci enim ullamcorper mauris, suscipit placerat mi odio et lorem. Vestibulum dui elit, porttitor rutrum, accumsan quis, dignissim eget, ligula. Proin mollis. Mauris hendrerit aliquam nec ipsum euismod mi consequat rutrum. Morbi erat dui, aliquet eu, iaculis quis, lobortis vel, leo. Aenean eget diam. Cum sociis natoque penatibus et magnis dis parturient montes, nascetur ridiculus mus. Cras dignissim lectus nec nulla. Donec tincidunt. Sed sed felis at dolor ornare pulvinar. Suspendisse quis justo non neque pulvinar mollis. Praesent id sapien. Sed posuere. Cras orci pede, euismod eu, congue vel, suscipit eu, ligula.

This is the main content.

Lorem ipsum dolor sit amet, consectetuer adipiscing elit. Praesent volutpat purus ut lectus. Sed molestie nulla sed enim. Integer ullamcorper, libero non molestie sodales, lacus leo tincidunt metus, vitae egestas tortor leo ac nunc. Aenean venenatis euismod neque. Class aptent taciti sociosqu ad litora torquent per conubia nostra, per inceptos himenaeos. Aliquam erat volutpat. In nunc. Sed vitae ipsum sit amet nibh tempus imperdiet. Ut sagittis urna sed dui. Mauris adipiscing erat vitae odio. Sed gravida mi sed mauris. Nam nec orci. Etiam adipiscing, erat non venenatis tempus, odio velit ornare felis, sit amet egestas est magna eget libero. Pellentesque condimentum tristique ipsum.

Morbi auctor, orci consectetuer dapibus interdum, nunc lorem dapibus massa, ac fringilla velit lacus at sem. Proin sit amet mauris eu velit semper posuere. Nam interdum, ante ac ornare interdum, metus orci iaculis risus, ut venenatis metus diam sit amet nibh. Proin congue nunc at nisl. Phasellus fermentum. Donec iaculis dui in orci. Sed sit amet tortor eget ante ultricies fermentum. Nulla quis lorem sit amet nunc ultricies cursus. Integer nulla. Cras at nisl bibendum nibh suscipit hendrerit. Etiam libero. Proin massa. Mauris lorem. Aliquam facilisis metus eget dui. In ultrices rhoncus odio. Nulla suscipit nibh a mauris. Donec laoreet congue nisl. Sed pellentesque dictum sem.

Cras in ligula eget lorem viverra dapibus. Sed leo. Ut ligula lacus, porttitor et, elementum at, adipiscing ac, nunc. Aenean tortor odio, rhoncus ac, molestie eu, venenatis nec, mauris. Donec tortor dolor, condimentum et, laoreet ac, elementum tristique, justo. Duis dictum eros quis libero molestie tempor. Nullam id leo. In augue. Donec sed eros nec ligula imperdiet elementum. Proin porta rhoncus lorem. Sed erat. Etiam pellentesque dolor sit amet turpis. Nunc sapien odio, consequat a, ornare vel, dictum sit amet, purus. Phasellus sagittis, nibh ac tristique euismod, pede nulla tincidunt nisl, sit amet scelerisque libero turpis quis sem. Donec mattis, nulla mollis molestie cursus, velit orci adipiscing lorem, eget convallis dolor tortor in turpis. Donec sit amet urna. Suspendisse condimentum dolor commodo lorem. Curabitur nec arcu. Morbi elementum massa et turpis.

This is the secondary content.

Nullam dolor. Nulla mauris quam, pulvinar sed, tristique et, elementum eget, neque. Etiam porttitor, urna id venenatis placerat, orci enim ullamcorper mauris, suscipit placerat mi odio et lorem. Vestibulum dui elit, porttitor rutrum, accumsan quis, dignissim eget, ligula. Proin mollis. Mauris hendrerit aliquam turpis. Aliquam nec ipsum euismod mi consequat rutrum. Morbi erat dui, aliquet eu, iaculis quis, lobortis vel, leo. Aenean eget diam. Cum sociis natoque penatibus et magnis dis parturient montes, nascetur ridiculus mus. Cras dignissim lectus nec nulla. Donec tincidunt. Sed sed felis at dolor ornare pulvinar. Suspendisse quis justo non neque pulvinar mollis. Praesent id sapien. Sed posuere. Cras orci pede, euismod eu, congue vel, suscipit eu, ligula. Nulla condimentum, mi in elementum lacinia, tellus nunc porttitor turpis, nec pulvinar leo metus sit amet arcu.

This is the footer.

FIGURE 4.7 With each of the sidebars floated to either side, the main content `div` simply takes up the remaining space in the middle.

You'll want to keep the same CSS used earlier on the footer to make sure it doesn't get overlapped by either of the sidebars above. The `clear: both` instead of `clear: right` declaration on the footer has come in handy, because there is now a left float as well as a right float above the footer. Without that `clear: both`, or if it was only a `clear: right`, the left-floated sidebar could overlap the footer.

Now that we have a float on the left side of the page, the three-pixel text jog becomes visible. This is a bug present in IE 6 and earlier that adds three pixels of extra space between a float and the non-floated adjacent content—sometimes outside both columns and sometimes as a gap within the non-floated column on the side next to the floated column. It was actually also triggered in the two-column example, but was simply not noticeable because it happened along the inside right edge of the non-floated sidebar, where the ragged ends of the lines of text hid it. If we had floated the main content `div` to the left instead, the gap would have appeared inside the

■ **NOTE:** The page showing this completed technique is liquid_ margins_threecol.html in the ch4_examples.zip file.

sidebar's left side, promptly ending after the bottom of the main content div, creating a noticeable "text jog" (**Figure 4.8**). In this three-column version, you can see the text jog within the non-floated main content div. You may choose to ignore this, but it is also possible to add hacks to your page to get rid of it if you like (see the sidebar at right).

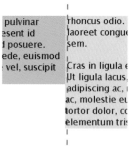

FIGURE 4.8 The text in the main content div is indented by three pixels along the full length of the sidebar div. As soon as the sidebar div ends, note how the text "jogs" back over three pixels to the left.

With the Extra Wrapper Div Adding a third column takes a little more work when you want the main content div to come first in the source. You can't just add another div below the main content and float it—at least, not if you intend for the sidebars to flank either side of the main content column, instead of both sitting together on the main side. This is because when the main content div comes first and is floated, the browser will move it first as far to the right or the left as possible. Then the browser will move the next div, and then the next. But the main content div is already up against one of the sides of the viewport, with no space left over for the second sidebar to sit in.

The solution is to think of creating a three-column layout as creating two two-column layouts, one nested inside of the other.

Once again, here's the div structure you'll use:

```
<div id="header"></div>
<div id="content-wrapper">
   <div id="content-main"></div>
   <div id="content-secondary"></div>
</div>
<div id="sidebar"></div>
<div id="footer"></div>
```

HACKING AWAY THE THREE-PIXEL TEXT JOG

Although the three-pixel text jog is just a small cosmetic problem that will only be seen in a declining browser, you may want to add a hack to your page to get rid of it. Here's what you do: assign side margins to the floats that are each three pixels smaller than you want the gap between the divs to be, set hasLayout (a made-up Microsoft DHTML property that cannot be turned on or off directly) on the non-float, and remove the side margins on the non-float. Here's what those styles look like with our example:

```
<!--[if lte IE 6]>
<style>
#sidebar {
margin-right: -3px;
}
#content-secondary {
margin-left: -3px;
}
#content-main {
zoom: 1;
margin: 0;
}
</style>
<![endif]-->
```

Since we want the gap between the sidebars and the main content div to be zero, right and left margin values that are three pixels smaller than this, -3px, are used on each of the floated sidebar divs. The zoom: 1 on the content-main div is one hasLayout trigger that can be used. hasLayout is a made-up Microsoft DHTML property, present in IE 7 and earlier, that affects the layout of blocks in relation to each other and often determines whether certain IE bugs show up. It is either "on" or "off," but it can't be set to either of these values directly. Instead, you use other CSS properties, such as width, height, and zoom, to trigger hasLayout. For more information on hasLayout, see the comprehensive article "On Having Layout" by Ingo Chao (www.satzansatz.de/cssd/onhavinglayout.html).

These styles need to be hidden from all browsers except IE 6 and earlier. Here, the <!--[if lte IE 6]> line starts a conditional comment to do this. *Conditional comments* are special types of comments that only IE can read. Because they are truly just HTML comments, all other user agents ignore their contents, so they never see these hacks. You can customize the syntax to target all versions of IE or only particular ones; see http://msdn.microsoft.com/en-us/library/ms537512.aspx for examples. This conditional comment block needs to be placed below the existing closing style tag in the head of the page in order to override those earlier styles.

The first two-column layout is made up of the content-wrapper and sidebar divs, using the exact same two-column layout method we discussed at the start of the chapter:

```
#content-wrapper {
    float: right;
    width: 75%;
    background: #98F5E8;
}
#sidebar {
    margin-right: 75%;
    background: #FFA480;
}
```

Next, create another two-column layout within the content-wrapper div itself:

```
#content-main {
    float: left;
    width: 75%;
    background: #F0EE90;
}
#content-secondary {
    margin-left: 75%;
    background: #9BF598;
}
```

You may notice in **Figure 4.9** that the sidebar divs don't match in width, even though both should have explicit widths of 25 percent. This is because the 25 percent is calculated based on the parent element, and each sidebar has a different parent. The sidebar div's parent is the body element, so it is going to be 25 percent as wide as the viewport. The content-secondary div, on the other hand, is nested within the content-wrapper div, which is only 75 percent as wide as the viewport. This means the content-secondary div is 25 percent of 75 percent, or roughly 19 percent of the viewport width.

If your design depends on the two sidebars having identical widths, despite their differing points of reference for calculating those widths, you'll need to resort to some algebra. Here's the formula for figuring it out:

width of column you want to match ÷ width of parent column = width of nested column

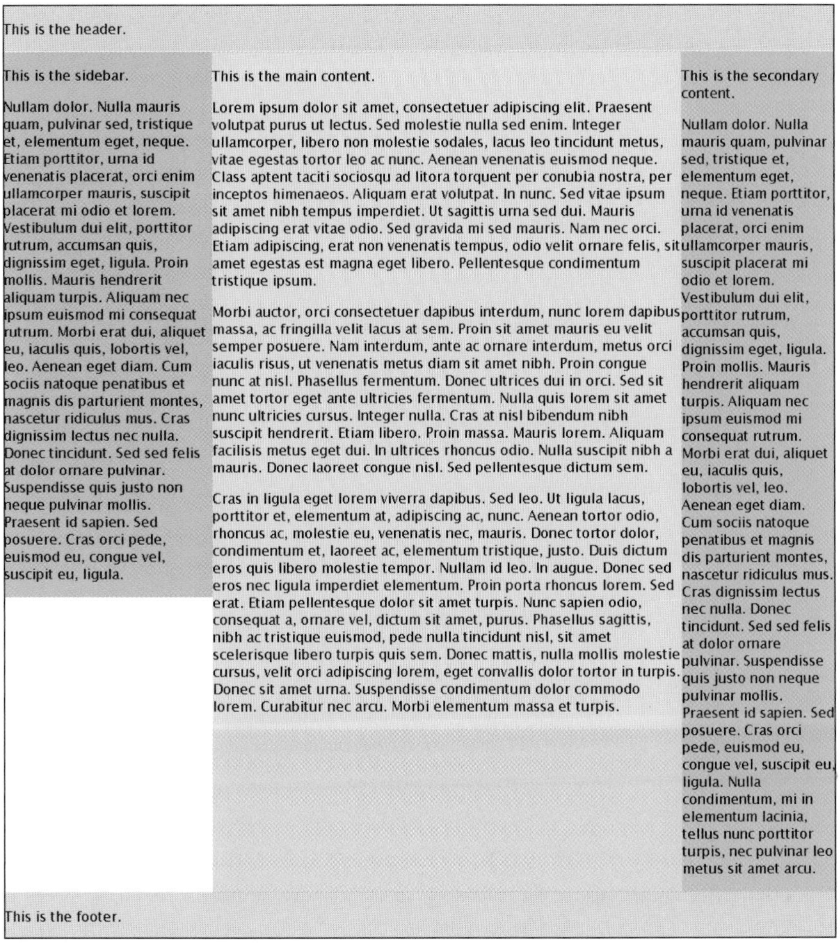

This is the header.

This is the sidebar.

Nullam dolor. Nulla mauris quam, pulvinar sed, tristique et, elementum eget, neque. Etiam porttitor, urna id venenatis placerat, orci enim ullamcorper mauris, suscipit placerat mi odio et lorem. Vestibulum dui elit, porttitor rutrum, accumsan quis, dignissim eget, ligula. Proin mollis. Mauris hendrerit aliquam turpis. Aliquam nec ipsum euismod mi consequat rutrum. Morbi erat dui, aliquet eu, iaculis quis, lobortis vel, leo. Aenean eget diam. Cum sociis natoque penatibus et magnis dis parturient montes, nascetur ridiculus mus. Cras dignissim lectus nec nulla. Donec tincidunt. Sed sed felis at dolor ornare pulvinar. Suspendisse quis justo non neque pulvinar mollis. Praesent id sapien. Sed posuere. Cras orci pede, euismod eu, congue vel, suscipit eu, ligula.

This is the main content.

Lorem ipsum dolor sit amet, consectetuer adipiscing elit. Praesent volutpat purus ut lectus. Sed molestie nulla sed enim. Integer ullamcorper, libero non molestie sodales, lacus leo tincidunt metus, vitae egestas tortor leo ac nunc. Aenean venenatis euismod neque. Class aptent taciti sociosqu ad litora torquent per conubia nostra, per inceptos himenaeos. Aliquam erat volutpat. In nunc. Sed vitae ipsum sit amet nibh tempus imperdiet. Ut sagittis urna sed dui. Mauris adipiscing erat vitae odio. Sed gravida mi sed mauris. Nam nec orci. Etiam adipiscing, erat non venenatis tempus, odio velit ornare felis, sit amet egestas est magna eget libero. Pellentesque condimentum tristique ipsum.

Morbi auctor, orci consectetuer dapibus interdum, nunc lorem dapibus massa, ac fringilla velit lacus at sem. Proin sit amet mauris eu velit semper posuere. Nam interdum, ante ac ornare interdum, metus orci iaculis risus, ut venenatis metus diam sit amet nibh. Proin congue nunc at nisl. Phasellus fermentum. Donec ultrices dui in orci. Sed sit amet tortor eget ante ultricies fermentum. Nulla quis lorem sit amet nunc ultricies cursus. Integer nulla. Cras at nisl bibendum nibh suscipit hendrerit. Etiam libero. Proin massa. Mauris lorem. Aliquam facilisis metus eget dui. In ultrices rhoncus odio. Nulla suscipit nibh a mauris. Donec laoreet congue nisl. Sed pellentesque dictum sem.

Cras in ligula eget lorem viverra dapibus. Sed leo. Ut ligula lacus, porttitor et, elementum at, adipiscing ac, nunc. Aenean tortor odio, rhoncus ac, molestie eu, venenatis nec, mauris. Donec tortor dolor, condimentum et, laoreet ac, elementum tristique, justo. Duis dictum eros quis libero molestie tempor. Nullam id leo. In augue. Donec sed eros nec ligula imperdiet elementum. Proin porta rhoncus lorem. Sed erat. Etiam pellentesque dolor sit amet turpis. Nunc sapien odio, consequat a, ornare vel, dictum sit amet, purus. Phasellus sagittis, nibh ac tristique euismod, pede nulla tincidunt nisl, sit amet scelerisque libero turpis quis sem. Donec mattis, nulla mollis molestie cursus, velit orci adipiscing lorem, eget convallis dolor tortor in turpis. Donec sit amet urna. Suspendisse condimentum dolor commodo lorem. Curabitur nec arcu. Morbi elementum massa et turpis.

This is the secondary content.

Nullam dolor. Nulla mauris quam, pulvinar sed, tristique et, elementum eget, neque. Etiam porttitor, urna id venenatis placerat, orci enim ullamcorper mauris, suscipit placerat mi odio et lorem. Vestibulum dui elit, porttitor rutrum, accumsan quis, dignissim eget, ligula. Proin mollis. Mauris hendrerit aliquam turpis. Aliquam nec ipsum euismod mi consequat rutrum. Morbi erat dui, aliquet eu, iaculis quis, lobortis vel, leo. Aenean eget diam. Cum sociis natoque penatibus et magnis dis parturient montes, nascetur ridiculus mus. Cras dignissim lectus nec nulla. Donec tincidunt. Sed sed felis at dolor ornare pulvinar. Suspendisse quis justo non neque pulvinar mollis. Praesent id sapien. Sed posuere. Cras orci pede, euismod eu, congue vel, suscipit eu, ligula. Nulla condimentum, mi in elementum lacinia, tellus nunc porttitor turpis, nec pulvinar leo metus sit amet arcu.

This is the footer.

FIGURE 4.9 The completed three-column layout using a wrapper `div`.

So, if we divide 75 into 25, we get a result of .3333, or 33.33 percent. We'll just round that to 33 percent, which means the width of content-main `div` needs to be 67 percent:

```
#content-main {
    float: left;
    width: 67%;
    background: #F0EE90;
}
#content-secondary {
    margin-left: 67%;
    background: #9BF598;
}
```

■ **NOTE:** The page showing this completed technique is liquid_margins_threecol_wrapper.html in the ch4_examples.zip file.

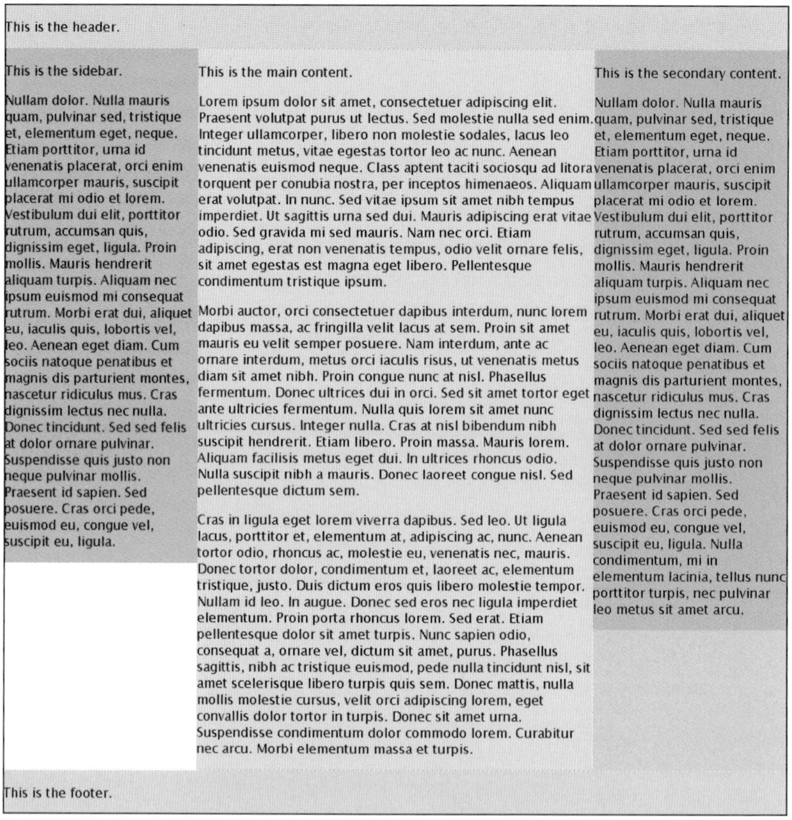

FIGURE 4.10 With the width of the nested content-main div decreased, the two sidebars now match in computed width.

This is the header.

This is the sidebar.

Nullam dolor. Nulla mauris quam, pulvinar sed, tristique et, elementum eget, neque. Etiam porttitor, urna id venenatis placerat, orci enim ullamcorper mauris, suscipit placerat mi odio et lorem. Vestibulum dui elit, porttitor rutrum, accumsan quis, dignissim eget, ligula. Proin mollis. Mauris hendrerit aliquam turpis. Aliquam nec ipsum euismod mi consequat rutrum. Morbi erat dui, aliquet eu, iaculis quis, lobortis vel, leo. Aenean eget diam. Cum sociis natoque penatibus et magnis dis parturient montes, nascetur ridiculus mus. Cras dignissim lectus nec nulla. Donec tincidunt. Sed sed felis at dolor ornare pulvinar. Suspendisse quis justo non neque pulvinar mollis. Praesent id sapien. Sed posuere. Cras orci pede, euismod eu, congue vel, suscipit eu, ligula.

This is the main content.

Lorem ipsum dolor sit amet, consectetuer adipiscing elit. Praesent volutpat purus ut lectus. Sed molestie nulla sed enim. Integer ullamcorper, libero non molestie sodales, lacus leo tincidunt metus, vitae egestas tortor leo ac nunc. Aenean venenatis euismod neque. Class aptent taciti sociosqu ad litora torquent per conubia nostra, per inceptos himenaeos. Aliquam erat volutpat. In nunc. Sed vitae ipsum sit amet nibh tempus imperdiet. Ut sagittis urna sed dui. Mauris adipiscing erat vitae odio. Sed gravida mi sed mauris. Nam nec orci. Etiam adipiscing, erat non venenatis tempus, odio velit ornare felis, sit amet egestas est magna eget libero. Pellentesque condimentum tristique ipsum.

Morbi auctor, orci consectetuer dapibus interdum, nunc lorem dapibus massa, ac fringilla velit lacus at sem. Proin sit amet mauris eu velit semper posuere. Nam interdum, ante ac ornare interdum, metus orci iaculis risus, ut venenatis metus diam sit amet nibh. Proin congue nunc at nisl. Phasellus fermentum. Donec ultrices dui in orci. Sed sit amet tortor eget ante ultricies fermentum. Nulla quis lorem sit amet nunc ultricies cursus. Integer nulla. Cras at nisl bibendum nibh suscipit hendrerit. Etiam libero. Proin massa. Mauris lorem. Aliquam facilisis metus eget dui. In ultrices rhoncus odio. Nulla suscipit nibh a mauris. Donec laoreet congue nisl. Sed pellentesque dictum sem.

Cras in ligula eget lorem viverra dapibus. Sed leo. Ut ligula lacus, porttitor et, elementum at, adipiscing ac, nunc. Aenean tortor odio, rhoncus ac, molestie eu, venenatis nec, mauris. Donec tortor dolor, condimentum et, laoreet ac, elementum tristique, justo. Duis dictum eros quis libero molestie tempor. Nullam id leo. In augue. Donec sed eros nec ligula imperdiet elementum. Proin porta rhoncus lorem. Sed erat. Etiam pellentesque dolor sit amet turpis. Nunc sapien odio, consequat a, ornare vel, dictum sit amet, purus. Phasellus sagittis, nibh ac tristique euismod, pede nulla tincidunt nisl, sit amet scelerisque libero turpis quis sem. Donec mattis, nulla mollis molestie cursus, velit orci adipiscing lorem, eget convallis dolor tortor in turpis. Donec sit amet urna. Suspendisse condimentum dolor commodo lorem. Curabitur nec arcu. Morbi elementum massa et turpis.

This is the secondary content.

Nullam dolor. Nulla mauris quam, pulvinar sed, tristique et, elementum eget, neque. Etiam porttitor, urna id venenatis placerat, orci enim ullamcorper mauris, suscipit placerat mi odio et lorem. Vestibulum dui elit, porttitor rutrum, accumsan quis, dignissim eget, ligula. Proin mollis. Mauris hendrerit aliquam turpis. Aliquam nec ipsum euismod mi consequat rutrum. Morbi erat dui, aliquet eu, iaculis quis, lobortis vel, leo. Aenean eget diam. Cum sociis natoque penatibus et magnis dis parturient montes, nascetur ridiculus mus. Cras dignissim lectus nec nulla. Donec tincidunt. Sed sed felis at dolor ornare pulvinar. Suspendisse quis justo non neque pulvinar mollis. Praesent id sapien. Sed posuere. Cras orci pede, euismod eu, congue vel, suscipit eu, ligula. Nulla condimentum, mi in elementum lacinia, tellus nunc porttitor turpis, nec pulvinar leo metus sit amet arcu.

This is the footer.

Creating Columns by Floating Everything

Another way to create column layouts with CSS is to float every single div.

Let's go back to our simple two-column example, where the main content div was floated to the right. You'll use the same CSS for the main content div, but remove the matching side margin from the sidebar div. You'll then need to add float and width values to the sidebar div:

■ NOTE: We actually could float the sidebar to the right as well, and it would end up in the same space it now sits. That's because float: right forces it to move as far to the right as it can, and the farthest to the right it can go is the left side of the main content column—right where it is now and where we want it.

```
#content-main {
    float: right;
    width: 75%;
    background: #F0EE90;
}
#sidebar {
    float: left;
    width: 25%;
    background: #FFA480;
}
```

To make sure the footer doesn't get overlapped by either of the columns above, keep using the same `clear: both` declaration that we've been using all along.

■ **NOTE:** The page showing this completed technique is named liquid_floats_twocol.html in the ch4_examples.zip file.

The two-column layout made by floating both of the columns looks exactly the same as if we had floated only one (as in Figure 4.5)—unless you look really closely or view the page at certain viewport widths in IE. All current browsers have some degree of trouble when you make widths of columns total exactly 100 percent, as our two columns do right now. Browsers have to translate every percentage dimension into a non-fractional number of pixels in order to display the page, which means they're often forced to round to the nearest full pixel. If the browser rounds down, you might get a one-pixel-wide gap, and if it rounds up, you might get a one-pixel-wide overlap (**Figure 4.11**).

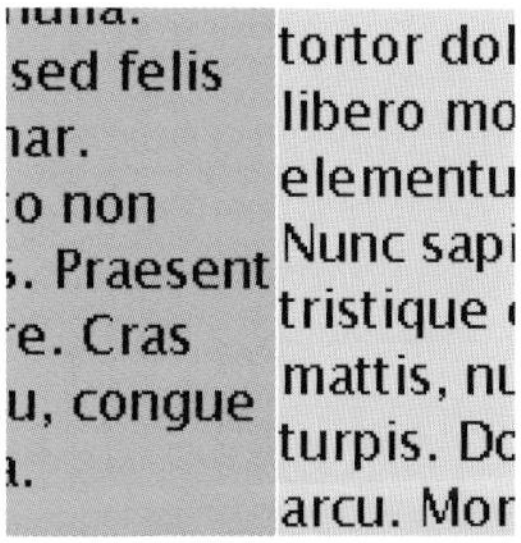

FIGURE 4.11 At certain viewport widths, rounded percentage measurements leave one-pixel-wide gaps between the columns.

In most designs, the one-pixel gap is neither noticeable nor detrimental to the design; it can often be worked around or—better still—ignored, if you, or your client, can tolerate that. The overlap is a bigger problem, simply because IE won't let it happen. Instead, it decides that the `div`s don't have room to sit side by side—since their combined width is the width of the viewport plus just one pixel—and it forces one to drop down beneath the other (**Figure 4.12**). This is often referred to as *float drop*. At certain window sizes the page will look perfectly fine, and at others it will appear that one column has completely disappeared.

To prevent that extra pixel from breaking the layout in IE, it's best to choose dimensions that add up to a tiny bit less than 100 percent:

```
#content-main {
    float: right;
    width: 74.9%;
    background: #F0EE90;
}
```

FIGURE 4.12 At certain window sizes in IE, it might appear that the sidebar has disappeared completely (left). Not until you scroll down do you see that the sidebar is still there, but dropped below the level of the main content column (right).

This stops the float drop in IE, but makes the one-pixel gap show up even more often in all browsers. There are a few ways we can deal with it:

+ **Ignore it.** If you've created a design that doesn't have to be "pixel perfect," as I promoted in Chapter 1, that tiny gap shouldn't be an issue for your design. For instance, you may choose not to have two solid blocks of color butted up against each other, as these sample layouts do. Even if you do have two differently colored columns touching each other, and you can't have even one pixel of space between them, all might not be lost: You will probably end up using a "faux column" effect to create the colored columns out of a single background image anyway, and a single image of course can't get gaps in it. We'll cover the faux column technique in Chapter 8.

+ **Move it to the outside by floating all the columns in the same direction.** The gap will be less noticeable if it shows up on the outside edge of one of the columns, instead of between the two. You can make this happen by changing the `float: left` on the sidebar to `float: right` instead. It will move as far to the right as it can go—in this case, jammed up against the left side of the main content column, so not even a pixel can squeeze between the two. Any pixels of space left over from rounding problems will show up on the left side of the sidebar instead. A one-pixel gap on the very edge of the browser window is noticeable only in the most precise of designs.

+ **Use a negative margin layout technique.** Margins with negative values are not only allowed by the CSS specification, they're quite useful. They can prevent you from having to declare widths on all your columns that add up to exactly 100 percent—the trigger for one-pixel gaps. Many negative margin layout techniques stop the gaps from occurring in standards-compliant browsers, but don't do the same for IE. Later in the chapter, I'll show you one that stops the gaps in all modern browsers. For now, let's stick with the floating-all-the-columns methods, and we'll come back to this alternative layout technique in a bit.

Of course, sometimes the anxiety over a one-pixel gap is moot, because we actually *want* a gap between the columns. To create a five-percent gap, as we did earlier in the chapter, we can simply reduce the width of either of the divs by five percent. This is safer than applying an actual margin value of five percent to the sides of one of the divs because it keeps the margin implicit instead of explicit. The gap will absorb any rounding inconsistencies the browser creates when calculating the explicit widths of the columns. It gives us breathing room.

BENEFITS OF FLOATING ALL THE COLUMNS

So far it may seem like this floating-all-the-divs method is more trouble than the first layout method we discussed, where we floated only one column and used side margins to move the other over. However, there are some perks to this second method.

One advantage to this method is that we avoid the three-pixel text jog bug. It occurs only between floated and non-floated adjacent content, and since all our divs are now floated, it's never triggered.

Another advantage is that each floated column creates a new block formatting context for itself. Basically, every block formatting context is an isolated container that controls the layout of the boxes within it, irrespective of any elements outside of it. It's handy to have every column in your layout be in a separate block formatting context, because this allows you to use the clear property within one of the columns—to clear, say, a floated image in the text—without that clear also clearing a totally separate floated column. It makes the clear property ignore the external columns and affect only the layout within its own block formatting context.

It's certainly possible to create a new block formatting context for each div using properties other than float, but not having to worry about setting some other CSS property just to get the clear property to work the way you want is a nice side effect of floating every single column. For more information on what block formatting context means and how it works, read "Control Block Formatting Context" at www.communitymx.com/abstract. cfm?cid=6BC9D.

ADDING A THIRD COLUMN

Creating a three-column layout when floating all the `div`s requires the same choice of compromise: do you prefer no extra `div`s or ideal source order?

If you want ideal source order and are thus comfortable adding that extra wrapper `div`, you'll use the same idea of creating two two-column layouts, one nested inside of another, as we did earlier. But this time, you simply float every `div`, instead of using side margins on the non-floated `div`s to create room for the floats:

```
#content-wrapper {
    float: right;
    width: 75%;
    background: #98F5E8;
}
#content-main {
    float: left;
    width: 67%;
    background: #F0EE90;
}
#content-secondary {
    float: right;
    width: 33%;
    background: #9BF598;
}
#sidebar {
    float: left;
    width: 25%;
    background: #FFA480;
}
#footer {
    clear: both;
    background: #DDDDDD;
}
```

■ **NOTE:** The page showing this completed technique is liquid_floats_ threecol_wrapper.html in the ch4_examples.zip file.

Although the width of the content-wrapper `div` is only 75 percent, make sure the widths of the `div`s inside it—the content-main and content-secondary `div`s—add up to 100 percent (unless you want a gap between them, in which case you'd decrease one of their widths accordingly). Remember, percentage widths are always relative to the declared width of their parent elements. When we make the nested `div`s add up to 100 percent, we're telling them to be 100 percent as wide as the content-wrapper `div`, not the viewport. If we change the width of the content-wrapper `div`, we don't need to make any adjustments to its children `div`s—they'll still fill up the whole width of the content `div` proportionally.

If you don't want to have that extra wrapper div in your (X)HTML, or you don't want to mess with algebra to get the two sidebars to match in width, you can reorder your source in one of two ways:

◆ Order the divs sidebar, content-secondary, content-main. Float the sidebar div left and both content-secondary and content-main right.

◆ Order the divs sidebar, content-main, content-secondary. Float all three either to the left (if you want the sidebar div on the left) or to the right (if you want it on the right).

Neither of these ordering options is ideal if the div we're calling content-main is truly your most important content and ought to come first in the source (although the second option is a little better than the first). But this may not be the case. For instance, you may have three feature boxes you want to line up on your home page. In this case, it makes sense for the box that's shown farthest to the left to be the first in the source, then the second leftmost box comes second in the source, and so on. The second ordering option, with all three divs floated to the left, would be ideal here.

FIGURE 4.13 On the Inmersio home page (www. inmersio.com), four columns are formed by floating each div to the left. The div farthest to the left is the first in the source, which is the most logical source order for this content.

But neither of these reordering options is ideal when we're dealing with the typical three-column layout for the page as a whole. That's when our next three-column layout method comes in.

Creating Columns with Floats and Negative Margins

The two liquid layout methods we've looked at so far, using side margins beside floats and floating all the divs, each have their pros and cons. Negative margin layout techniques often avoid many of the cons of both: they provide ideal source order without the three-pixel text jog or the float drops that can happen in IE. Some negative margin techniques can also prevent the one-pixel gaps between columns that we've seen in standards-compliant browsers, and some even eliminate the need for extra wrapper divs, as we've used in our three-column methods.

However, negative margin techniques have their own unique downsides. They're difficult to wrap your head around and can require some tricky math. Their increased complexity can lead to new problems in IE that we haven't yet encountered, such as invisible or completely out-of-place columns. These IE bugs can be hacked, but adding hacks is yet another layer of complexity. You need to test negative margin layouts heavily in many different browsing scenarios to make sure they don't fall apart.

There are a myriad of variations to negative margin layout techniques, but they all share some basic features:

1. Space is created on the side or sides of the main content `div` using positive margin or padding values.

2. The main content `div` is floated and given 100 percent of the remaining width.

3. The sidebar or sidebars that follow the main content `div` in the source are pulled to the side by a negative margin, which effectively negates the space they would otherwise take up, allowing them to move up beside the main content `div` and preventing float drops.

It's hard to explain in the abstract, so let's walk through one type of negative margin layout so you can see in general how they work and decide if they might be right for your site. The steps for this technique are a little more involved than those for the previous layout methods we've gone through, so hang on tight.

EASIER NEGATIVE MARGIN TECHNIQUES

The negative margin technique outlined here is actually a bit harder to grasp (though not really harder to implement) than some others out there. That's because it's a fully liquid layout, and fully liquid negative margin layouts tend to be more buggy, primarily in IE, than fixed-width or hybrid layouts. Most negative margin layout demos that you will find online use hybrid layouts, with fixed-width sidebars and a liquid middle column, which tends to fit very well with negative margin techniques. The tutorial "In Search of the Holy Grail" at www.alistapart.com/articles/holygrail showcases an excellent hybrid negative margin layout. It can be adapted to work with fully liquid layouts, but requires a little more tricky math, needs extra hacks added to get it to work in IE 6 and 7 (it doesn't work at all in IE 5.x), and even then exhibits the one-pixel gap in IE (though not in other browsers). Still, it's a great way to orient yourself to how negative margin layouts work, and perfectly suitable if you want hybrid instead of fully liquid.

Before working on the CSS for our negative margin layout, we need to add an extra wrapper div around the main content column in the HTML:

```
<div id="header"></div>
<div id="content-wrapper">
    <div id="content-main"></div>
</div>
<div id="content-secondary"></div>
<div id="sidebar"></div>
<div id="footer"></div>
```

This extra div is the main downside of this particular layout, but one that I consider quite minor given its accompanying strengths.

The wrapper div needs to be floated and assigned a width of 100 percent. The main content div within it will have space on either side of it, though, using margins set to the width of the sidebars:

```
#content-wrapper {
    float: left;
    width: 100%;
    background: #98F5E8;
}
#content-main {
    margin: 0 25%;
    background: #F0EE90;
}
#content-secondary {
    width: 25%;
    background: #9BF598;
}
#sidebar {
    width: 25%;
    background: #FFA480;
}
```

So far, the divs stack from top to bottom as normal (**Figure 4.14**). We can float the sidebars to either side, but that won't get them to move up beside the main content div, since content-wrapper is taking up 100 percent of the available viewport width. That's where the negative margins become necessary—they allow the divs to overlap, despite the lack of room, so they can sit on the same line with each other.

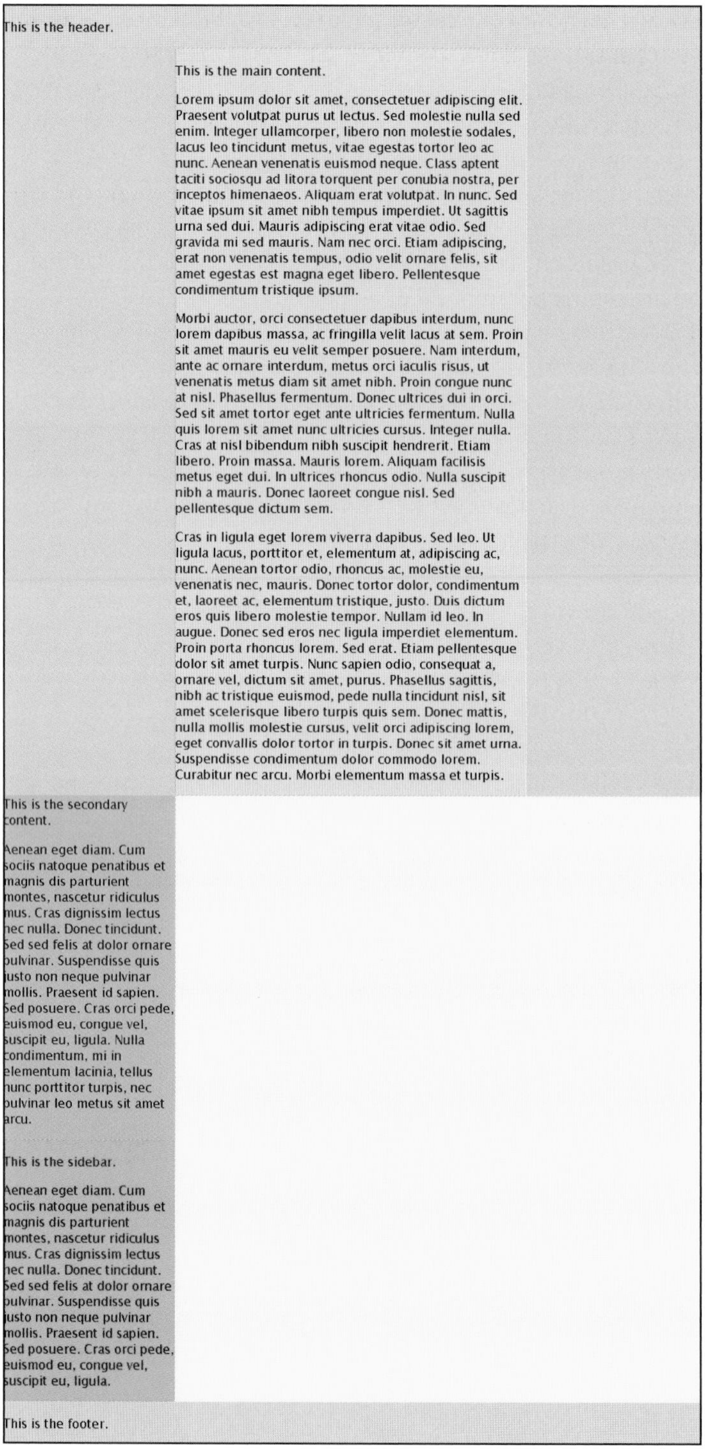

FIGURE 4.14 The main content `div` has space beside it for the two sidebars to sit in, but they are still sitting in their default positions below the main content `div` because they follow it in the source.

This is the header.

This is the main content.

Lorem ipsum dolor sit amet, consectetuer adipiscing elit. Praesent volutpat purus ut lectus. Sed molestie nulla sed enim. Integer ullamcorper, libero non molestie sodales, lacus leo tincidunt metus, vitae egestas tortor leo ac nunc. Aenean venenatis euismod neque. Class aptent taciti sociosqu ad litora torquent per conubia nostra, per inceptos himenaeos. Aliquam erat volutpat. In nunc. Sed vitae ipsum sit amet nibh tempus imperdiet. Ut sagittis urna sed dui. Mauris adipiscing erat vitae odio. Sed gravida mi sed mauris. Nam nec orci. Etiam adipiscing, erat non venenatis tempus, odio velit ornare felis, sit amet egestas est magna eget libero. Pellentesque condimentum tristique ipsum.

Morbi auctor, orci consectetuer dapibus interdum, nunc lorem dapibus massa, ac fringilla velit lacus at sem. Proin sit amet mauris eu velit semper posuere. Nam interdum, ante ac ornare interdum, metus orci iaculis risus, ut venenatis metus diam sit amet nibh. Proin congue nunc at nisl. Phasellus fermentum. Donec ultrices dui in orci. Sed sit amet tortor eget ante ultricies fermentum. Nulla quis lorem sit amet nunc ultricies cursus. Integer nulla. Cras at nisl bibendum nibh suscipit hendrerit. Etiam libero. Proin massa. Mauris lorem. Aliquam facilisis metus eget dui. In ultrices rhoncus odio. Nulla suscipit nibh a mauris. Donec laoreet congue nisl. Sed pellentesque dictum sem.

Cras in ligula eget lorem viverra dapibus. Sed leo. Ut ligula lacus, porttitor et, elementum at, adipiscing ac, nunc. Aenean tortor odio, rhoncus ac, molestie eu, venenatis nec, mauris. Donec tortor dolor, condimentum et, laoreet ac, elementum tristique, justo. Duis dictum eros quis libero molestie tempor. Nullam id leo. In augue. Donec sed eros nec ligula imperdiet elementum. Proin porta rhoncus lorem. Sed erat. Etiam pellentesque dolor sit amet turpis. Nunc sapien odio, consequat a, ornare vel, dictum sit amet, purus. Phasellus sagittis, nibh ac tristique euismod, pede nulla tincidunt nisl, sit amet scelerisque libero turpis quis sem. Donec mattis, nulla mollis molestie cursus, velit orci adipiscing lorem, eget convallis dolor tortor in turpis. Donec sit amet urna. Suspendisse condimentum dolor commodo lorem. Curabitur nec arcu. Morbi elementum massa et turpis.

This is the secondary content.

Aenean eget diam. Cum sociis natoque penatibus et magnis dis parturient montes, nascetur ridiculus mus. Cras dignissim lectus nec nulla. Donec tincidunt. Sed sed felis at dolor ornare pulvinar. Suspendisse quis justo non neque pulvinar mollis. Praesent id sapien. Sed posuere. Cras orci pede, euismod eu, congue vel, suscipit eu, ligula. Nulla condimentum, mi in elementum lacinia, tellus nunc porttitor turpis, nec pulvinar leo metus sit amet arcu.

This is the sidebar.

Aenean eget diam. Cum sociis natoque penatibus et magnis dis parturient montes, nascetur ridiculus mus. Cras dignissim lectus nec nulla. Donec tincidunt. Sed sed felis at dolor ornare pulvinar. Suspendisse quis justo non neque pulvinar mollis. Praesent id sapien. Sed posuere. Cras orci pede, euismod eu, congue vel, suscipit eu, ligula.

This is the footer.

Let's say we were to float the content-secondary div to the left, so it was sitting right up against the left side of the viewport. That's exactly where it's sitting even before being floated, but making it a float makes it want to move up beside the floated content-wrapper div if it can fit there. If we then give it a left margin value of 25 percent, it would push 25 percent to the right, or 25 percent *away* from the left side. If we give it a *negative* 25 percent margin instead, it simply does the opposite: it moves *to* the left, out of the visible area of the window, since it is only 25 percent wide itself. But, think of the viewport like Christopher Columbus did the Earth: it's not flat, so if you go off one side, you come back on the other. When you push the content-secondary div off the left side of the viewport, it pops onto the right side of the viewport, overlapping the content-wrapper div (**Figure 4.15**). This happens only if it's floated, however; without the float on both content-secondary and content-wrapper, they wouldn't be able to sit on the same line. Floating on both divs is what gets content-secondary to move up, and the negative margin is what gets it to overlap content-wrapper:

```
#content-secondary {
    float: left;
    width: 25%;
    margin-left: -25%;
    background: #9BF598;
}
```

You need to do a similar thing for the sidebar div. Float it to the left, and it sits in the exact horizontal position that we want—it just needs space to be able to move up. We need to use a negative margin again to allow an overlap and create that space. We can't use a value of 25 percent again, because that would put it right where content-secondary is, overlapping it. Instead, it needs to make one complete circuit behind the viewport and back to its original spot, so a value of negative 100 percent is what we need:

```
#sidebar {
    float: left;
    width: 25%;
    margin-left: -100%;
    background: #FFA480;
}
```

■ **NOTE:** If you use Adobe Dreamweaver to edit pages, you'll find that it has an awful time trying to render negative margin layouts in Design View. This layout has its columns displaced, and the content of the two sidebars is completely uneditable in Design View. Unfortunately, there's no fix—just submit it as a bug to Adobe at www.adobe.com/cfusion/mmform/index.cfm?name=wishform; hopefully they'll get it fixed in the next release!

FIGURE 4.15 With the float and negative margin in place, the secondary content div can move up and overlap the content wrapper div. Since the main content has a gap to its right created by a margin, the overlap doesn't actually cover any content, just the blue background color of the content wrapper div.

FIGURE 4.16 The float and negative margin on the sidebar div gets it to move up and overlap the content wrapper div, completing the layout of the three columns.

With all three columns in place, the only thing left to do is clear the footer, so that when one or both of the sidebar divs are longer than the main content div, they don't overlap the footer. Unfortunately, the clear property alone isn't enough to get IE 6 and earlier to stop the overlap of the content-secondary div over the footer completely, but adding position: relative to the footer—a common IE hack—fixes this without harming any other browsers:

```
#footer {
    position: relative;
    clear: both;
    background: #DDDDDD;
}
```

PROBLEMS WITH THE HEADER DIV IN IE 6 AND EARLIER

We don't have one in this example layout, but it's very common to use a wrapper div around all the divs as a whole, from the header through the footer, usually as a vehicle for a background image or to limit the overall width of the layout. If you do add a wrapper div to this particular negative margin layout, you may find that your header div disappears in IE 6 and earlier. To fix this, add a hasLayout hack to the wrapper div like zoom: 1 or any width value.

And with that, our negative margin layout is complete. Although the logic behind the CSS can be difficult to understand at first, the amount of CSS used to create the layout is not really any greater than the other layout methods we've gone over, so once you understand how it works, it can be just as quick to create a negative margin layout as any other type.

■ **NOTE:** The page showing this completed technique is liquid_negative_threecol.html in the ch4_examples.zip file.

Keeping the Layout from Spanning the Whole Viewport

You now have a number of liquid layout techniques to choose from in building your pages. So far, all of the examples shown have spanned the entire viewport width, but they don't have to be set up this way. Any one of these layouts can be adapted to take up a smaller percentage of the window, using a variety of methods.

Changing Column Widths

One way to have a layout span less than the entire viewport is to simply reduce the widths of individual columns within the layout so they no longer equal 100 percent. If you're using the floats-with-matching-side-margins method, this works only if the float is on the left. If the float is on the right, as it was in our very first example, the non-floated column will stick to the left side of the viewport in its default location, and the right-floated column will stick to the right side, together still spanning the full width of the viewport, simply with a big gap in between.

■ **NOTE:** The page showing this completed technique is liquid_margins_twocol_reduced1.html in the ch4_examples.zip file.

Besides changing the float direction, you'll need to add widths to the previously width-less sidebar, header, and footer:

```
#header {
   width: 90%;
```

```
        background: #DDDDDD;
    }
    #content-main {
        float: left;
        width: 65%;
        background: #F0EE90;
    }
    #sidebar {
        width: 25%;
        margin-left: 65%;
        background: #FFA480;
    }
    #footer {
        clear: both;
        width: 90%;
        background: #DDDDDD;
    }
```

FIGURE 4.17 The layout now takes up only 90 percent of the viewport.

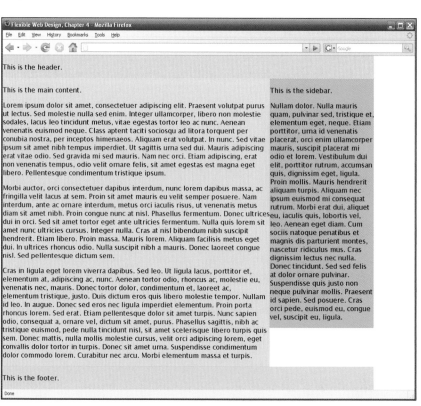

If you need the sidebar to be on the left, as it was in the original floats-with-matching-side-margins example, it will need to be the floated column, which means it will need to switch places with the main content div in the source.

If you're floating all the columns, you'll first want to get them all floated in the same direction. They can all be floated left or right, but this corresponds with whether the entire reduced-width layout sticks to the left or right side of the viewport, and it can look pretty odd to have it stuck to the right side. Of course, floating both columns left also means that if you want the sidebar to be on the left side of the main content column, it needs to precede it in the source. If you don't want to make that compromise, here's how it would work with right floats:

```
#header {
    float: right;
    width: 90%;
    background: #DDDDDD;
}
#sidebar {
    float: right;
    width: 25%;
    background: #FFA480;
}
#content-main {
    float: right;
    width: 65%;
    background: #F0EE90;
}
#footer {
    clear: both;
    float: right;
    width: 90%;
    background: #DDDDDD;
}
```

In both of these cases, the layout no longer takes up the entire viewport width, although it still adjusts in size proportionally to the viewport. However, the layouts are not centered within the viewport. There's nothing wrong with this, but many layouts are designed to be centered. If this applies to yours, read on.

Assigning Side Margins

If you assign margins that match in width on both sides of the layout, you're creating equally sized gaps on both sides of the layout, and that's exactly what centering is.

■ **NOTE:** The page showing this completed technique is named liquid_floats_twocol_reduced1.html in the ch4_examples.zip file.

FIGURE 4.18 With both columns floated right, the reduced-width layout will stick to the right side of the viewport.

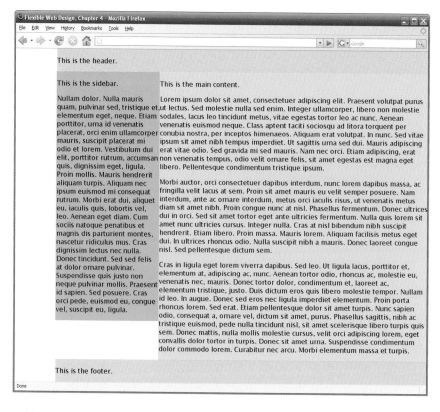

Taking our first reduced-width example, where the main content div was floated left and the sidebar had a matching left margin, you would apply a left margin to the main content div and increase the left margin on the sidebar accordingly. The header and footer would need margins applied to both sides:

```css
#header {
    width: 90%;
    margin: 0 5%;
    background: #DDDDDD;
}
#content-main {
    float: left;
    width: 65%;
    margin-left: 5%;
    background: #F0EE90;
}
#sidebar {
    width: 25%;
    margin-left: 70%;
    background: #FFA480;
}
```

```
#footer {
    clear: both;
    width: 90%;
    margin: 0 5%;
    background: #DDDDDD;
}
```

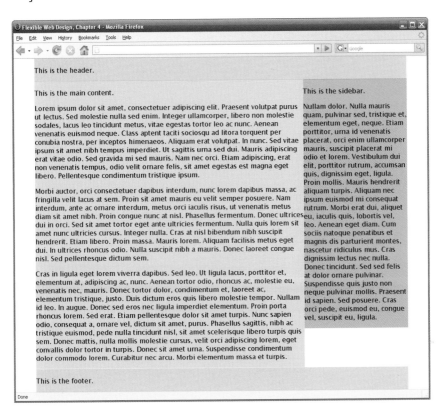

FIGURE 4.19 The layout still takes up only 90 percent of the viewport, but is now centered, because the extra 10 percent is split equally on both sides using five-percent side margins.

Using side margins makes it possible to keep the sidebar on the left without having to switch the source order—just switch the main content back to floating right and give it a right margin instead. To create a matching space on the left side of the sidebar, add a left margin in addition to the right margin it already has that makes room for the float:

■ **NOTE:** The page showing this completed technique is liquid_margins_twocol_reduced2.html in the ch4_examples.zip file.

```
#sidebar {
    margin-right: 65%;
    margin-left: 5%;
    background: #FFA480;
}
```

```
#content-main {
    float: right;
    width: 65%;
    margin-right: 5%;
    background: #F0EE90;
}
```

FIGURE 4.20 By switching the direction of the float on the main content `div` and changing the side margins on the sidebar `div`, you can keep the same source order but move the sidebar back to the left side.

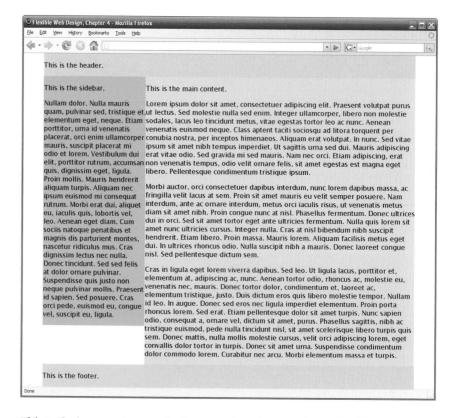

This technique works exactly the same for a layout where all of the columns are floated. Just apply a right margin to the rightmost `div`, a left margin to the leftmost `div`, and both left and right margins to `div`s that span the entire width, like headers, footers, navigation bars, and other single-column items.

Often when you add side margins to a float, you're going to trigger the doubled float margin bug in IE 6 and earlier. These browsers will double the value of the margin set on the same side that the float is facing (**Figure 4.21**). So, a right margin will be doubled on a right float, and a left margin will be doubled on a left float. To fix this problem, just apply `display: inline` to the float. It doesn't hurt any other browsers—it's nonsensical but semantically valid CSS, so other browsers just ignore it—so there's no need to hide it through the use of a separate IE-only style sheet or other hack.

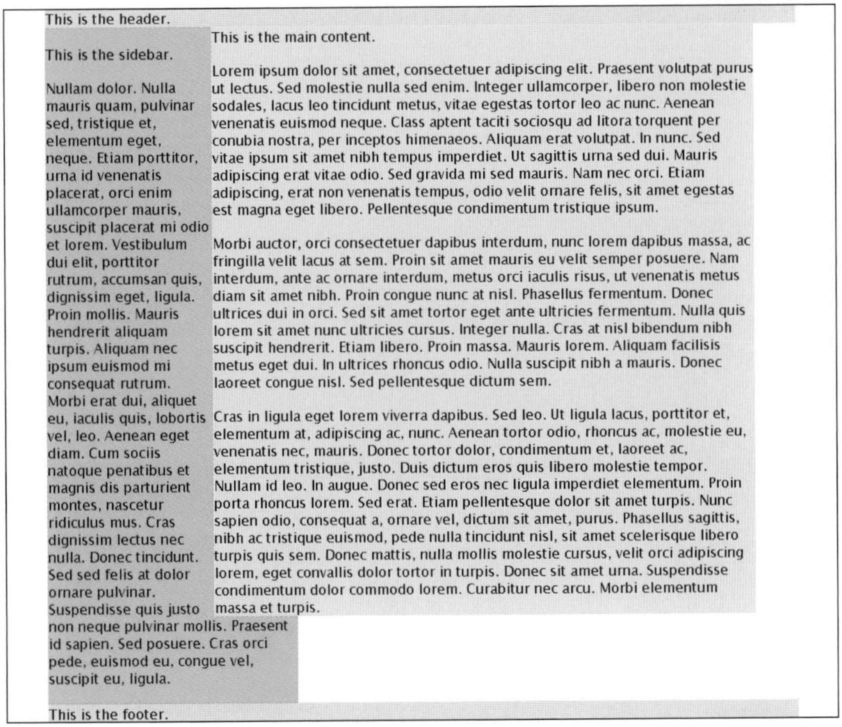

FIGURE 4.21 The five-percent right margin on the right-floated main content div is doubled to 10 percent in IE 6 and earlier, so it sits too far to the left.

There's an even easier way to add these side margins to achieve centering: nest all the divs in a single wrapper div, and apply the margins to that div:

```
<div id="wrapper">
    <div id="header"></div>
    <div id="content-main"></div>
    <div id="sidebar"></div>
    <div id="footer"></div>
</div>
```

Although this wrapper div is not necessary for centering a layout, as we've seen, it often becomes necessary later when you want to apply background images to the design, so adding it at this point is not a bad idea.

When you add the wrapper, you'll need to remove the reduced widths and the side margins of the divs nested within it, so that they fill up the entire wrapper div. Then, apply equal left and right margins to the wrapper div, using whatever unit you like:

```
#wrapper {
    margin: 0 5%;
}
#header {
    background: #DDDDDD;
```

```
}
#content-main {
    float: left;
    width: 75%;
    background: #F0EE90;
}
#sidebar {
    margin-left: 75%;
    background: #FFA480;
}
#footer {
    clear: both;
    background: #DDDDDD;
}
```

FIGURE 4.22 Margin values in percentages adjust in width based on the browser window, just as width values in percentages do.

 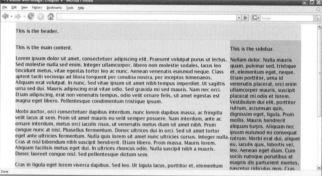

■ **NOTE:** Although the code example above shows the float-with-matching-sidebar method, you can use the exact same CSS on the wrapper in layouts where all columns are floated. This technique works the same no matter what float layout method is being used within the wrapper.

■ **NOTE:** The page showing this completed technique is liquid_margins_twocol_reduced_wrapper1.html in the ch4_examples.zip file.

Margin values in percentages, like the five percent used here, keep the gaps proportional to the viewport.

Values in pixels can be used as well to create fixed-width space on either side of the layout. The layout itself still adjusts to the viewport, but it always sits a fixed number of pixels away from either side:

```
#wrapper {
    margin: 0 50px;
}
```

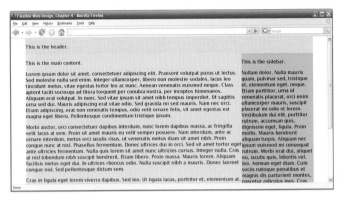 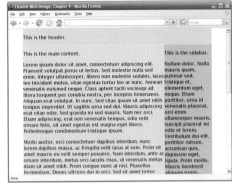

Assigning a Percentage Width to the Wrapper

FIGURE 4.23 Margin values in pixels create gaps of the same widths, no matter what size the window is.

Another great use of a wrapper `div` is to set the overall width of the layout. You can simply assign a percentage width to the wrapper to constrain the entire layout to your chosen portion of the viewport:

```
#wrapper {
    width: 90%;
}
```

You don't need to change any of the percentage values of the `div`s inside the wrapper, because they are relative to their parent. The 100 percent that they add up to now means 100 percent of the wrapper `div`, not the viewport. Thus, if your wrapper is set to 80 percent, don't try to make the `div`s inside add up to 80 percent. Each time you set a width on a parent element, you're creating a brand new yardstick for what represents 100 percent and giving the child `div`s a new point of reference to measure against.

Assigning a width to the wrapper does not by itself center the layout. As with all the centering examples we've gone through so far, you need equally sized margins on each side to do this. You could use percentage value margins again, such as 10 percent on each side of an 80-percent-wide wrapper, but to avoid adding up to 100 percent as much as possible and triggering rounding errors, a simpler way is to use the value of `auto` for both side margins:

```
#wrapper {
    width: 90%;
    margin: 0 auto;
}
```

Basically, this tells the browser to take up whatever space is left, and since both sides are equally set to *auto*, the space will be equally divided on both sides. This has the added advantage that if you later change the width of the wrapper, you don't have to remember to change the width of the side margins as well. One less thing to change means one less chance for error, however small.

■ **NOTE:** The page showing this completed technique is liquid_margins_twocol_reduced_wrapper2.html in the ch4_examples.zip file.

Site-Building Exercise: Creating the Shelter's Inner-Page Layout Structure

In this exercise, you'll build the liquid layout structure of the inner pages of the Beechwood Animal Shelter site. In the next chapter, you'll tackle the construction of the home page—a somewhat more advanced layout because of the additional design elements it contains.

FIGURE 4.24 The design of the inner pages of the Beechwood Animal Shelter site. In this exercise, you'll create the two-column layout structure and pave the way for the graphic elements that you'll add in later chapters.

You'll work with the exercise files from this book's companion web site at www.flexiblewebbook.com. Download and unzip the file ch4_exercise.zip.

Preparing the Page

Open the file programs-start.html in your text or code editor of choice. The file already contains all the content of the Our Programs page, marked up semantically, but no divs to form the structure of the layout.

1. Enter a new line below the opening body tag, and type the following:

   ```
   <div id="header">
   ```

2. Locate `<h1>Our Programs</h1>` several lines down in the HTML. Enter a new line above this, and type `</div>` to close the header div you just created.

3. Enter a new line between the closing div tag you just typed and `<h1>Our Programs</h1>`. Type the following:

   ```
   <div id="content-wrapper">
   <div id="content-main">
   ```

4. Immediately following the h1 element is a single paragraph. Locate its closing tag and enter a new line beneath it. Type the following to close the main content div and its wrapper that you just created:

   ```
   </div>
   </div>
   ```

5. Enter a new line beneath the last closing div tag you just typed, and type the following:

   ```
   <div id="nav-secondary">
   ```

6. Locate `<p>&copy; 2008 Beechwood Animal Shelter</p>` right before the end of the page. Enter a new line above this, and type `</div>` to close the secondary navigation div you just created.

7. Enter a new line after the closing div tag you just typed, and type:

   ```
   <div id="footer">
   ```

8. Enter a new line after `<p>&copy; 2008 Beechwood Animal Shelter</p>`. Type `</div>` to close the footer div you just created.

■ **TIP:** As an optional step, you may want to indent the markup within each of the divs you added to make the HTML easier to read.

You've now added all the basic structural `div`s that you'll need to create the layout. The HTML within the `body` tags should look like this (most of the content has been removed to highlight the `div` placement):

```
<div id="header">
    <ul>
        <li>Skip to Main Content</li>
        ...
        <li><a href="/about/">About the Shelter</a></li>
    </ul>
</div>
<div id="content-wrapper">
    <div id="content-main">
        <h1>Our Programs</h1>
        ...
    </div>
</div>
<div id="nav-secondary">
    <ul>
        <li><a href="animal-rescue.html">Animal Rescue</a></li>
    ...
        <li><a href="#">Headline Three</a> <span>Date</span></li>
    </ul>
</div>
<div id="footer">
    <p>&copy; 2008 Beechwood Animal Shelter</p>
</div>
```

Adding Base Styles

■ **TIP:** As mentioned earlier, it's often easiest to develop CSS embedded in the head of a single page, and then move it to an external style sheet when it's completed.

Now it's time to start applying the CSS that will turn this single-column page into a multi-column layout. First, though, you need to add a few base styles.

1. In the head of the page, enter a new line between `<title>Our Programs | Beechwood Animal Shelter</title>` and the closing head tag. Type the following:

   ```
   <style type="text/css">
   </style>
   ```

   You'll add the CSS for the page between these `style` tags.

2. Enter a new line between the opening and closing `style` tags. Add a rule for the `body` element to set some base properties for the page:

```
body {
    margin: 0;
    padding: 0;
    font: 88% "Lucida Sans Unicode", "Lucida Grande", sans-
serif;
    line-height: 1.4;
}
```

Only the `margin` and `padding` properties affect the layout of the page; the `font` and `line-height` properties are just there for appearance's sake.

3. Add background colors to the `div`s to see where each lies as you change their positions on the page. Add the following rules:

```
div {
    padding: 1px 0;
}
#header, #footer {
    background: #EFEFEF;
}
#content-main {
    background: #CFC;
}
#nav-secondary {
    background: #FCF;
}
```

The first rule, for all `div` elements, adds one pixel of padding inside the top and bottom of each `div` to stop margin collapsing: it keeps the margins of the interior elements from escaping from the `div`s and creating gaps between their colored bands. It's simply another visual aid to help you while moving the `div`s around.

> **■ NOTE:** The lack of a unit of measurement on the line-height value is not a mistake. Unitless line-height values are not only allowed, they're usually ideal. Learn more at http://meyerweb.com/eric/thoughts/2006/02/08/unitless-line-heights in Eric Meyer's blog.

> **■ NOTE:** For a brief refresher on margin collapsing, see "What's the point of one pixel of padding?" on page 90.

FIGURE 4.25 With background colors in place, it's easy to see where each `div` lies in relation to the others on the page. So far, the page is simply a single-column liquid layout.

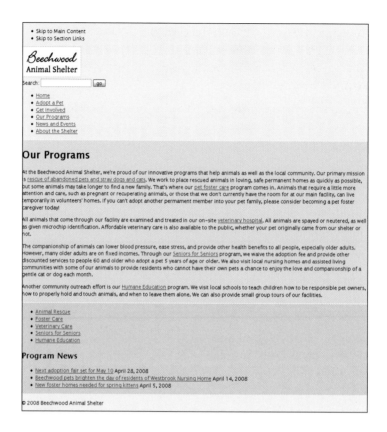

Creating the Two-Column Layout

Now you'll add the styles to actually create the layout. Any of the float layout methods described earlier in the chapter could be used, but we'll use a negative margin method here, in order to make the layout more adaptable to the design embellishments that will be coming in later chapters.

1. Add the following rule inside the `style` tags in the `head` of the page:

```
#content-wrapper {
    float: left;
    width: 100%;
    padding: 0;
}
```

Only the `float` and `width` properties are necessary for the layout. The padding simply overrides the earlier padding set on all `div`s, so that an empty pixel of space isn't shown above the main content `div`, which has its own padding also set.

2. Modify the `#content-main` rule you created earlier to add space for the navigation sidebar to sit in:

```
#content-main {
    margin-left: 20%;
    background: #CFC;
}
```

3. Modify the `#nav-secondary` rule you created earlier to move the `div` into the space left by the margin you just added:

```
#nav-secondary {
    float: left;
    width: 20%;
    margin-left: -100%;
    background: #FCF;
}
```

4. There's already a grouped rule for the header and footer together, but add a separate rule for just the footer, so it can clear the sidebar:

```
#footer {
    clear: both;
}
```

All of the `div`s should now be in their proper places (**Figure 4.26**). Verify this by opening the file in several different browsers. Try changing the size of the browser window as well as the font size, and make sure the layout holds together at a variety of different settings. If you narrow your window enough, the content in the sidebar will start to overflow, but other than that there should be no layout problems in any of the major browsers, including IE 6 and earlier.

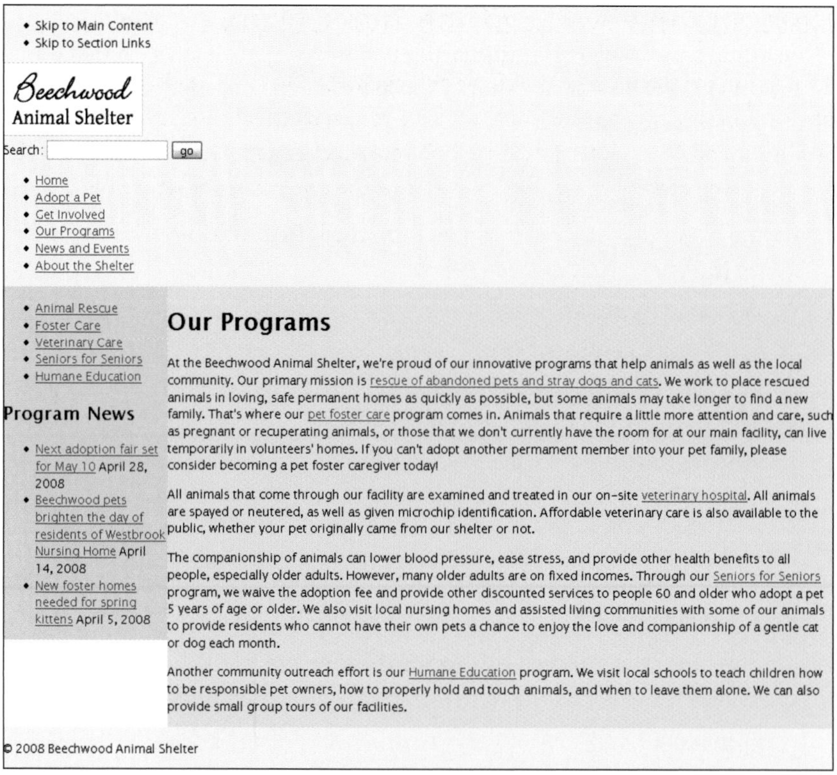

FIGURE 4.26 The nav-secondary div is now a sidebar on the left side of the page.

TEST EARLY, TEST OFTEN...TEST IE LAST

It's important to test your pages in as many browsers as possible, but make sure that you test in more standards-compliant browsers first. Get the page working correctly in browsers like Firefox, Safari, and Opera before moving on to—and addressing the shortcomings of—less capable browsers. To put it bluntly, test in just about anything other than Internet Explorer first, and then test in IE and worry about its bugs. It's much easier to code for the standard and then hack against IE's bugs than it is to code for IE's bugs and then try to hack other browsers into imitating those often unpredictable and illogical bugs. The latter is usually impossible to do, and just costs you a lot of time retooling your IE-specific CSS to get it working in a wider range of browsers.

As long as you test often in IE, it's not too hard to make the adjustments you need along the way to accommodate it, even if you are accommodating the more standards-compliant browsers first.

Reducing the Width of the Two Columns

The design for the interior pages of the Beechwood Animal Shelter site doesn't have the two main columns spanning the entire width of the viewport, though the header and footer do. You'll need to make a change to both the HTML and the CSS to create the space on either side of the two main columns.

■ **NOTE:** Using margin: 0 5% would have worked just as well to center the div. You can use whichever you like.

1. Locate `<div id="content-wrapper">` in the HTML and enter a new line above it. Type `<div id="wrapper">`.

2. Locate `<div id="footer">` and enter a new line above it. Type `</div>` to close the wrapper `div` you just created.

3. In the `style` section in the `head` of the page, add the following new rule:

```
#wrapper {
    width: 90%;
    margin: 0 auto;
}
```

This restricts the width of the two main columns to only 90 percent of the viewport (**Figure 4.27**), but keeps them centered in the remaining space.

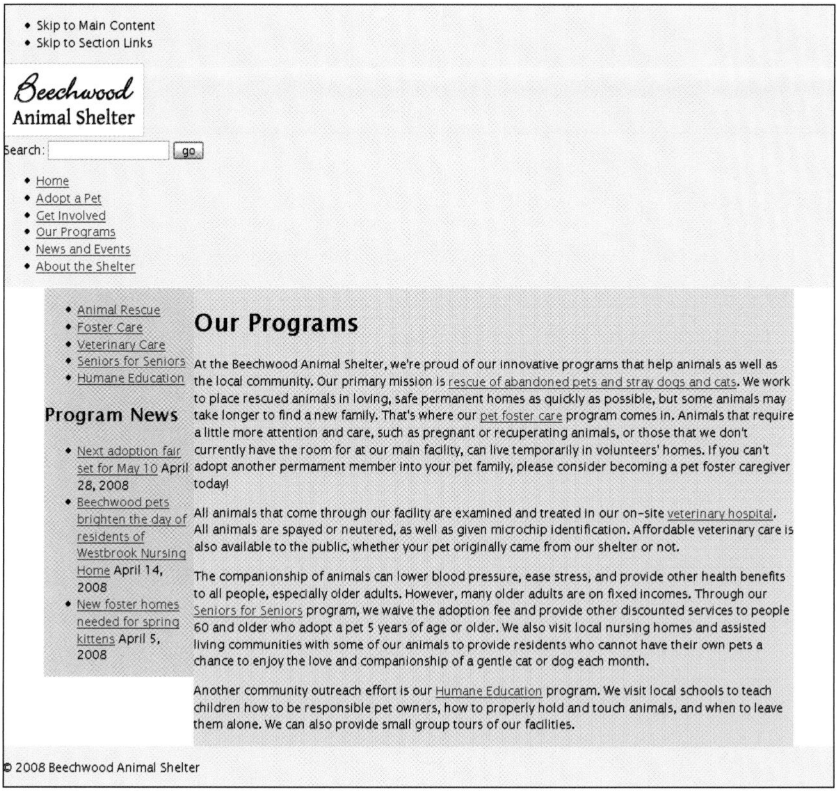

FIGURE 4.27 The two columns are still proportionally the same sizes, but now take up only 90 percent of the viewport width.

4. IE 6 miscalculates the placement of the nav-secondary `div` now that its wrapper has a percentage width set on it (**Figure 4.28**). To correct this, add a conditional comment targeting IE 6 only, directly below the closing `style` tag in the `head`:

```
<!--[if IE 6]>
<style>
#nav-secondary {
    margin-left: -90%;
}
</style>
<![endif]-->
```

This must be placed after the other `style` element in the `head` in order to override the earlier styles.

FIGURE 4.28 IE 6 miscalculates the placement of the nav-secondary `div` when the wrapper `div` has a percentage width set on it. Other versions of IE do not exhibit this bug.

To refresh your knowledge of conditional comments, see "Hacking away the three-pixel text jog" on page 101.

Your page should now look like Figure 4.27 (on the previous page) in all major browsers. To compare your work to the completed exercise, see the file programs-end.html in the files you extracted from ch4_exercise.zip.

Building Elastic Layout Structures

Each of the techniques for liquid layouts that we discussed in the previous chapter can be adapted to work for elastic layouts. Sometimes it's as easy as changing percentage dimensions to ems. However, the way that nested em measurements are computed differs from that of percentages, so a simple one-to-one switch doesn't always work. In this chapter, you'll learn what an em is, how it's computed, and how to choose proper em measurements for your sites. We'll apply this knowledge of ems to adapt the liquid layouts from the previous chapter. In the exercise at the end of the chapter, we'll create the structure of the Beechwood Animal Shelter home page.

Switching Dimensions to Ems

Creating an elastic layout is not the same as just creating a liquid layout with ems in place of percentages for the dimensions. Ems are computed very differently from percentages, so it's essential that you understand how they work before you can effectively create an elastic layout.

What is an Em?

If you read about the definition of the em in typography web sites and books, you may quickly become confused with all the jargon and history surrounding the term. Don't worry about all that. In terms of CSS dimensions, an em simply means the font size of the current element. Jon Tan puts it well in his article "The Incredible Em & Elastic Layouts with CSS" (http://jontangerine. com/log/2007/09/the-incredible-em-and-elastic-layouts-with-css):

> One em equals the vertical space needed for any given letter in a font, regardless of the horizontal space it occupies. Therefore: If the font size is 16px, then 1em = 16px.

Because fonts are measured by the vertical space of the character blocks but most characters are taller than they are wide, another way to approximate the size of an em is the width of two characters. So, a width value of 40 ems will come out to roughly 80 characters across.

Nesting Em Measurements

In the previous chapter, you saw how the percentage dimensions of nested divs compounded on one another. If you had a parent div with a width of 75 percent, and you wanted its child div to be 25 percent as wide as the viewport, you had to set the width of the child div to 33 percent, since 33 percent of 75 equals 25. If both the parent and child divs were given widths of 75 percent, they would not match in width.

Ems don't necessarily compound this same way. The em dimensions of the child div pay no attention to the em dimensions of the parent div. They pay attention only to the font size of the current div, not its parent's width or even its parent's font size. If both the parent and child divs were given widths of 75 ems, they *would* match in width, as long as both divs had the same computed font size—either because the font size was set to the same absolute measurement, or because they both inherited the same font size from ancestor elements.

That's one reason why you can't just take the liquid layouts we used earlier and switch every percentage dimension to its corresponding em value. You no longer need to do the math to figure out nested values.

All of what we've talked about so far applies only when ems are used as the unit of measurement for dimension values, such as width, height, and margin. Different calculation rules apply when ems are used as the unit of measurement for font sizes. When using ems as the value for font sizes, instead of for dimensions, you do need to be careful about how the computed values compound on one another. For instance, let's say your browser's default font size is 16 pixels (as most are), and you have a `div` on your page with its font size set to .88 em. All the text within the `div` will be 88 percent of 16 pixels, or 14 pixels. If you then have a paragraph nested within that `div`, and its font size is not allowed to inherit but instead is set explicitly to .88 em as well, it will not have a font size of 14 pixels. Instead, it will be computed as 88 percent of the `div`'s 14-pixel text, or 12 pixels.

But again, compounding isn't an issue when using ems as dimension values. When used as a width, height, margin, or other dimension, the em always refers to the current element's font size. Nevertheless, because the font size determines what pixel measurement an em computes to, you do need to know how em font sizes compound in order to correctly choose em dimensions.

AVOIDING COMPOUNDED EM FONT-SIZE MEASUREMENTS

To avoid nesting em font-size values—as well as percentage font-size values—always set your font sizes on as few elements as necessary, and take advantage of inheritance whenever possible. Start by determining the base font size at which you want the majority of your text to be seen, and set that size on the body element. All of the structural `div`s, as well as text elements like paragraphs and lists, will inherit this size and don't need to have font sizes set explicitly on them. Then, set font sizes just on elements whose text you want to be larger or smaller than the base font size. For instance, set your headings to larger percentages or greater-than-one em values. Since the headings will never be nested inside each other, and the only other items they might be nested in don't have font sizes explicitly set on them, this is a safe place to put font sizes to avoid compounding them.

Picking Em Measurements

Before switching your dimensions over to ems, you need to consider:

◆ What font size is currently in use on an element.

◆ How nested em values will or will not affect each other.

◆ How many characters you want to appear across a line of text.

◆ What pixel size you want the ems to compute to.

The first two considerations in the list above can help you determine how many pixels and text characters your em values are going to compute to, but they won't make your decision about the "proper" number of ems to use. This is completely up to you. You either choose an em value because you want it to translate into a particular pixel measurement at a particular text size, or you choose an em value because you want a certain number of text characters to appear across each line of text no matter the text size.

PICKING LINE LENGTHS

Choosing an em value based on the number of text characters it will translate to is the most common route. After all, optimizing line lengths for readability is one of the major reasons to choose an elastic layout in the first place, as we discussed in Chapter 1. Line lengths of 75 to 100 characters are considered easier to read onscreen than shorter line lengths. This would translate to roughly 37 to 50 ems for the width of your main block of text, since an em is always roughly two characters wide. Of course, unless you are only doing a single column layout, your overall em width will be larger than this once you add on the width of the side columns to those 37 to 50 ems for the main content column.

Set the width of your side columns according to the content within them. For instance, if you have a navigation menu forming one side column and you don't want the text within it to overflow or wrap, simply figure out how many characters are in the longest word and set the em value of that column to half that number of characters. If your side column instead contains narrative text, you may want to set it to a slightly larger em value to make reading a bit easier.

PICKING PIXEL EQUIVALENCES

Choosing an em value based on the number of pixels you want it to translate to is not as common as choosing values based on line lengths. This is because it kind of defeats the purpose of elastic layouts to do so: If you're so concerned about achieving a particular pixel measurement, why not stick with a fixed-width layout instead? Also, you can almost never depend on your entire audience having the same text size in their browsers, so trusting that your em measurements are going to come out to particular pixel measurements is dangerous. However, that doesn't mean that you should ignore the pixel equivalences of ems altogether. It's useful to know how many pixels your elastic layout is going to take up at different text sizes so that you can tweak measurements to make horizontal scrollbars less likely.

For instance, let's say you have a two-column elastic layout that is 50 ems wide overall, with the main column being 40 ems wide and the sidebar 10. At most user's default text size of 16 pixels, 50 ems comes out to 800 pixels wide. That means that people with 16-pixel text, viewing your site with screen resolutions of 800 by 600, will get a horizontal scrollbar. This may not be a concern for you, depending on your audience and for whom you want to optimize, but if you would like to avoid this, you can simply drop the width of the main content column to 37 ems. This gives the overall layout a width of 47 ems, which is equal to 752 pixels at a text size of 16 pixels. Most users with 800 by 600 screen resolutions will not get a horizontal scrollbar with these measurements.

One technique that some people use to make computing the pixel equivalences of ems easier is to first set the font size on the body element to 62.5 percent, which comes out to 10 pixels when the user has a default of 16 pixels. Having 10 as your base font size makes it very easy to figure out what each em measurement is going to come out to in pixels—40 ems is 400 pixels, 64 ems is 640 pixels, and so forth—and what em font sizes are going to come out to in pixels when you set font sizes on elements that need to differ from the base size, such as headings and footer text. Further, a base size of 10 helps you quickly determine the proper em or percentage values necessary to achieve particular pixel values. For instance, with a base font size of 10 pixels, setting a value of 140 percent or 1.4 ems on h1 elements means the browser will show them in 14-pixel text. You don't have to worry about the rounding differences that would occur between different browsers if you were starting with a base font size of 16 pixels. (For example, since 16 pixels times 140 percent equals 22.4, should the browser round that to 22 pixels or 23 pixels? There's no right answer, according to the CSS specification, so inconsistencies crop up between browsers.)

However, setting your base font size to 10 pixels has a lot of disadvantages as well. Most importantly, it's just really small text; even if you don't have a vision impairment, that's going to be hard to read. It also doesn't respect user preferences to set your fonts 62.5 percent smaller than they wanted. You could argue that setting any font size smaller than 100 percent is not

■ **NOTE:** Remember that all the pixel measurements in this example are dependent on the text size being 16 pixels on the divs that have the em values set on them. If you've decreased the text size, for example, through a universal font-size rule on the body element, you'll need to recalculate the pixel equivalences with your particular text size. Also, users with defaults other than 16 pixels will of course get different pixel sizes.

respecting user preferences, but at least setting it to something like 88 percent isn't so far off as to be completely out of the ballpark of the user's default. Web design is always a balancing act.

■ **NOTE:** Believe it or not, setting a font size smaller than the user's default could actually make the text larger than some user's defaults, if they have minimum font sizes in place. To read about this additional disadvantage to the 62.5 percent font-size trick, see the article "Sensible type sizing on the web" (www.bergamotus.ws/misc/sensible-css-text-sizing.html).

You could set your base font size to 62.5 percent to make pixel computations easier, and then reset all your text larger to make up for these disadvantages, but this gets really tricky. You can't set the larger font sizes on the layout divs, because that defeats the whole purpose of setting it to 10 pixels in the first place: Now all the text within those divs is a larger size, so you can't set em widths for those divs based on a starting point of ten, nor can you assign relative sizes to certain pieces of text within the divs like headings and have the nice base of 10 to start from. What *will* work is to set font sizes on all the individual text elements, such as paragraphs, headings, and lists, rather than the divs themselves. But since many of these text elements can be nested within each other, you're going to run into problems with compounded font sizes, as we talked about earlier in the chapter. To counteract the compounding effect, you'll have to add even more lines of CSS, setting the nested elements back up to the correct font size. You end up with a really bloated and confusing style sheet—and setting the base to 10 is supposed to ease your work, not add to it.

Given all this, I'm not a fan of the 62.5-percent-font-size-on-the-body trick, and we won't be using it here. I've mentioned it simply because it continues to be popular today and I don't want you thinking I've overlooked a really useful and common CSS trick! Instead, the examples in this chapter will not have any font size set on the body, in order to keep it at users' defaults, while the exercise sections at the end of each chapter use a font size of 88 percent on the body to size the text down a little bit without getting too far from users' defaults. We'll pick em measurements based more on line lengths than on pixel equivalences.

Creating Elastic Columns Using Floats

Now that you have a better idea of how ems work, let's start using them to create elastic layouts.

When we made liquid layouts in the last chapter, creating multi-column layouts was a matter of stopping the default top-to-bottom stacking of some of the divs to create side-by-side columns instead. We didn't have to worry about making the divs liquid, since they, like all block elements, are liquid by default. The process of switching the divs from being liquid to being elastic is going to require a little more work.

But first, there are a couple things you need to know about the examples shown in this chapter.

Refresher: About This Chapter's Examples

First, all of the examples will use the same basic div structure from the last chapter, where we worked on liquid layouts. Here it is again, to refresh your memory:

```
<div id="header"></div>
<div id="content-main"></div>
<div id="sidebar"></div>
<div id="footer"></div>
```

Second, as in the last chapter, I've applied some basic CSS for visual formatting to the page—mostly background colors on the divs so that you can see where each one lies in the examples shown in the figures. This visual formatting does *not* include a font size on the body or any of the divs, so we'll be assuming the common default font size of 16 pixels.

Finally, just as before, we'll start out with two-column structures to demonstrate the basic techniques, and then move on to adding more columns. I'm not going to cover all of the layout methods in as much detail as in the last chapter, simply because they contain many of the same steps and quirks, so make sure you're familiar with the previous chapter before delving further into this one.

■ NOTE: Each of the completed example files is available for download from this book's companion web site at www.flexiblewebbook.com. Download the file ch5_examples.zip to get the complete set. I'll let you know which file goes with which technique as we go along.

Creating Columns with Floats and Matching Side Margins

As with liquid layouts, a quick and easy way to create multiple elastic columns is to float the div or divs that you want to be on the edges of the page either to the right or the left, and then give the remaining div a matching margin facing the float to make room for it.

Since content-main is first in the source, it will be the float in this case:

```
#content-main {
    float: right;
    width: 37em;
    background: #F0EE90;
}
```

This gives us two columns, but only the right-hand one is elastic (**Figure 5.1**). So what we have at this point is not a fully elastic layout, but instead a liquid-elastic hybrid. This is because divs are liquid by default, so without setting any width on the sidebar div, it's going to continue adjusting in width to the viewport.

FIGURE 5.1 The right column is elastic; it gets bigger as the text size gets bigger and doesn't change in size when the window size changes. The left column is liquid; it takes up whatever space is left in the viewport.

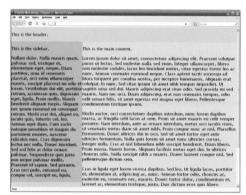

To make the layout fully elastic, assign a width to the sidebar `div`:

```
#sidebar {
    width: 10em;
    background: #FFA480;
}
```

Though this makes the sidebar elastic, it also creates a gap between the columns at many viewport sizes (**Figure 5.2**). This is because `div`s sit on the left side of the viewport by default, and simply adding a width to the sidebar `div` does nothing to change this default behavior. The main content column, on the other hand, has been floated to the right, so it will always hug the right side of the viewport, and the two `div`s will always sit as far from each other as they can.

This isn't usually the look you want in a multi-column layout. To get both `div`s sitting next to each other, without both being floats, you need to switch the `float` value from right to left:

```
#content-main {
    float: left;
    width: 37em;
    background: #F0EE90;
}
```

You also need to add a left margin to the sidebar `div` that is equal to or larger than the width of the content-main `div`:

```
#sidebar {
    width: 10em;
    margin-left: 37em;
    background: #FFA480;
}
```

This side margin was irrelevant when content-main was floated right, as both `div`s then wanted to sit as far from each other as possible, but it is needed now.

Both columns are now elastic and sit next to each other at all times (**Figure 5.3**). But the header and footer are not elastic yet; they continue to fill the width of the viewport. To make them match up with the combined width of the columns, give them both widths of 47 ems:

```
#header {
    width: 47em;
    background: #DDDDDD;
}
#footer {
    width: 47em;
    background: #DDDDDD;
}
```

DEALING WITH THE THREE-PIXEL TEXT JOG—AGAIN

In Chapter 4, you saw how IE 6 and earlier add three extra pixels of space between a float and adjacent non-floated content. There, this showed up as a "text jog:" the text within the non-floated column was shifted over three pixels from the edge of the float, and then shifted back into its correct position once the float ended. In this example, the extra three pixels show up not as a text jog but rather as a gap between the two columns. Despite the difference in appearance, it's the same bug, with the same hack to fix it. Should you want to apply this optional hack to this page, here's what it would look like, within conditional comments so only IE 6 and earlier can see it:

```
<!--[if lte IE 6]>
<style>
#sidebar {
    zoom: 1;
    margin: 0;
}
#content-main {
    margin-right: -3px;
}
</style>
<![endif]-->
```

FIGURE 5.3 Both columns are now not only elastic, but sit next to each other at all times.

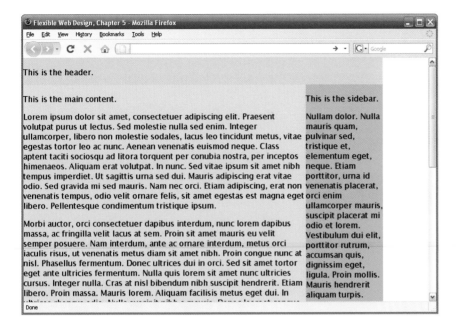

FIGURE 5.4 The header (and footer, not shown) are elastic as well, matching the width of the combined main and sidebar columns instead of filling the viewport.

Also, you should add the `clear` property to the footer to make sure the floated column never overlaps it:

```
#footer {
    clear: both;
    width: 47em;
    background: #DDDDDD;
}
```

This actually isn't necessary in this particular page, because the non-floated sidebar is longer than the floated main content column. The sidebar will always be longer because both columns are elastic; the text will never wrap differently, and the columns will both always keep their same relative dimensions to each other. But it's a good idea to have the `clear` property on the footer when building a real site. You never know which column is going to be longest from page to page, or when a text change will switch one column from being the longest to being the shortest, or if a tall floated image will wrap around text at the bottom of a `div`.

■ **NOTE:** The page showing this completed technique is elastic_margins_twocol.html in the ch5_examples.zip file.

KEEPING THE SIDEBAR ON THE LEFT

Switching the main content from floating right to floating left certainly solved the problem of the big gap between the columns, but it is still possible to keep the sidebar on the left with this layout method. You'll need to do some tinkering in the (X)HTML, though.

Keeping the sidebar on the left with an extra wrapper div. The first option is to add a wrapper around all the `div`s:

```
<div id="wrapper">
    <div id="header"></div>
    <div id="content-main"></div>
    <div id="sidebar"></div>
    <div id="footer"></div>
</div>
```

Give this wrapper `div` a width equal to the combined width of the columns (this also means you don't need to set that width individually on the header and footer anymore):

```
#wrapper {
    width: 47em;
    background: #98F5E8;
}
#header {
    background: #DDDDDD;
}
#footer {
    clear: both;
    background: #DDDDDD;
}
```

You can then float content-main to the right and get rid of the margin on the sidebar altogether:

```
#content-main {
    float: right;
    width: 37em;
    background: #F0EE90;
}
#sidebar {
    width: 10em;
    background: #FFA480;
}
```

CENTERING THE LAYOUT

Now that you have a wrapper `div` in your layout, you can use the auto-side-margins centering technique described in the "Keeping the Layout from Spanning the Whole Viewport" section of Chapter 4. All you have to do is add `margin: 0 auto;` to the `#wrapper` rule, and your design will be centered horizontally within the viewport instead of stuck against the left side. The other centering methods described in Chapter 4 won't work with elastic layouts.

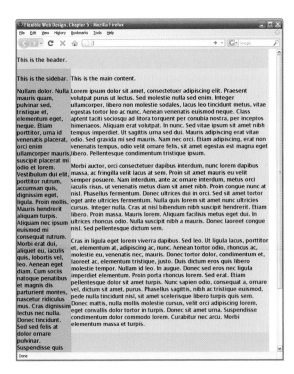

FIGURE 5.5 The sidebar is now on the left side of the main content column. The blue background of the new wrapper div shows behind both columns.

KEEPING FLOATS CONTAINED

If you were making this layout without a footer nested within the wrapper, and the non-floated sidebar was shorter than the main content column, you'd notice that the background color of the wrapper would not show behind both columns. This is correct behavior based on float theory: Floats are removed from the flow of the page, so the wrapper div acts as if the content-main div is not there and lets it overflow out of the bottom of the wrapper.

This doesn't happen in the current layout because the footer div, which sits below the main content column due to the clear property, is not floated and is within the wrapper, so the wrapper stretches down to contain it.

This also wasn't an issue in any of the layouts in Chapter 4, because in all of those the wrapper divs were floated. When you float an element, it automatically expands to hold children floats as well. This is the simplest way to contain floats: float the wrapper as well.

There are lots of other ways you could get the wrapper to contain the floated content-main div, however. Read more about them in "Methods for Containing Floats" at Ed Eliot's blog (www.ejeliot.com/blog/59).

This works great—except in IE 6 and earlier, where the three-pixel text jog severely disrupts the layout. Although this bug was present before the wrapper was added, it was merely a small cosmetic problem then. Now, with the wrapper `div` set to exactly the combined width of the columns, there's no breathing room for those extra three pixels, so IE 6 and earlier drop the sidebar down the page (**Figure 5.6**).

FIGURE 5.6 With the three extra pixels that IE 6 and earlier add, the two columns don't have room to sit side by side within the wrapper, so the second `div`—the sidebar—drops down the page.

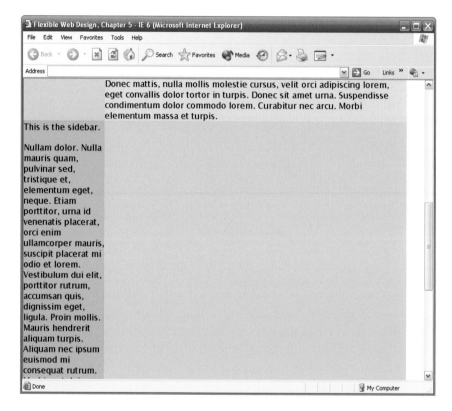

■ NOTE: The dropped sidebar `div` would be considered a "float drop," as described in Chapter 4, even though the sidebar itself is not a float. In this case, the float is causing the drop, as opposed to being the `div` that itself is dropped. The common usage of the term "float drop" includes both of these things.

One way to avoid this bug is to make the width of the wrapper `div` larger than the combined width of the two columns inside. This creates a small gap between the two columns, but in some designs, you want a gap anyway, so this isn't problematic. If you must have the two columns right next to each other, you can add a hack for IE 6 and earlier. Add the following just below the closing `style` tag in the *head* of the page, or below the `link` or `@import` directive to your external style sheet:

```
<!--[if lte IE 6]>
<style>
#sidebar {
    zoom: 1;
    margin: 0;
}
```

```
#content-main {
   margin-left: -3px;
}
</style>
<![endif]-->
```

Even in non-IE browsers, having a wrapper add up to exactly the width of the columns can be a little problematic. Any time you use relative measurements, like ems, you're depending on the browser to round them into an even number of pixels. Rounding inconsistencies are always possible. For instance, if the browser rounds the widths of the two columns inside the wrapper down, but rounds the width of the wrapper up, you'll be left with an empty pixel of space between the two columns. (The Safari browser seems to be the most prone to this in elastic layouts.) This is simply a tiny cosmetic problem, but it's still a disadvantage to keep in mind.

Keeping the sidebar on the left without an extra wrapper div. To avoid rounding problems and the dropped column in IE 6 and earlier, you'll need to use a different method to keep the sidebar on the left. Ditch the wrapper div and move the sidebar div before the content-main div in the source:

```
<div id="header"></div>
<div id="sidebar"></div>
<div id="content-main"></div>
<div id="footer"></div>
```

This is not ideal source order, of course, but it does allow you to make the sidebar div be the floated column, while content-main has the matching side margin:

```
#sidebar {
   float: left;
   width: 10em;
   background: #FFA480;
}
#content-main {
   width: 37em;
   margin-left: 10em;
   background: #F0EE90;
}
```

Now the columns will always sit right up against each other. If any rounding inconsistencies add or subtract an extra pixel, that pixel will end up to the right of the main content column, where it will be practically imperceptible. The three-pixel gap is still present in IE 6 and earlier using this method, as it occurs any time you have non-floated content next to a float, but it doesn't cause any columns to drop down—it's been relegated to "small cosmetic annoyance" status.

■ **NOTE:** The page showing this completed technique is elastic_margins_twocol_leftsidebar1.html in the ch5_examples.zip file.

■ **NOTE:** You may be able to see an extra pixel to the right of the columns due to rounding inconsistencies if you look really closely at the right edge of the main content column compared to the header and footer: they'll differ from each other by one pixel in width. But don't sweat it: not only is this very hard to notice, it will happen only at certain text sizes, and even then probably just in Safari.

■ **NOTE:** The page showing this completed technique is elastic_margins_twocol_leftsidebar2.html in the ch5_examples.zip file.

USING THE body TO STOP THE DROP

It's actually possible to create a three-column elastic layout without a wrapper div, but it requires placing a width or min-width on the body element (you'll learn about min-width in Chapter 6). There's nothing wrong with doing this, but it doesn't work for most layouts, since you often want to place a background color or image on the body that will fill the entire viewport, instead of being restricted to a certain width. Using a wrapper div also allows us to use more ideal source order. So, we won't be going over how to use the body element in place of a wrapper div to create three-column elastic layouts.

ADDING A THIRD COLUMN

Unlike with liquid layouts, where adding a wrapper div is optional, you really do need to add an extra wrapper div to create a third column in an elastic layout. That's because you can't float one div to the left and one to the right and then leave the main content column in the middle to fill in the rest of the space. All three columns need to have widths assigned and need to be oriented to one or the other side of the viewport. When the viewport is narrower than the combined width of the two floated divs, they can no longer sit side by side, so the one later in the (X)HTML source will drop down. This is just normal float behavior.

Adding a third column with ideal source order. One way to add the extra wrapper is to use the same div structure used for the liquid layout:

```
<div id="header"></div>
<div id="content-wrapper">
    <div id="content-main"></div>
    <div id="content-secondary"></div>
</div>
<div id="sidebar"></div>
<div id="footer"></div>
```

Just as before, what we're basically doing is creating a three-column layout out of two two-column layouts—one nested inside of the other. The first two-column layout is made up of the content-wrapper and sidebar divs, using the exact same two-column layout method we discussed at the start of the chapter:

```
#content-wrapper {
    float: left;
    width: 47em;
```

```
    background: #98F5E8;
}
#sidebar {
    width: 10em;
    margin-left: 47em;
    background: #FFA480;
}
```

The combined width of these two columns is 57 ems, not 47 as it was in our two-column version, so you need to increase the widths of the header and footer divs to match:

```
#header {
    width: 57em;
    background: #DDDDDD;
}
#footer {
    clear: both;
    width: 57em;
    background: #DDDDDD;
}
```

Next, create another two-column layout within the content-wrapper div itself:

```
#content-main {
    float: right;
    width: 37em;
    background: #F0EE90;
}
#content-secondary {
    width: 10em;
    background: #9BF598;
}
```

Unlike with the liquid layout version of this layout, there's no need to do any math to figure out what width to set the content-secondary div to in order to make it match in width with the sidebar div—just set both to 10 ems, and they'll be the same size onscreen (**Figure 5.7**). You don't have the same compounding measurements problem that arose with nesting percentage measurements. Remember, though, that this holds true only when the two divs in question have the same computed font size. If one of the two divs had a different font size set, or inherited, an em would compute to a different number of pixels in each div, so they would come out to different widths visually.

FIGURE 5.7 The two side-bars match in width, even though the right column is nested within another div.

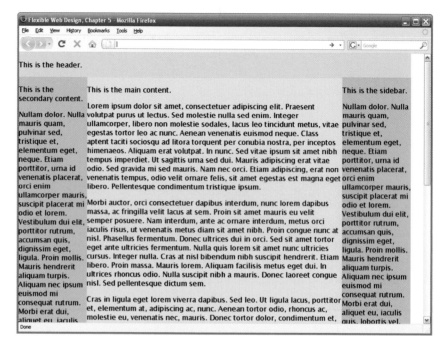

■ **NOTE:** The page showing this completed technique is elastic_margins_threecol1.html in the ch5_examples.zip file.

There's one more piece of business to attend to before we can call this layout finished, though: IE 6 and earlier. Once again, the three-pixel text jog causes a column to drop down, this time the content-secondary div. Here's the hack to fix the float drop, as well as the three-pixel gap that appears between the content-wrapper and sidebar divs:

```
<!--[if lte IE 6]>
<style>
#sidebar, #content-secondary {
    zoom: 1;
    margin: 0;
}
#content-wrapper {
    margin-right: -3px;
}
#content-main {
    margin-left: -3px;
}
</style>
<![endif]-->
```

Adding a third column with compromised source order. There's another method for creating a three-column elastic layout involving a wrapper div, but this time the wrapper is placed around all of the divs in the body:

```
<div id="wrapper">
    <div id="header"></div>
    <div id="content-secondary"></div>
    <div id="content-main"></div>
    <div id="sidebar"></div>
    <div id="footer"></div>
</div>
```

The source order isn't as ideal in this scenario, because the secondary content must come before the more important main content in the (X)HTML. Still, there may be times when the most important content on your page is not in the middle column of your design, but rather in the left column, with secondary content following in the columns to the right. Or, as we talked about in the last chapter, you may have three equally important feature boxes you want to display in three columns, and it makes sense for the one shown farthest to the left to be the first in the source, then the second leftmost box to be second in the source, and so on. So, in some cases, this source order may actually be the best choice for your particular content and design.

Give this wrapper div a width equal to the combined width of the columns. This also means you don't need to set that width individually on the header and footer anymore:

```
#header {
    background: #DDDDDD;
}
#wrapper {
    width: 57em;
    background: #98F5E8;
}
#footer {
    clear: both;
    background: #DDDDDD;
}
```

Next, float the content-secondary div to the left with a width of 10 ems:

```
#content-secondary {
    float: left;
    width: 10em;
    background: #9BF598;
}
#content-main {
    float: left;
```

■ **TIP:** In this example, you could do away with the wrapper div entirely and just use the body element—it already wraps around all the divs— for the same purpose. It wouldn't solve the source order problems, but would give you one less div to worry about. However, it also means one less "hook" where you can attach CSS backgrounds and other styles.

```
    width: 37em;
    background: #F0EE90;
}
#sidebar {
    width: 10em;
    margin-left: 47em;
    background: #FFA480;
}
```

■ **NOTE:** Even though the extra space gives IE enough room to bring the third column back up on a level with the other two, it doesn't actually cure the bug. Once the column moves up, you'll still see the three-pixel gap between the content-main and sidebar columns. You can hack away this small cosmetic problem if you wish.

Make sure the same float, width, and margin values are on the content-main and sidebar `divs` as you used in the two-column, right-sidebar version. The only exception to this is the left margin value on the sidebar, which must be increased from 37 to 47 ems to make room for the combined width of the two columns to its left.

This successfully completes the layout in browsers other than IE 6 and earlier, where the familiar float drop occurs. Luckily, in this layout it's much easier to avoid any hacks and just work around the bug than it was in layouts earlier in the chapter. If you increase the width of the wrapper by just .5 em, you give IE enough room to pull that column back up:

```
#header {
    width: 57em;
    background: #DDDDDD;
}
#wrapper {
    width: 57.5em;
    background: #98F5E8;
}
#footer {
    width: 57em;
    clear: both;
    background: #DDDDDD;
}
```

■ **NOTE:** The page showing this completed technique is elastic_margins_threecol2.html in the ch5_examples.zip file.

Unlike in earlier layouts, this extra space will not be added between the columns, but to the right of all three (**Figure 5.8**). If you have a background color or pattern on the wrapper, this extra space inside the right edge of the wrapper will be noticeable, but if not, no one will ever know that extra space is there, especially if you set the header and footer widths back to the regular 57 ems. And of course, if the extra space *is* disruptive of your design, you can always hack the three-pixel text jog as usual—it's just nice to avoid hacks when possible.

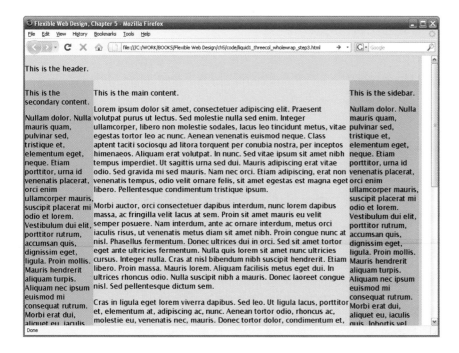

FIGURE 5.8 Although the extra space is visible here because the wrapper has a blue background, in many designs you would not have a background on the wrapper, making the space imperceptible.

Creating Columns by Floating Everything

Just as with liquid layouts, you can float every single `div` to create multi-column elastic layouts.

Let's go back to our simple two-column example, where the main content `div` was floated to the left. You'll use the same CSS for the main content `div`, but remove the matching side margin from the sidebar `div`. You'll then need to float the sidebar `div` to the left as well:

```
#content-main {
    float: left;
    width: 37em;
    background: #F0EE90;
}
#sidebar {
    float: left;
    width: 10em;
    background: #FFA480;
}
```

The two-column layout made by floating both of the columns looks exactly the same as if we had only floated one—until you narrow your window past the combined width of the two columns. Then, the sidebar drops down (**Figure 5.9**).

■ **NOTE:** Although having a column drop down the page is not desirable in most designs, it can be used as a design feature, not a flaw. To learn why you might want to let columns drop down, see "Alternative Ways to Limit Flexibility" in Chapter 6.

FIGURE 5.9 When the viewport is narrower than the combined width of the two floats, the later one drops down to the first spot on the page where it can fit.

■ **TIP:** Don't forget to remove the width values from the header and footer when you add a wrapper around them with its own width. Setting the width in one place—on the wrapper—keeps you from having to remember to change it in three places down the road.

■ **NOTE:** The page showing this completed technique is elastic_floats_twocol.html in the ch5_examples.zip file.

This happens for the same reason that we couldn't create a three-column elastic layout without an extra wrapper div: normal float behavior. When the viewport is too narrow to fit both floats side by side, the later one drops down. This didn't happen in the liquid layout where every div was floated, because the viewport was never narrower than 100 percent (the combined width of the two columns): such a thing would be impossible. When you're dealing with ems or pixels, however, it's quite easy for the viewport to get smaller than the combined width of your columns.

So, just as with the three-column version, the solution is to add a wrapper div around all the divs and set its width to the combined width of the columns inside—in this case, 47 ems. You don't need to worry about making the width a little larger to give IE 6 and earlier some breathing room—the three-pixel text jog is never triggered in layouts where all the columns are floated.

Adding the wrapper also makes it easy for you to get the sidebar back on the left if you want—simply float both divs to the right instead. No changes to the (X)HTML are needed.

ADDING A THIRD COLUMN

Since you already have a wrapper in place for the two-column version of the float-all-the-divs layout, it's easy to add a third column. Just add the new div before the main content div in the source, as we did before with the floats-and-matching-margins three-column layout:

```
<div id="wrapper">
    <div id="header"></div>
    <div id="content-secondary"></div>
    <div id="content-main"></div>
    <div id="sidebar"></div>
    <div id="footer"></div>
</div>
```

Then, simply float the content-secondary div to the left. Make sure to increase the width of the wrapper div by the width of this new div as well:

```
#wrapper {
    width: 57em;
    background: #98F5E8;
}
#content-secondary {
    float: left;
    width: 10em;
    background: #9BF598;
}
#content-main {
    float: left;
    width: 37em;
    background: #F0EE90;
}
#sidebar {
    float: left;
    width: 10em;
    background: #FFA480;
}
```

That's all there is to it. There's no need to add any hacks for IE or worry about float drops. The completed layout will look just like Figure 5.7.

As I said earlier, this source order isn't ideal if the div we're calling content-main is truly your most important content. If you want to get content-main back before the other columns in the source, use a wrapper around just the content-main and content-secondary divs:

```
<div id="header"></div>
<div id="content-wrapper">
    <div id="content-main"></div>
    <div id="content-secondary"></div>
</div>
<div id="sidebar"></div>
<div id="footer"></div>
```

■ **NOTE:** The page showing this completed technique is elastic_floats_threecol1.html in the ch5_examples.zip file.

Set the width of content-wrapper to 47 ems, and add widths back to the header and footer `div`s as well, since they no longer have anything wrapping around them to constrain their widths:

```
#header {
    width: 57em;
    background: #DDDDDD;
}
#content-wrapper {
    width: 47em;
    background: #98F5E8;
}
#footer {
    clear: both;
    width: 57em;
    background: #DDDDDD;
}
```

Next, add the `float` properties. You should already have the sidebar and content-secondary `div`s floating to the left. Float content-wrapper to the left as well, and switch the `float: left` declaration on content-main to `float: right` instead:

```
#content-wrapper {
    float: left;
    width: 47em;
    background: #98F5E8;
}
#content-main {
    float: right;
    width: 37em;
    background: #F0EE90;
}
#content-secondary {
    float: left;
    width: 10em;
    background: #9BF598;
}
#sidebar {
    float: left;
    width: 10em;
    background: #FFA480;
}
```

■ **NOTE:** The page showing this completed technique is elastic_floats_threecol2.html in the ch5_examples.zip file.

The completed three-column layout will look exactly as it did when the wrapper was around all three columns, but this version has a more optimal source order for the majority of situations.

NO ELASTIC NEGATIVE MARGIN LAYOUT?

In the last chapter, you learned how to create a liquid layout using floats and negative margins. We won't be going over a negative margin technique to create an elastic layout in this chapter—not because such a technique can't be used for elastic designs, but simply because there's no advantage to using negative margin techniques over the techniques you've learned so far in this chapter. There's no need to introduce the extra layer of complexity that negative margin layouts bring when the simpler methods work just as well.

Site-Building Exercise: Creating the Shelter's Home Page Layout Structure

In this exercise, you'll build the elastic layout structure of the home page of the Beechwood Animal Shelter site. Although the inner page of the site that we built in the last chapter was liquid, it's fine to mix different layout types throughout a site if you wish. Plus, we need to get some practice building real elastic pages somewhere!

You'll work with the exercise files from this book's companion web site at www.flexiblewebbook.com. Download and unzip the file ch5_exercise.zip.

Preparing the Page

Open the file home-start.html in your text or code editor of choice. The file already contains all the content of the home page, marked up semantically. It also contains a few of the `div`s we used in the last chapter—header, wrapper, and footer—so you don't have to worry about adding these again. You will, however, need to add the structural `div`s *inside* the wrapper `div`.

If you look at the layout of the elements in **Figure 5.10**, you can see that the home page is made up of several two-column layouts nested within each other. Each shaded box in Figure 5.10 denotes a column, and each column has to be made out of one or more block-level elements, such as a `div`, paragraph, or list. You'll add those block elements now.

FIGURE 5.10 The home page is made up of several two-column layouts nested within each other. Each column is denoted with a shaded box.

1. Enter a new line below the opening tag for the wrapper div, and type the following:

   `<div id="banner">`

2. On the next line is the single paragraph of text in the banner. Locate the closing p tag, and enter a new line below it. Type **</div>** to close the banner div you just created.

3. Enter a new line between the closing div tag you just typed and the img element below it. Type the following:

   `<div id="ads">`

4. On the next line are two img elements. After the second one, enter a new line. Type **</div>** to close the ads div you just created.

5. Enter a new line between the closing div tag you just typed and the img element below it. Type the following:

   `<div id="story">`

6. Immediately following the `img` element is an `h2` element, and then a paragraph. Locate the paragraph's closing tag, and enter a new line beneath it. Type **</div>** to close the story `div` you just created.

7. Enter a new line between the closing `div` tag you just typed and the `h2` element below it. Type the following:

   ```
   <div id="adopt-pets">
   ```

8. Immediately following the `h2` element is a `ul` element. Locate its closing tag and enter a new line beneath it. Type the following to open a new `div` nested within the adopt-pets div:

   ```
   <div id="search-pets">
   ```

9. Following this new `div` tag you created is a paragraph and then a form. Locate the form's closing tag, and type the following to close both the adopt-pets and search-pets `div`s:

   ```
   </div>
   </div>
   ```

■ **NOTE:** We're not adding a `div` around the `ul` element because it is a block-level element that can form its own column without the need for a `div`. You'll see how later.

■ **TIP:** As an optional step, you may want to indent the markup within each of the `div`s you added to make the HTML easier to read.

You've now added all the basic structural `div`s that you'll need to create the layout. The HTML within the wrapper `div` should look like this (most of the content has been removed to highlight the `div` placement):

```html
<div id="banner">
    <p>Beechwood Animal Shelter is a no-kill animal rescue...</p>
</div>
<div id="ads">
    <img src="images/feature-fair.png"...>
</div>
<div id="story">
    <img src="images/story.jpg" width="86" height="86" alt="">
    ...
</div>
<div id="adopt-pets">
    <h2>Adopt me!</h2>
    <ul>
        ...
    </ul>
    <div id="search-pets">
        <p>These are just a few of the hundreds of dogs and
cats...</p>
        <form>
            ...
        </form>
    </div>
</div>
```

Adding Base Styles

These base styles from the previous chapter's exercise have been preserved for the home page:

```
body {
    margin: 0;
    padding: 0;
    font: 88% "Lucida Sans Unicode", "Lucida Grande", sans-serif;
    line-height: 1.4;
}
div {
    padding: 1px 0;
}
#header, #footer {
    background: #EFEFEF;
}
```

You'll now need to add background colors to the new divs to see where each lies as you change their positions on the page. Add the following rules within the style section in the head of the page:

```
#banner {
    background: #CFC;
}
#ads {
    background: #FCF;
}
#story {
    background: #FFC;
}
#adopt-pets {
    background: #CFF;
}
#search-pets {
    background: #CCF;
}
```

Creating the Columns

Now you'll add the styles to actually create the columns. We'll use both the floats-with-matching-side-margins and all-floats methods on the various two-column layouts that make up this page's design.

1. Add the following rule to the `style` section in the `head` of the page:

   ```
   #wrapper {
       width: 54em;
       margin: 0 auto;
   }
   ```

   This sets the overall width of the layout between the header and footer `div`s to 54 ems and centers it horizontally in the viewport. Putting a width on the wrapper keeps you from having to set a width on the banner `div` or any other blocks inside the wrapper that you want to be a single, full-width column, as well as establishing the limits for the widths of the other columns nested within.

2. Modify the `#ads` rule you created earlier to move that `div` into place on the left side of the layout:

   ```
   #ads {
       float: left;
       width: 13em;
       background: #FCF;
   }
   ```

3. Modify the `#story` rule you created earlier to get that `div` out of the way of the ads `div`:

   ```
   #story {
       float: right;
       width: 41em;
       background: #FFC;
   }
   ```

4. Make the same modification to the `#adopt-pets` rule for the same purpose:

   ```
   #adopt-pets {
       float: right;
       width: 41em;
       background: #CFF;
   }
   ```

5. There's already a grouped rule for the header and footer together, but add a separate rule for just the footer, so it can clear both the floated `div`s above it:

   ```
   #footer {
       clear: both;
   }
   ```

   This completes the outermost two-column layout (**Figure 5.11**). You now need to create the two-column layouts within the story `div` and the adopt-pets `div`.

> ■ **NOTE:** Since the font size on the body is set to 88 percent, most people would be viewing this page with a font size of about 14 pixels (given the browser default of 16 pixels that most people never change). With 14-pixel text, the width of 54 ems comes out to 756 pixels.

FIGURE 5.11 The outermost two-column layout is in place.

6. In the `style` section in the `head` of the page, add the following new rules:

    ```
    #story img {
        float: left;
    }
    #story h2,
    #story p {
        margin: 0 0 0 100px;
    }
    ```

This is a little sneak-peek at hybrid layouts: You've created a left column that has a fixed width, and then used side margins on the adjacent blocks to move them out of the way of the left column and create an elastic right column. You'll learn more about hybrid layouts in the next chapter.

7. Add another new rule in the `style` section to create the left column inside the adopt-pets `div`:

```
#adopt-pets ul {
    float: left;
    width: 14em;
}
```

Because the `ul` element is a block element itself, it can be floated without the need for a `div`. And, since it's the only `ul` inside the adopt-pets `div`, it can be targeted in the CSS with a descendant selector, instead of having to add an `id` attribute to the `ul` in the HTML.

8. Modify the `#search-pets` rule you created earlier, to get that `div` out of the way of the floated `ul` and create the right column:

```
#search-pets {
    margin-left: 15em;
    background: #CCF;
}
```

The two nested two-column layouts are now complete (**Figure 5.12**). To compare your work to the completed exercise, see the file home-end.html in the files you extracted from ch5_exercise.zip.

To test the elasticity of the design, open the page in a browser and change the text size up and down to watch it expand and contract proportionally in size. (Make sure not to use the browser's zoom function to test this, as that makes everything look elastic even if it is not.)

Don't worry that the images in the leftmost column don't scale right now and can therefore get cut off when the text size is very small. Also, don't worry about the funky appearance of the list of pets to adopt. For now, we're just focusing on making elastic columns. You'll learn how to style elastic *content* to go inside those columns in later chapters.

FIGURE 5.12 The two nested two-column layouts—the photo by the "happy ending" story and the list of pets by the search form—are now in place.

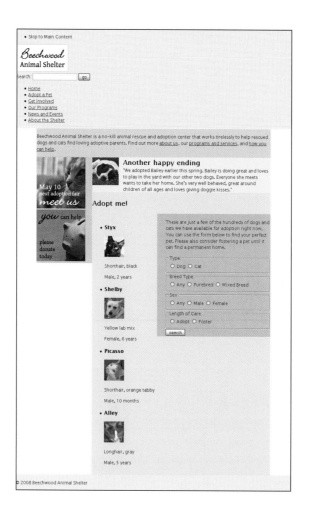

6

Putting Limits on Flexibility

You now know how to create liquid and elastic layouts that adapt to individual users' web browsing setups. But sometimes you want layouts that aren't quite so adaptable. It's possible to compromise between a fixed-width layout and a 100-percent liquid or elastic layout using a number of techniques that limit the degree of flexibility that your design has.

Building Hybrid Layouts

■ **NOTE:** Each of the completed example files is available for download from this book's companion web site at www.flexiblewebbook.com. Download the file ch6_examples.zip to get the complete set. I'll let you know which file goes with which technique as we go along.

As we discussed in Chapter 1, hybrid layouts mix units of measurements between columns. You can add one or more fixed-width columns onto your existing liquid or elastic layout to create a design that is still flexible overall—just to a lesser degree than fully liquid or elastic layouts.

There are so many combinations of column types you can make to create hybrid layouts, but we'll go over two of the most common:

* Fixed sidebars with a liquid center column
* Fixed sidebars with an elastic center column

Fixed Sidebars with a Liquid Center Column

One very popular type of hybrid layout has a liquid main content column, with the sidebar or sidebars given fixed pixel widths. One reason for this style's popularity is probably because it's generally a very easy type of layout to create. Another reason might be because readability is usually not nearly so important for sidebars, which generally aren't text-heavy, as it is for the main content column. Thus, it may be less imperative to make the sidebars liquid, which may free up the design to do some different things that couldn't be achieved in an all-liquid layout (such as using full-width, fixed-width image ads in the sidebar).

USING FLOATS WITH MATCHING SIDE MARGINS

The general idea behind liquid-fixed hybrid layout methods is that you assign widths in pixels to the sidebars but leave a width off the main content column entirely. This allows the main content column to simply take up whatever space is left in the viewport or wrapper div after the sidebars are accounted for—it will always be some different, variable percentage in width.

A CASE FOR FLEXIBLE SIDEBARS

Just because your sidebars don't contain a lot of text doesn't mean there wouldn't be any benefit to making them liquid or elastic. For instance, someone using large text might get only one or two words per line in a narrow side column, or, even worse, have really long words overflowing out of the column. In this particular case, an elastic column might be the best option. It can also sometimes be easier to keep all the columns liquid or all the columns elastic—mixing units of measurements in a single layout can sometimes result in difficult math or lots of extra structural divs.

Because the main content column doesn't have a declared width, you can't float it—you'll just use the matching-side-margins method to get it out of the way of the sidebars, which will be floated to either side. For a two-column layout where the sidebar is on the left side of the page, the CSS might look like this:

```
#sidebar {
    float: left;
    width: 200px;
}
#content-main {
    margin-left: 200px;
}
```

■ NOTE: Remember that any page where you have floats next to non-floats, as we do here, suffers from the three-pixel text jog bug in IE 6 and earlier. See the explanation in Chapter 4 if you want to hack it away.

If you wanted to add a third column on the right side of the page, you'd just float it in the opposite direction, and give content-main a matching margin on that side as well:

```
#sidebar {
    float: left;
    width: 200px;
}
#content-secondary {
    float: right;
    width: 250px;
}
#content-main {
    margin: 0 250px 0 200px;
}
```

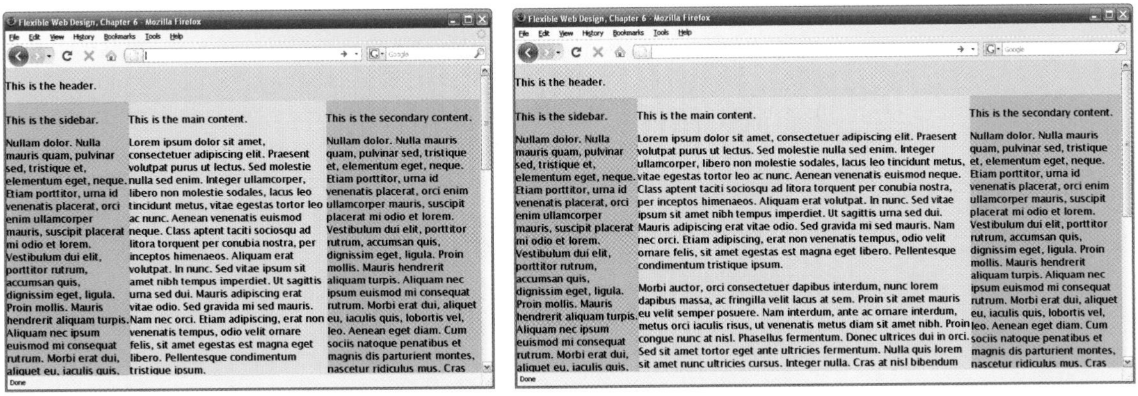

FIGURE 6.1 The sidebars always remain a fixed width, with the center column simply taking up whatever percentage of the viewport is left.

Because, in the (X)HTML, floats have to precede the non-floated content that you want to appear adjacent to them, both the sidebar and content-secondary divs must come before the content-main div in this method.

■ NOTE: The page showing this completed technique is liquid-fixed_threecol.html in the ch6_examples.zip file.

COMBINING LIQUID AND ELASTIC COLUMNS IN ONE LAYOUT

Although all of the hybrid examples we're going over incorporate fixed-width columns, it's perfectly acceptable to combine liquid and elastic columns into a single hybrid layout. This type of layout wouldn't *limit* flexibility, of course, just change the type of flexibility in use—which is why we're not covering it here.

Elastic columns are kind of like fixed-width columns, in that they have a fixed pixel width for any given text size in use by visitors to the site, so the liquid-fixed hybrids we're covering here are your best point of comparison for liquid-elastic hybrids. You'd use the same methods for liquid-elastic hybrids as with liquid-fixed hybrids, simply switching out pixel widths and margins for em widths and margins.

If you want content-main to come before the sidebars in the source, it's going to have to be floated and given a width as well. But, as we already discussed, the percentage width that the main content column is going to take up is going to constantly change as the viewport width changes, so there's no single value we can assign to the div to make this work. The solution is to use a negative margin layout method instead.

LIQUID-FIXED HYBRID LAYOUTS USING NEGATIVE MARGINS

In Chapter 4, you learned about how negative margins combined with floats can produce layouts that allow the main content div to come first in the source when simpler layout methods fail to do so. We can adapt the same fully liquid negative margin layout from that chapter to be a liquid-fixed hybrid instead.

You'll use the same (X)HTML as before, and just make a couple small changes to the CSS. Here's the complete, original CSS from the fully liquid version in Chapter 4:

```
body {
    margin: 0;
    padding: 0;
    font-family: "Lucida Sans Unicode", "Lucida Grande",
sans-serif;
}
div {
    padding: 1px 0;
}
#header {
    background: #DDDDDD;
}
#content-wrapper {
```

```
    float: left;
    width: 100%;
    background: #98F5E8;
}
#content-main {
    margin: 0 25%;
    background: #F0EE90;
}
#content-secondary {
    float: left;
    width: 25%;
    margin-left: -25%;
    background: #9BF598;
}
#sidebar {
    float: left;
    width: 25%;
    margin-left: -100%;
    background: #FFA480;
}
#footer {
    position: relative;
    clear: both;
    background: #DDDDDD;
}
```

The first modification you need to make, of course, is to change the widths of the two sidebars to pixel measurements:

```
#content-secondary {
    float: left;
    width: 250px;
    margin-left: -25%;
    background: #9BF598;
}
#sidebar {
    float: left;
    width: 200px;
    margin-left: -100%;
    background: #FFA480;
}
```

Then, change the margin values on content-main to match and make room for the two sidebar columns:

```
#content-main {
    margin: 0 250px 0 200px;
    background: #F0EE90;
}
```

Next, you need to change the negative margin values to place the columns in the correct spots. When the content-secondary div had a width of 25 percent, it made sense to use a left margin value of negative 25 percent. This pushed the content-secondary div 25 percent off the left side of the viewport, so it would pop back around the right side. It would always sit 25 percent over from the right side of the viewport, and since it was 25 percent wide, the whole column fit perfectly there.

Now, however, the negative 25 percent margin doesn't correspond with the pixel width of content-secondary. The negative margin will still push it to the left, but depending on your viewport width, it may not be big enough to push it entirely out of the viewport so it can pop back on the right side. Only when 25 percent is bigger than 250 pixels—the width of the column—will this happen.

To fix this, change the negative margin on content-secondary to exactly match its width:

```
#content-secondary {
    float: left;
    width: 250px;
    margin-left: -250px;
    background: #9BF598;
}
```

This value pushes content-secondary exactly 250 pixels—its width at all times—off the left side of the viewport, so it always pops back on the right side and shows fully. Since content-main has a positive right margin of 250 pixels as well, there is space already there in which to let content-secondary sit without overlapping content-main.

When you make this change, not only does content-secondary pop into place, but so does the sidebar div, even though we haven't changed its margin value from negative 100 percent. This is because a value of negative 100 percent still makes the column do a complete circuit of the viewport, ending up back where it started. If content-secondary had not been in the way, the sidebar column would have started out up against the left side of the screen (which you may remember from Chapter 4), which is exactly where we want it to be. The negative margin simply moves it up to sit beside content-main. The resulting layout will look just like Figure 6.1, just with more ideal source order.

PREVENTING THE LAYOUT FROM SPANNING THE WHOLE VIEWPORT WIDTH

Both of the liquid-fixed layout examples you've seen so far span the entire viewport width. This isn't required, of course—just like with fully liquid

■ **NOTE:** Remember in Chapter 4 I mentioned a negative margin technique that works well for hybrid layouts? Now's your chance to use it! If you want this other, somewhat simpler option (it doesn't even require an extra wrapper div), check out "In Search of the Holy Grail" at www.alistapart.com/articles/holygrail.

■ **NOTE:** The page showing this completed technique is liquid-fixed_threecol_negative.html in the ch6_examples.zip file.

layouts, you can restrict the overall width to create empty space on either side of the design.

The most effective way to reduce the amount of the viewport taken up by the overall layout is to nest all the `div`s inside a wrapper `div`. Then, simply assign it a percentage width:

```
#wrapper {
    width: 80%;
}
```

If you want the layout to be centered within the viewport, add equal margin values on each side of the wrapper:

```
#wrapper {
    width: 80%;
    margin: 0 auto;
}
```

This works for both the negative margin and matching-side-margin layouts.

Fixed Sidebars with an Elastic Center Column

An elastic-fixed hybrid layout is a completely different beast than a liquid-fixed hybrid, because with elastic-fixed layouts, you have to assign every single column an explicit width. You can't leave off a width on the main content column to just have it take up the rest of the space. That means you have to use somewhat different techniques than you would with liquid-fixed layouts.

The easiest way to create an elastic-fixed hybrid is to use the same matching-side-margins method we used on the liquid-fixed hybrid, but add a width to content-main:

```
#sidebar {
    float: left;
    width: 200px;
    background: #FFA480;
}
#content-main {
    width: 35em;
    margin-left: 200px;
    background: #F0EE90;
}
```

This works fine for two-column layouts (**Figure 6.2**). If you want the sidebar on the right instead, just move content-main first in the source and make it the float instead. The sidebar `div` will get the matching left margin.

■ **NOTE:** The page showing this completed technique is elastic-fixed_twocol.html in the ch6_examples.zip file.

FIGURE 6.2 The sidebar width remains fixed no matter what the text size, but the main content column expands and contracts proportionally to the text size.

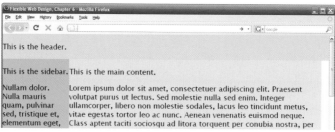

If you want to add a third column, it gets a bit tricky. You can't just add the extra `div` before content-main and float it to the right. Doing so would make it stick to the right side of the viewport, not the right side of content-main, and the latter is probably the look you're going for (**Figure 6.3**). Even worse, if the viewport is not large enough to fit all three columns side by side, the right column will overlap the non-floated main content column (**Figure 6.4**). If you float the main content column, it will no longer get overlapped, but instead will drop down the page when there's not enough room.

FIGURE 6.3 The right-floated green column goes as far to the right as it can— up against the right side of the viewport—instead of staying up against the side of the middle column.

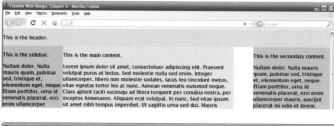

FIGURE 6.4 When the window is too small to fit all three columns side by side, the right column will overlap the background of the non-floated middle column.

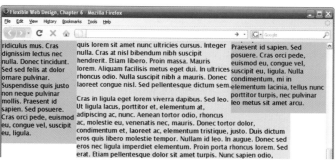

The only way to add a third column without these problems—without using a negative margin technique, which we'll go over shortly—is to cheat a little bit. First, add a div named content-wrapper after the sidebar div, and nest first content-secondary and then content-main inside the new div:

```
<div id="header"></div>
<div id="sidebar"></div>
<div id="content-wrapper">
    <div id="content-secondary"></div>
    <div id="content-main"></div>
</div>
<div id="footer"></div>
```

Then, assign a width in ems to content-wrapper—some value larger than the em width you want for the main content column—as well as a left margin value matching the width of the sidebar div:

```
#content-wrapper {
    width: 45em;
    margin-left: 200px;
    background: #98F5E8;
}
```

This creates the outermost two-column layout. You'll create another two-column layout inside content-wrapper by floating content-secondary to the right and giving content-main a matching right margin:

```
#content-secondary {
    float: right;
    width: 250px;
    background: #9BF598;
}
#content-main {
    margin-right: 250px;
    background: #F0EE90;
}
```

■ **NOTE:** The page showing this completed technique is elastic-fixed_threecol.html in the ch6_examples.zip file.

The reason I say this is cheating a little bit is that content-main doesn't have a particular em width assigned to it. It will still act elastic, as you can see in **Figure 6.5**, because it's nested inside another elastic div. But it won't be a consistent em width wide—you can also see in Figure 6.5 that the number of words on each line in the main content column varies. This is because the wrapper with the assigned em width contains a fixed-width div; the fixed number of pixels of this div will correspond to a varying number of ems depending on the font size, so the remaining ems left over for the main content column will also vary. Therefore, the resulting three-column layout *is* an elastic-fixed hybrid, but it's not quite the same as having one column with an explicit, constant em width stuck between two fixed-pixel-width columns.

FIGURE 6.5 The main content column varies in width with the text size, but doesn't maintain a consistent proportion in regard to it.

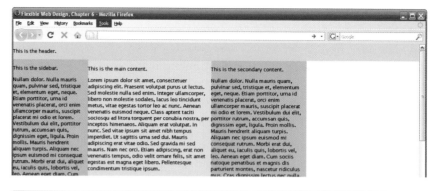

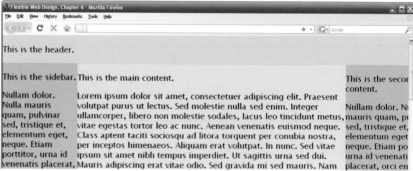

The only way to create an elastic-fixed hybrid where the main content column has a constant em width is to use a negative margin technique. Before we move on to another layout technique, though, there may be a couple more aesthetic adjustments you'd like to make to these first two elastic-fixed layout examples.

FINE-TUNING THE APPEARANCE WITH A WRAPPER div

You may have noticed that none of the elastic-fixed layouts we've created so far have been centered horizontally in the viewport, but instead have been aligned to the left side of the screen. For the liquid-fixed layouts we discussed earlier, changing this alignment was as easy as adding a wrapper div with a width and a margin: 0 auto; declaration.

The elastic-fixed layouts we've gone over so far, however, do not have wrapper divs already in place. While it's easy to add the divs as well as their relevant margin: 0 auto; declarations, doing so is not enough to make the layouts centered; the wrappers need to have widths assigned to them in order to be centered. But here's the catch: You can't assign widths, because you can't know the sum of em and pixel measurements. Without explicitly declared widths, the wrapper divs will simply remain in their default liquid state and fill up the entire viewport width.

The lack of wrapper `divs`—as well as the inability to know the sum of em and pixel measurements—is also the cause for another visual quirk you might not have liked in the elastic-fixed layouts: The header and footer `divs` don't match the combined width of the columns, but instead fill the entire viewport width. In some designs, including the design for our Beechwood Animal Shelter site, this is what you want, but many times it is not.

Both the lack of centering and the lack of alignment between the header and footer `divs` and the columns can be changed by adding a wrapper `div` with not only `auto` side margins, but also a `display: table;` declaration:

```
#wrapper {
    display: table;
    margin: auto;
    background: #98F5E8;
}
```

A `display` value of `table` makes the `div` act just like a regular (X)HTML table with no width assigned: It will be only as wide as its content inside dictates. This is often referred to as "shrinkwrapping," since instead of expanding to fill the entire available space, the block element shrinks as small as it can.

> ■ **NOTE:** You can use a value of `table-cell` or `table-row` as well for the shrinkwrapping effect, but only a value of `table` allows the `div` to also be centered horizontally in the viewport.

HYBRID LAYOUTS WITH FIXED-WIDTH CENTERS AND ELASTIC SIDEBARS

In a hybrid layout, you don't have to make the main content column the flexible one; you can make it fixed-width, if you like, with liquid or elastic sidebars. While this isn't as typical as the types of hybrid layouts we've gone over so far, it's certainly a viable option. Hybrid layouts with fixed-width center columns and elastic sidebars are more common, and probably more useful, than those with liquid sidebars, simply because people usually want to make sidebars expand with their text—to keep things like navigation elements from wrapping—instead of with the width of the window.

Creating hybrid layouts with fixed-width centers and elastic sidebars is basically the same as creating the elastic-fixed layouts we've been going over in this section. You simply swap the pixel measurements with em ones, and vice versa. Elastic-fixed and fixed-elastic hybrids share the same quirks and challenges with source order, wrapper `divs`, and the like, making the identical techniques and limitations necessary for both.

FIGURE 6.6 Adding a wrapper div with display set to table and auto side margins makes the header and footer match the combined width of the columns and also centers the entire layout.

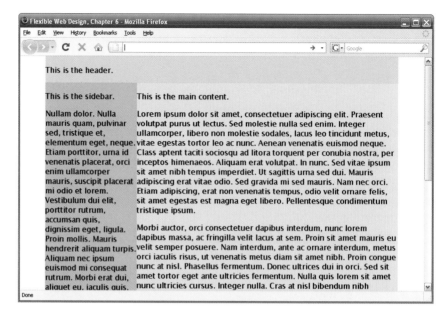

■ **NOTE:** The page showing this completed technique is elastic-fixed_centered.html in the ch6_examples.zip file.

Unfortunately, IE versions 7 and earlier do not support any of the table-related display values, even though they've been part of the CSS 2 specification for many years. (IE 8 does support these values.) This may be something you can live with, as your page probably won't look "broken" without the centering and the header and footer width matchup, and IE users will thus never know they're seeing something a little different from what everyone else sees. But if you can't live with this difference in IE, this is yet another reason to use a negative margin layout for elastic-fixed hybrids.

ELASTIC-FIXED HYBRID LAYOUTS USING NEGATIVE MARGINS

The negative margin layout we've been using all along works fine for an elastic-fixed hybrid if you have only two columns and want the sidebar to be on the left side of the page. First, just remove content-secondary from both the (X)HTML and the CSS. Then, remove the right margin from content-main and add an em width to it:

```
#content-main {
    width: 35em;
    margin: 0 0 0 200px;
    background: #F0EE90;
}
#sidebar {
    float: left;
    width: 200px;
    margin-left: -100%;
    background: #FFA480;
}
```

You get the same basic elastic-fixed, two-column layout that comes from not using negative margins (it looks just like Figure 6.2), but with a more logical source order.

But this particular negative margin layout doesn't work when you want to add a third column to the right side of the elastic main content column. That's because this technique places the right column up against the right side of the viewport (or an overall wrapper `div`, if present) and not up against the right side of the main content column. This is fine when the main content column is liquid and just takes up all the space left over once the side margins are accounted for, but not when it's elastic, as the space remaining to the right of the elastic column may be larger or smaller than the pixel width of the right column. Just as you saw in Figures 6.3 and 6.4, the right column will either leave a gap between itself and the middle column or it will overlap the middle column.

However, there are other negative margin layout methods you can use. Start with almost the same (X)HTML as that of the negative margin layout we've been using so far—just move the wrapper to surround all the `div`s, instead of just the main content `div`:

```
<div id="wrapper">
    <div id="header"></div>
    <div id="content-main"></div>
    <div id="content-secondary"></div>
    <div id="sidebar"></div>
    <div id="footer"></div>
</div>
```

In the previous negative margin layout, you used side margins on the content-main `div` to create space for the two sidebars to sit in. In this negative margin layout, you'll use side padding instead, and you'll place it on the wrapper, not on content-main:

```
#wrapper {
    padding: 0 250px 0 200px;
    background: #98F5E8;
}
```

You also need to place a width on the wrapper `div` equal to the width you want content-main to be:

```
#wrapper {
    width: 30em;
    padding: 0 250px 0 200px;
    background: #98F5E8;
}
```

■ **NOTE:** The page showing this completed technique is elastic-fixed_twocol_negative.html in the ch6_examples.zip file.

■ **NOTE:** To center this layout, you would simply add `margin: 0 auto;` to the #wrapper rule.

If you look at the page in a browser now, you'll see that all of the `div`s are exactly 30 ems wide at all times, and all have fixed-pixel space to either side of them (**Figure 6.7**). This is what we want for content-main, but it's not what we want for any of the other `div`s. We'll take care of the size and placement of the content-secondary and sidebar `div`s shortly by assigning them pixel widths and negative margins. But what about the header and footer `div`s? They're in the right place, but we don't want the empty space on their sides. We can't just assign them widths, since there's no way to know the sum of 30 ems, 250 pixels, and 200 pixels.

The solution is to use negative margins, on both sides of the `div`s, that match the positive margins set on the wrapper `div`:

```
#header,
#footer {
    margin: 0 -250px 0 -200px;
    background: #DDDDDD;
}
```

These negative margins basically pull out the edges of the `div`s, instead of pushing them in and away from the inner boundary of the wrapper `div`, as positive margin values would do.

Now you can turn your attention to the two sidebars. Assign pixel widths to each, and float one to the right and one to the left:

```
#content-secondary {
    float: right;
    width: 250px;
    background: #9BF598;
}
#sidebar {
    float: left;
    width: 200px;
    background: #FFA480;
}
```

Now that the footer `div` has floats above it, make sure to assign it a `clear` value:

```
#footer {
    clear: both;
}
```

These changes get the content-secondary and sidebar `div`s sitting side by side, but they're still below the content-main `div` because they follow it in the source, and they're not at the edges of the wrapper because of the wrapper `div`'s padding (**Figure 6.8**).

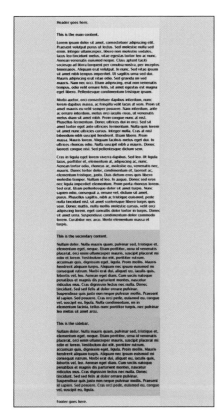

FIGURE 6.7 The blue space is ready to receive the sidebars, but so far all the `divs` are stuck within the 30-em width of the wrapper.

FIGURE 6.8 The sidebar and secondary content columns are now *sized* correctly, but not yet *placed* correctly.

USING GROUPED SELECTORS FOR EFFICIENCY

The rule assigning negative side margins to the header and footer `divs` uses a grouped selector; both the `#header` and `#footer` selector are combined together, separated with a comma. Using grouped selectors is a good idea when you have identical values for multiple `divs`. In this case, if you later change the width of one or both sidebars, you'll have fewer places to also update the margin values on other `divs`. You'll also use fewer lines of CSS, keeping the file size down.

To fix the latter problem of the sidebars not being against the edges of the wrapper `div`, use negative margins in the same direction as each float to pull them out into the spaces left by the wrapper's padding:

```
#content-secondary {
    float: right;
    width: 250px;
    margin-right: -250px;
    background: #9BF598;
}
#sidebar {
    float: left;
    width: 200px;
    margin-left: -200px;
    background: #FFA480;
}
```

This works because negative margins have the opposite effect as positive ones; positive margin values would have pushed the `div`s further away from the edges of wrapper, inward, while negative ones pull them outward.

The sidebars are now in the correct places horizontally, but not vertically—they still are below content-main (**Figure 6.9**).

The first step to allowing the two sidebars to move up beside the main content column is to make the content-main `div` a float as well, since three floats will all sit side by side if they have enough room. You'll also need to give content-main a width of 100 percent so it will always exactly fill up the 30-em width of the wrapper `div`:

```
#content-main {
    float: left;
    width: 100%;
    background: #F0EE90;
}
```

KEEP THOSE GUTTERS CLEAR!

To create gaps between the three columns, simply increase the padding on the wrapper `div`, and then increase the negative margin values to match. For instance, right padding of 300 pixels on the wrapper, followed by a `margin-right` value of negative 300 pixels on the content-secondary `div`, will create a 50-pixel space between the 250-pixel-wide content-secondary `div` and the content-main `div`.

FIGURE 6.9 Negative margins pull the two sidebars over the empty padding of the wrapper `div`.

These changes allow the sidebars to move up on the same level with content-main—but now the sidebar `div` overlaps the main content column (**Figure 6.10**). This is because of its negative margin. If you had three regular floats in succession—a left float, a right float, and then another left float—the second left float would sit between the two previous floats, as long as it had room there, not to the left of the first left float. The sidebar `div` is this second left float, so it wants to sit between content-main and content-secondary. But there's no space for it there, as content-main fills up the width of the wrapper `div` entirely—unless a negative margin allows the sidebar `div` to overlap the wrapper `div`'s padding. The negative margin allows the sidebar `div` to move up, but once it's up there, the negative margin also allows the sidebar to sit 200 pixels to the left of where it normally would—between content-main and content-secondary. Thus, it overlaps content-main by 200 pixels.

FIGURE 6.10 The green sidebar is in the correct spot, but the orange sidebar overlaps the main content column.

To fix this, you need to move the sidebar `div` over to the left an additional 30 ems—the width of the content-main `div`. You can't adjust the `margin-left` value in the `#sidebar` rule to do this, as you can't know the sum of 200 pixels plus 30 ems. But you can use a negative right margin on the content-main `div` to do the same thing:

```
#content-main {
    float: left;
    width: 100%;
    margin-right: -30em
    background: #F0EE90;
}
```

Another `margin-right` value that will have exactly the same effect is 100 percent, as this instructs the browser to move the sidebar `div` over by the full width of the content-main `div`:

```
#content-main {
    float: left;
    width: 100%;
    margin-right: -100%;
    background: #F0EE90;
}
```

Either value—30 em or 100 percent—works, but 100 percent is a little more efficient. This way, you set the width of content-main in only one place—on the wrapper `div`—and then make reference to that width using the value of

100 percent elsewhere. If you need to change the 30-em value later, you'll only have to do it in one place.

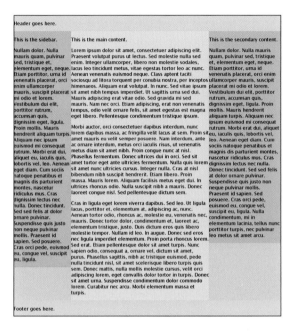

FIGURE 6.11 The completed elastic-fixed layout using negative margins.

This completes the layout for more standards-compliant browsers, but there are a few quirks seen elsewhere that we need to take care of. The first is in IE 6 and earlier: The doubled float margin bug places the content-secondary `div` too far to the right, so it seems to disappear entirely. To fix this, just add `display: inline;` to the `#content-secondary` rule.

USING DESIGN-TIME STYLE SHEETS IN DREAMWEAVER

If you don't want the extra styles correcting Dreamweaver's Design View problems mucking up your main style sheet, you could add them to a Design-time style sheet instead. This is a Dreamweaver feature that allows you to create a special style sheet that only Dreamweaver uses in Design View—it's not uploaded to your site or used by any browsers. Unfortunately, Dreamweaver doesn't allow you to apply a Design-time style sheet to an entire site, so if you wanted it to fix the display of all of your pages, you'd have to apply it to each page individually. The only way to work around this is to apply the Design-time style sheet to a template—all pages based on the template will automatically have the Design-time style sheet applied. For more information on using the Design-time style sheets feature, see Dreamweaver Help.

■ **NOTE:** The page showing this completed technique is elastic-fixed_threecol_negative.html in the ch6_examples.zip file.

Second, in Dreamweaver's Design View, this page is completely uneditable because you cannot click inside any of the divs. If you use Dreamweaver and want to fix this, you'll need to add position: relative; to the rules for each of the three column divs. This then has the side effect of making the sidebar div disappear from Design View entirely. Adding position: relative; to the #wrapper rule fixes this. These changes don't help Dreamweaver place the divs in the correct places, but at least they allow you to click inside the divs to edit content. (Don't ask me why position: relative helps, though—there's no CSS reason for it, and I just stumbled on it accidentally!)

Adding Minimum and Maximum Widths

Another way to limit the flexibility of your layouts—whether they're fully liquid or elastic or just hybrids—is to use the CSS min-width and max-width properties to set minimum and maximum widths for the entire layout or individual columns.

Protecting Your Users, Designs, and Content

In an ideal world, every design would be able to adapt to every width or text size at which users could realistically want to view it. And users would choose only the browser widths or text sizes that were optimized for their ease of viewing.

Reality, however, is not so kind to us web designers. Most users don't know how to customize their browsing setup to optimize it for their own particular needs. Many people can do basic customizations, such as maximizing or resizing browser windows, but they may choose settings that make it harder, not easier, for them to use many web pages well.

■ **NOTE:** Remember to check out the report "Actual Browser Sizes" at http://baekdal.com/reports/actual-browser-sizes, mentioned in Chapter 1, for more information on what window sizes people use to browse the web.

For instance, most Windows users maximize their browsers, regardless of whether viewing pages at that size is most comfortable for them. The tendency to maximize happens to a lesser degree as screen resolutions increase, but even at very large resolutions like 1680 by 1050, a few people still maximize. It's possible that some of these people are consciously choosing this browser window size because it works best for them; for example, if they have a very large font size because of a vision impairment, they may prefer really large windows in order to view more words across each line. But it's likely that most of these users are not maximizing at such ridiculous widths because they actually want web pages to stretch out that far. Rather, most people do so out of habit, because they don't like seeing any of their cluttered desktop peeking out from behind a non-maximized window, or for other reasons having nothing to do with their browsing experience. At such large sizes, liquid layouts can become very hard to read if the user's text isn't very large, as the lines of text get stretched to several hundred characters per line.

At the other end of the scale, there are people who view web pages on small-screen, handheld devices like mobile phones. Since it's unlikely your design for desktop browsers will look any good at only a couple hundred pixels wide, it's best to create a separate style sheet for handheld devices using the media type handheld. Unfortunately, many mobile phones do not support handheld style sheets and instead will render the page using the regular screen style sheet, which can result in a big mess as content overflows and overlaps.

Not only can both of these extremes in width make your sites very hard to use, they can also make them very unattractive. Although you learned in Chapter 2 how to make designs that look good at a large range of sizes, it's still a range—it has a beginning and an end. It's pretty tough to create designs that can work at both 200 pixels and 1600 pixels wide.

That's the point of minimum and maximum widths. They protect your content from becoming unreadable as it overlaps at super-small window sizes. They protect your users from extreme browsing-scenario choices that hurt their ability to read and use your site well. And they protect your designs from becoming awkward and ugly at extreme sizes.

Choosing min-width and max-width values

Once you've decided why you want to implement minimum and maximum widths, you can determine the min- and max-width values that suit your pages and your users.

PIXELS

The most common values that people pick for min- and max-width values are in units of pixels. For instance, you might decide you don't want your design to get any smaller than 600 pixels or any larger than 1200 pixels.

In some cases, it makes a lot of sense to use pixel values. It may simply be impossible to get your design to work any smaller or larger than certain pixel values. Or, you may have a single column that you have to limit to a particular pixel width because it contains fixed-width content, such as large images, and can't be allowed to get any smaller than this content.

In many cases, however, the decision to use pixel min- and max-width values is rather arbitrary. A designer may simply not like the appearance of the page outside of a certain pixel range. But I encourage you to not be concerned whether the page looks "great" at the ends of the range, but rather that it doesn't look "broken" and is still functional and usable. Your design may indeed look prettier at 750 pixels wide than at 600, but if it's not broken at 600, you may as well let it get that small instead of setting a min-width of 750 pixels. The smaller min-width probably won't be seen by very many people, but those few who do need to browse at the smaller size will appreciate not having a horizontal scrollbar, and will never know—nor probably care—that they could be seeing a slightly prettier version of the page.

PERCENTAGES

Percentage values can often be just as arbitrary as pixel values. When they're used as the max-width for elastic designs, however, they make a lot of sense.

Elastic designs are very prone to horizontal scrollbars, because the entire design gets larger with the text without any regard for the viewport size. You may be fine with allowing the horizontal scrollbars—I've heard from some visually impaired users who use very large font sizes that they'd rather have horizontal scrollbars than be limited to the viewport and thus only have a couple words on a line. After all, the point of using an elastic layout is to optimize the line lengths of the text, so using a max-width to then change the line lengths and instead accommodate the viewport kind of defeats the purpose.

But if you do think stopping the horizontal scrollbars is best for your content and your users, you can do so by applying a max-width of 100 percent to the entire layout. This limits the entire layout to 100 percent of the viewport width, so it never generates a horizontal scrollbar. Alternatively, you can apply the 100-percent max-width to just the main content column, so that even though you will still get a horizontal scrollbar at larger font sizes, it will happen less frequently, and the main content itself will always fit within the viewport. Users will never have to scroll back and forth horizontally to read the main content—only to navigate between the different columns of the design.

USING min-height **AND** max-height

You can constrain the height of blocks just as easily as widths, using the min-height and max-height properties. These properties aren't really any more applicable to flexible layouts than to other types of layouts, however, so we won't be covering them in this book. Most of the time, you want to let your text determine the height of boxes, instead of imposing limits on height, so that text doesn't overflow.

EMS

The problem with liquid layouts is not horizontal scrollbars, but rather really short or really long lines of text. You can avoid both of these problems by using em values for `min-` and `max-width`, thereby limiting the width to a certain number of text characters. For instance, you could set an overall `min-width` of 30 ems and an overall `max-width` of 60 ems. This keeps people who are browsing with really large windows but small font sizes from getting outrageously long lines of text, while also allowing the text to fill the viewport for those users who browse with really large windows because they have large font sizes. The design will still be liquid, not elastic, but will simply stop adjusting to the viewport size after the width reaches a certain number of text characters.

Another great use of an em `min-width` in liquid designs is on sidebars. You may have a sidebar that contains a navigation menu with large words that could overflow out of the column at very small window sizes or if the user has specified very large text. Both problems can be avoided if you set a `min-width` in ems on the sidebar column that will accommodate the number of characters in the longest word in that column.

Using the `min-width` and `max-width` Properties

Now that you know why `min-width` and `max-width` are important and how to choose appropriate values, let's go over how to actually add them to your pages.

APPLYING THE PROPERTIES TO THE OVERALL PAGE

If you want to constrain the overall width of your design, you can apply the `min-width` and `max-width` properties to either a wrapper `div` or the `body` element. Here's a simple example of using `min-` and `max-width`, in pixels, on a wrapper `div` of a liquid layout:

```
#wrapper {
    min-width: 500px;
    max-width: 1000px;
    background: #98F5E8;
}
#header {
    background: #DDDDDD;
}
#content-main {
    float: right;
    width: 75%;
    background: #F0EE90;
}
```

```
#sidebar {
    margin-right: 75%;
    background: #FFA480;
}
#footer {
    clear: both;
    background: #DDDDDD;
}
```

Though pixel values usually aren't the best choice for `min-` and `max-width` values, they allow you to easily see how these properties work, which can be instructive. In the first image in **Figure 6.12**, the layout entirely fills the viewport (which is 750 pixels wide at the moment). In the second image, the layout has narrowed quite a bit—it's still liquid—but has stopped narrowing at 500 pixels wide and is instead generating a horizontal scrollbar. In the third image, the layout has widened significantly, but has stopped at 1000 pixels wide, leaving empty space to its right.

If you want the layout to be centered in the viewport after the maximum width is reached, simply add `margin: 0 auto;` to the element that has the `min-` and `max-width` set on it (in this case, the wrapper `div`).

FIGURE 6.12 Using `min-` and `max-width` on the wrapper, the columns of this liquid layout still expand and contract with the browser window, but only within the specified range.

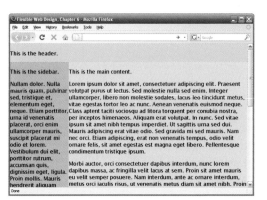

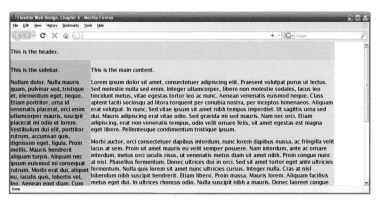

In case you're wondering, you don't have to use both `min-` and `max-width` at the same time: You can choose one or the other. If you do decide to use both together, it's fine to mix values between the two. For instance, you might want to set just a `max-width` of 100 percent on an elastic layout, or you might also want to add a `min-width` in pixels to keep it from getting smaller than a certain piece of fixed-width content you need to accommodate.

You can also use `min-` and `max-width` in conjunction with the `width` property. For example, in Chapter 4 we set a width of 90 percent on the wrapper `div` of a liquid layout in order to limit the amount of the viewport it took up. We could add a `min-` and `max-width` onto the wrapper as well:

```
#wrapper {
    width: 90%;
    min-width: 30em;
    max-width: 60em;
    margin: 0 auto;
}
```

I've switched to em values here instead of pixels since ems are more suited to limiting the width of liquid layouts. Regardless of the actual `min-` and `max-width` values used, however, the value of the `width` property will apply when the layout is between its minimum and maximum widths, and then the `min-` and `max-width` will kick in at the appropriate extremes (**Figure 6.13**).

When choosing which element to apply the `min-` and `max-width` to, you'll want to keep in mind how you want the page to look after those minimum and maximum widths are reached. If you need certain background colors or graphics to fill the remaining space, you may have to put the properties on a different element or even add a second wrapper `div`.

For instance, let's say you have a liquid layout that has a wrapper `div` around just a certain part of the page. If you apply a `max-width` to this wrapper `div`, its background color will not fill any space beyond that `max-width`. If you do want the background color to always fill the entire viewport behind that section of the page, you'd need to either move the `max-width` onto an element nested one level down from the wrapper `div`—such as a second, nested wrapper `div`—or move the background color one level up from the wrapper `div`—such as onto the `body` element. This second option of moving the background color to the `body` may not work if the wrapper's background color is only supposed to show behind a certain portion of the page, not the entire page, so you may have to add that second wrapper `div` within the first one just to hold the `max-width` value.

■ **NOTE:** The page showing this completed technique is minmax_overall_liquid.html in the ch6_examples.zip file.

FIGURE 6.13 With a width of 90 percent in addition to `min-` and `max-width` values, the layout will only ever fill the viewport when it has reached its minimum width.

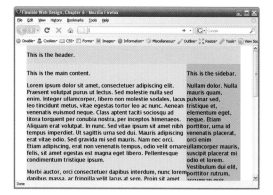

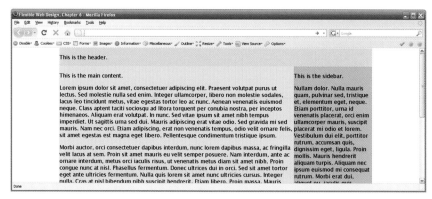

FIGURE 6.14 To get the yellow background color of the main content `div` to fill the space after its `max-width` is reached, another `div` had to be nested within it. The outer one holds the background color, the inner one the `max-width` value.

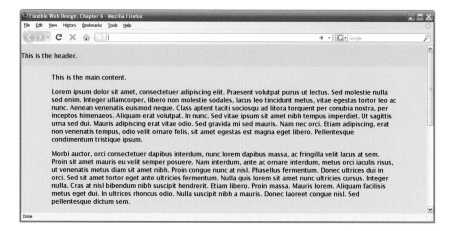

Sometimes it takes even more tweaking to your (X)HTML and CSS to add minimum and maximum widths. For instance, let's say you wanted to add a `min-width` of 500 pixels and a `max-width` of 100 percent to the basic two-column elastic layout from Chapter 5. You could add these values right onto the body element, or add a wrapper around all the divs and put them on that wrapper:

```
body {
    min-width: 500px;
    max-width: 100%;
    margin: 0;
    padding: 0;
    font-family: "Lucida Sans Unicode", "Lucida Grande",
sans-serif;
}
div {
    padding: 1px 0;
}
#header {
    width: 47em;
    background: #DDDDDD;
}
#content-main {
    float: left;
    width: 37em;
    background: #F0EE90;
}
#sidebar {
    width: 10em;
    margin-left: 37em;
    background: #FFA480;
}
#footer {
    clear: both;
    width: 47em;
    background: #DDDDDD;
}
```

The min- and max-width values would successfully limit the width of the body element, but the body element doesn't determine the width of the elastic columns inside it, so those columns are still able to grow larger and smaller without restriction (**Figure 6.15**). Unlike the liquid layout examples given thus far, the elastic columns are paying no attention to the width of their parent element to determine their own widths, so they go on shrinking and expanding without any limits.

FIGURE 6.15 Despite the max-width of 100 percent on the body, the layout is still allowed to exceed the width of the viewport and generate a horizontal scrollbar.

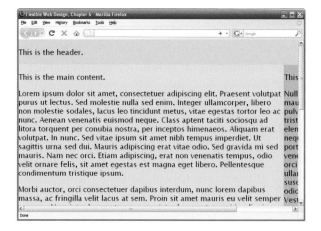

To change this, first add a width to the body element, in ems, to set the overall elastic width of the layout, and then remove the widths from the header and footer divs:

```css
body {
    width: 47em;
    min-width: 500px;
    max-width: 100%;
    margin: 0;
    padding: 0;
    font-family: "Lucida Sans Unicode", "Lucida Grande",
sans-serif;
}
#header {
    background: #DDDDDD;
}
#footer {
    clear: both;
    background: #DDDDDD;
}
```

Then, you need to get rid of the em widths on the columns inside. Instead, you want those columns to adjust to the width of their parent element. To do this, the columns must have widths in percentages:

```css
#content-main {
    float: left;
    width: 79%;
    background: #F0EE90;
}
#sidebar {
    margin-left: 79%;
    background: #FFA480;
}
```

To get the value of 79 percent for both the width of content-main and the matching left margin on the sidebar, I simply divided 37 ems (the old value) into 47 ems (the total width of the layout set on the body element). 37 is roughly 79 percent of 47, so this percentage value gives us the same elastic width on the main content column as before. Note that I've also removed the width entirely from the sidebar div; the sidebar will simply take up whatever space is left over, which again will roughly equal its old width of 10 ems.

Since the parent element, the body, has a width set in ems, the columns inside will still be elastic, but they will base their elasticity on the width of their parent instead of their own set widths. Once they're dependent on the parent for width, they'll also be constrained by that parent's min- and max-width values (**Figure 6.16**).

NOTE: The page showing this completed technique is minmax_ overall_elastic.html in the ch6_examples.zip file.

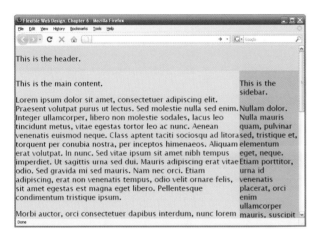

FIGURE 6.16 Now the layout cannot get wider than the viewport, no matter how large the text is, so it will never generate a horizontal scrollbar.

APPLYING THE PROPERTIES TO INDIVIDUAL COLUMNS

You use the same CSS to apply min- and max-width to individual columns as you do to the entire layout. In theory, all you have to do is pick the div you want to limit the width of, and add the appropriate min- and max-width values.

In reality, however, you will probably have to do a lot more tweaking to your CSS and (X)HTML to get these minimum and maximum widths to play well with the other, unrestricted columns. For instance, here's our basic liquid layout created with a matching side margin on the side of the float, plus a min- and a max-width added to the main content column:

```
#content-main {
    float: right;
    width: 75%;
    min-width: 500px;
    max-width: 800px;
```

```
   background: #F0EE90;
}
#sidebar {
   margin-right: 75%;
   background: #FFA480;
}
```

Again, I've used pixels for the values in the first example here simply because it makes it easy to see how the values are working.

The `margin-right` value of 75 percent will no longer match up with the width of the floated content-main `div` at all times. When the `min-width` is reached, the content-main `div` will exceed a width of 75 percent, causing it to overlap the sidebar, and when the `max-width` is reached, the content-main `div` will be less than 75 percent wide, leaving a gap between the columns (**Figure 6.17**). There's no way to create a minimum or maximum *margin* value, only minimum and maximum widths and heights, so any layout method that depends on matching up a margin with a float's width is not going to work as-is when you add a `min-` or `max-width` on one of the columns.

FIGURE 6.17 When the main content column reaches its minimum width, it overlaps the sidebar. When it reaches its maximum width, it leaves a gap between itself and the sidebar.

Depending on what you hope to accomplish, you may need only small revisions to your original (X)HTML and CSS in order to get the `min-` or `max-width` to work. For instance, in the layout shown in Figure 6.17, if you wanted to add only a `max-width` to the main content column, without that gap appearing, you could manage this quite easily by adding another `div` within the content-main `div`, and just applying the `max-width` to this new `div`:

```
<div id="content-main">
   <div id="content-main-inner">
      <p>This is the main content.</p>
      ...
   </div>
</div>
```

```
#content-main {
    float: right;
    width: 75%;
    background: #F0EE90;
}
#content-main-inner {
    max-width: 800px;
}
#sidebar {
    margin-right: 75%;
    background: #FFA480;
}
```

This allows the background color of the main content column to continue filling 75 percent of the viewport no matter what, while only the content inside it is stopped from growing past 800 pixels wide (**Figure 6.18**).

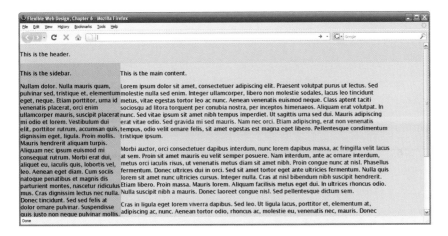

FIGURE 6.18 Once the `max-width` on the main content column is reached, it stays up against the sidebar with no gap, and its background color simply fills in the space on the right side of the viewport.

However, these changes do nothing to accommodate a minimum width on the main content column. In cases like this, you will probably have to switch to a different layout type altogether in order to get `min-` and `max-width` to work on an individual column. Negative margin layouts are your best bet here. The new negative margin layout you learned earlier in this chapter, where the sidebars stick to the sides of the main content column instead of the sides of the viewport, can easily accommodate a minimum and maximum width on the main content column. Here's that same elastic-fixed hybrid layout with a `min-` and `max-width` applied to the wrapper `div`, which determines the width of the content-main `div`:

■ **NOTE:** The page showing this completed technique is minmax_single_liquid.html in the ch6_examples.zip file.

```
#wrapper {
    width: 30em;
    min-width: 300px;
```

```
    max-width: 600px;
    padding: 0 250px 0 200px;
    background: #98F5E8;
}
#content-main {
    float: left;
    width: 100%;
    margin-right: -100%;
    background: #F0EE90;
}
#content-secondary {
    display: inline;
    float: right;
    width: 250px;
    margin-right: -250px;
    background: #9BF598;
}
#sidebar {
    float: left;
    width: 200px;
    margin-left: -200px;
    background: #FFA480;
}
```

■ **NOTE:** The page showing this completed technique is minmax_single_elastic-fixed.html in the ch6_examples.zip file.

Because this layout uses padding on the outside of the wrapper div to create the space for the sidebars, there will always be exactly 250 pixels of space right next to each side of the main content column, with no chance of the main content column overlapping the sidebars or leaving a gap between itself and them, as we saw in Figure 6.17.

This particular negative margin layout method doesn't have to be restricted to just elastic-fixed hybrids, by the way. You can use it for any type of layout you want. But be aware that not every variation works as well with min- and max-width on the main content column. For instance, a design with a liquid center and fixed-width sidebars works just as well with min- and max-width on the center column, but a fully liquid design does well only with a max-width (a min-width starts pushing the left sidebar off the left side of the viewport, with no way to access it with a scrollbar).

There are almost infinite variations in layout types and columns you might want to apply min- and max-width to—either together or separately—so we can't go over every scenario here. Just keep in mind that you might have to play around with your layout quite a bit to get it to accept a min- or max-width on a single column as opposed to the entire layout. Plan this in from the beginning, instead of trying to add it later, and you'll have a much easier time finding the layout that will give you the effect you want.

Incompatibility in IE 6 and Earlier

The min-width and max-width properties are not supported at all in IE 6 and earlier; these browsers simply ignore them. While this used to be a big problem that kept people from using min- and max-width—and even flexible layouts—at all, it doesn't need to be a big stumbling block nowadays, and here's why.

While IE 6 still comprises a significant portion of browser share on most sites, its usage has drastically fallen compared with a couple years ago, and will only continue to fall in the future. IE 5.5 and 5.0 make up only a tiny percentage of the browser share on most sites, and on some they've disappeared entirely.

Also remember that min- and max-width are only of benefit to the people who go beyond the minimum and maximum widths; in other words, only users who browse with extreme font or window sizes will "experience" them. These people probably make up a very small percentage of your overall users anyway, and when you consider that that small percentage is a subset of the also small number of IE 6 and earlier users, you're talking about a very tiny group of people who are affected by the lack of min- and max-width support.

BROWSER MARKET SHARE

Browser market share is hard to establish with certainty, but the statistics from Net Applications (http://marketshare.hitslink.com/report.aspx?qprid=0) are generally well-trusted. In August 2008, Net Applications reported the total market share of IE 6 at 25.17% and IE 5.5 and 5.0 at 0.06% each. In August 2007, IE 6 claimed 44.86% of the total market, and in August 2006 (the farthest back Net Applications browser share reports go), IE 6 dominated the market with an 80.16% share. (To find statistics from many other sources, search on "usage share of web browsers" in Wikipedia.)

It's important to be aware of your own sites' unique browser-share statistics, though, and not rely too much on generic reports for the entire market. For instance, many of the sites I've worked on in the past have been targeted to elementary schools and government agencies, both of which tend to lag behind in the versions of the browsers they use. Pay attention to your own browser-share statistics using a web analytics tool—but I will bet you anything that even if IE 6 makes up a larger percentage of your visitors than what is reported for the total market, it's still a much smaller portion than it used to be.

Not only that, but those who are affected by the lack of support will probably never know they're missing anything. In many cases, `min-` and `max-width` is not strictly necessary in order to use the site—they just make things look a little nicer and keep the text a little easier to read. Unless your site looks broken or is unreadable at the extremes this tiny group of people is browsing at, they're never going to know anything is wrong, and will just have a less optimized but still usable experience on your site.

For all these reasons, I don't think the lack of support for `min-` and `max-width` in IE 6 and earlier is much to worry about anymore. It certainly shouldn't stop you from using `min-` or `max-width` for all the other more modern and standards-compliant browsers, nor should it stop you from creating flexible layouts in the first place.

But I do recognize that there are times when you must have `min-` or `max-width` in these browsers. Your particular site may have a lot more IE 6 or IE 5.x users than most, and it may have more than the average number of people browsing at extremes. If your design is truly unreadable or "broken" at certain sizes that a significant portion of your audience will experience, you'll need to address this. Even if you don't have many people who will be affected, or you don't have a design that looks all that bad at an extreme, you may be forced to address the lack of support because your boss (or client) happens to browse with IE 6 with a maximized window at 1680 by 1050 and just can't stand how the design looks.

In such sticky situations, there is hope. There are a number of scripting techniques that can simulate or add `min-` and `max-width`. While explaining how to write JavaScript or IE's proprietary expressions is beyond the scope of this book—and I wouldn't be the person to do it anyway—you can learn more about a few of these techniques, and find links to download code, at www.flexiblewebbook.com/bonus.

Alternative Ways to Limit Flexibility

Besides using hybrid layouts or adding minimum and maximum width, there are other CSS techniques that you can use to limit the degree of flexibility in a web page design. Though usually not as user-friendly or universal in the types of designs they work with, these alternative techniques deserve a brief mention.

Using the overflow Property

You saw in Chapter 2 how scrollbars on an overly large image could be used to keep text adjusting to smaller viewport widths while still allowing large images into the page. This effect is created using the CSS overflow property.

To make scrollbars show up only when needed, use overflow: auto; on the element that contains the overly large content. If the image is the content you want to make scrollable, you need to first put it inside a containing element, like a div, and then apply the overflow property to that container:

```
<div class="image">
    <img src="styx.jpg" width="560" height="371" alt="my cat
Styx">
</div>

div.image {
    overflow: auto;
}
```

When the entire image can fit within its container, no scrollbars will be seen, but when it would need to overflow, the appropriate type of scrollbar—horizontal or vertical, or both—will appear (**Figure 6.19**). This lets the overall layout be flexible, while individual elements can remain more rigid.

■ **NOTE:** The page showing this completed technique is overflow_ image.html in the ch6_examples.zip file.

FIGURE 6.19 A horizontal scrollbar appears only on the piece of content that needs it.

The overflow property can be used on blocks of text just as well as on images. For instance, let's say you had a liquid layout with a middle column that you wanted to stop shrinking at 400 pixels. You could accomplish this with a min-width of 400 pixels on the middle column, but what if you wanted the right column to still show on the screen after this minimum width was reached? Using `min-width` alone would generate a horizontal scrollbar in the browser as a whole that you would have to use to access the right column.

You could combine `min-width` with `overflow` to add the horizontal scrollbar to the middle column only. First, you'd need to add another `div` within the `div` for the middle column:

```
<div id="content-main">
    <div id="content-main-inner">
        <p>This is the main content.</p>
        ...
    </div>
</div>
```

■ **NOTE:** The page showing this completed technique is overflow_ text.html in the ch6_ examples.zip file.

Then, set the `overflow` property on the outer `div`, and the `min-width` on the inner `div`:

```
#content-main {
    overflow: auto;
    float: left;
    width: 67%;
}
#content-main-inner {
    height: 400px;
    min-width: 400px;
}
```

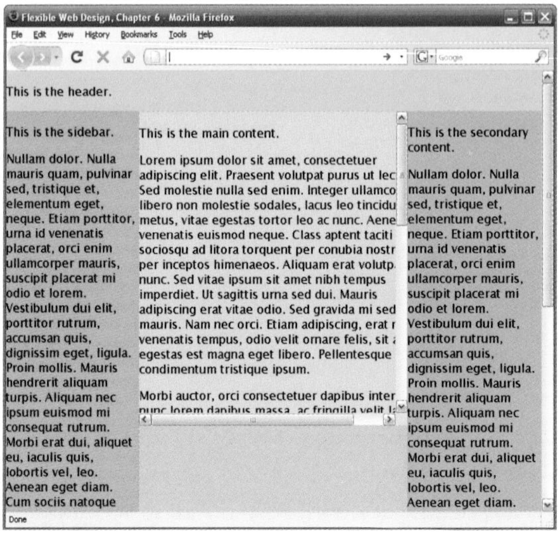

FIGURE 6.20 A vertical and horizontal scrollbar kick in when both the height and width of the content within the middle column are too large.

I've added a height value to the inner `div` as well as a minimum width because I want to increase the chances that the horizontal scrollbar, which is placed at the bottom of the `div`, is visible within most users' viewports without their having to scroll down the page. Without that height, the `div` would be as tall as the content dictated, and users may never notice that there is a horizontal scrollbar at the bottom of that column. The content may simply look cut off on the right side (**Figure 6.21**). Even if a user discovers the horizontal scrollbar at the bottom, he would have to scroll down—using the browser scrollbar—to access it, and then scroll to the side—using the area-specific scrollbar—and finally scroll back up to finish reading the line of text he started from. He would have to keep doing this over and over again in order to read the text.

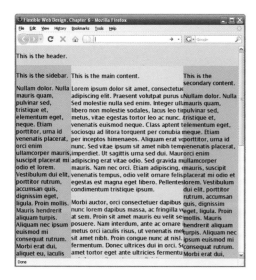

FIGURE 6.21 When the height of the scrollable area exceeds the viewport, no horizontal scrollbar is visible on the middle column, and its content looks cut off on its right side with no way to access the remainder.

This is one of the dangers in generating scrollbars on individual sections of the page: They can be very annoying to use—much more so that regular browser scrollbars. Use the `overflow` property for area-specific scrollbars very sparingly, preferably on small areas that don't have a ton of content the user will need to look through. Make sure, when you do use the `overflow` property, that you test it thoroughly to make sure it will be usable by your audience.

Letting Columns Drop

In some of the many layouts we've gone over, we've had to change the CSS or the (X)HTML to keep columns from dropping down the page when the window is narrowed. For instance, this layout with all three columns floated will drop the third column (the sidebar) when the window is narrowed past a width of 57 ems (**Figure 6.22**):

■ **NOTE:** The page showing this completed technique is columndrop.html in the ch6_examples.zip file.

```
#content-secondary {
    float: left;
```

```
    width: 10em;
    background: #9BF598;
}
#content-main {
    float: left;
    width: 37em;
    background: #F0EE90;
}
#sidebar {
    float: left;
    width: 10em;
    background: #FFA480;
}
```

FIGURE 6.22 The orange sidebar, which normally sits to the right of the yellow main content column, instead drops down the page when there isn't room for it to the right of the main content column.

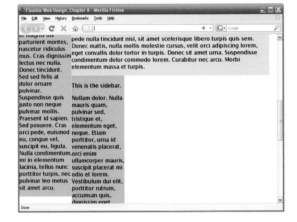

If you continue to narrow the window past a width of 47 ems, the second column, content-main, will also drop down. In most designs, this isn't what you want to happen, and you can prevent it by either changing the layout method or adding a width or minimum width to the body element or wrapper div. But some designs are made to allow columns to drop as another way to accommodate the differing viewport widths of their users. For instance, The Accessible Art Fair Geneva web site at http://accessibleart.ch/ is not liquid, but still accommodates a wide range of viewport widths by allowing the third column to drop under the second, and then both the second and third columns to drop under the first, when the window is narrowed (**Figure 6.23**). Though this leaves gaps on the right side of the design at certain viewport widths, the gaps are never so large as to look like mistakes, and the design accommodates the varying positions of the second and third columns without any problems. Other examples of designs where columns drop down on purpose and gracefully are the hybrid CSS Beauty web site (www.cssbeauty.com) and the liquid How Deep is the Ocean web site (http://howdeepistheocean.com).

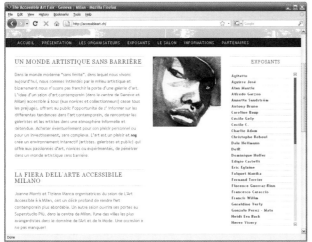

To create a layout where a column drops down, all you need to do is place more than one float on the same line, and then make sure that the viewport is allowed to get smaller than the combined width of the floats. In the example code posted above, the viewport can get smaller than the combined width of the floats because there is no wrapper around the floats with a width set on it. On the How Deep is the Ocean web site, the viewport can get smaller than the combined width of the floats because the main content column, the column furthest to the left, has a `min-width` set on it in pixels. When it reaches its `min-width`, it takes up more than its declared 50-percent width, so there is no longer enough space left over for the other two columns to fit on the same line.

It doesn't have to be the rightmost column that drops first. Whichever float comes last in the source will drop down first. It's as simple as that. For instance, if you had right and left sidebars in a three-column layout placed ahead of the center main content `div` in the (X)HTML, and all three `div`s were floated, the main content column would be the first one to drop down.

Again, this isn't an approach that will work for everyone, and you'll need to test it thoroughly if you do decide to implement it. But it's another technique that you can add to your repertoire as a way to create layouts that adapt to the viewport size without being quite as flexible as a fully liquid layout would be.

FIGURE 6.23 At larger window widths, this design has three columns. At smaller window widths, the third column drops under the second, creating a two-column design that fits within the viewport without a horizontal scrollbar.

Site-Building Exercise: Limiting the Flexibility of the Shelter's Pages

You've already built the layouts for the Beechwood Animal Shelter home and inner pages. You'll now modify each of them to limit their flexibility: The home page will become a hybrid layout, and the inner page will have a minimum and maximum width assigned.

You'll work with the exercise files from this book's companion web site at www.flexiblewebbook.com. Download and unzip the file ch6_exercise.zip.

Modifying the Programs Page

Open the file programs-start.html in your text or code editor of choice. This is the same page as the final version of the Programs page you completed in Chapter 4.

To get a minimum and maximum width working on this page, the only thing you need to change is the CSS; no changes to the HTML are necessary. Since this is a liquid layout that could suffer from overly long or short line lengths, you'll use ems as the unit of measurement for the minimum and maximum widths.

Locate the #wrapper rule inside the style tags in the head of the page, and add min- and max-width properties to match the following:

```
#wrapper {
    width: 90%;
    min-width: 40em;
    max-width: 65em;
    margin: 0 auto;
}
```

This sets the minimum and maximum widths of the overall layout, not individual columns, but you can figure out what this will make the minimum and maximum widths be for each column by looking at the percentage of the wrapper div that each takes up. Look at the #nav-secondary rule:

```
#nav-secondary {
    float: left;
    width: 20%;
    margin-left: -100%;
    background: #FCF;
}
```

This rule makes the left sidebar 20 percent as wide as the wrapper `div`. This means the sidebar's `min-width` will effectively be 8 ems, which is 20 percent of the overall `min-width` of 40 ems. This `min-width` should be sufficient for the sidebar, where the longest word is nine characters—or about 5 ems—long.

The main content column, which takes up the remainder of the width in the wrapper `div`, will thus have a `min-width` of 32 ems (80 percent of the overall `min-width` of 40 ems). Remember that a range of roughly 37 to 50 ems creates what is considered the most readable onscreen line lengths for the majority of people. 32 ems is just a bit smaller than the bottom of this range to allow for those people who have special needs that might make shorter line lengths more preferable, without being so far out of the range as to pose a problem for the majority.

You can make the same calculations on the `max-width` value of 65 ems—20 percent of 65 is 13 ems for the sidebar, and 80 percent is 52 ems for the main content column. Again, this should be readable for the majority while still allowing a large range of widths to accommodate people's varying needs.

There's no way to know what pixel widths this translates into, as it will be different for each user based on his or her own text size. But most users have 16-pixel text, and this page reduces that by 88 percent (in the `body` rule), meaning most people will see 14-pixel text. With 14-pixel text, the `min-width` of 40 ems will be 560 pixels wide, and the `max-width` of 65 ems will be 910 pixels wide.

To compare your work to the completed Programs page for this exercise, see the file programs-end.html in the files you extracted from ch6_exercise.zip.

FIGURE 6.24 The Programs page can get no narrower than 40 ems (about 560 pixels with the text size shown), nor wider than 65 ems (about 910 pixels here).

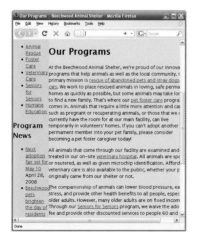

Modifying the Home Page

Open the file home-start.html in your text or code editor of choice. This is the same page as the final version of the home page you completed in Chapter 5.

Right now, all of the columns in this page are elastic. The leftmost column really ought to be fixed-width, however, as it contains fixed-width images. It's possible to make those images scale using CSS, as you'll learn in Chapter 9, but since the images contain text, they probably won't look very good scaled by the browser.

FIGURE 6.25 At small text sizes, the left column gets too narrow to hold the fixed-width images inside it, so the images overflow and look cut off.

The tricky thing about this particular elastic-fixed hybrid layout is that the banner div needs to match the combined width of the two columns below it: the left fixed-width column and the right elastic column. There's no way to know what this combined width value is, as the pixels it translates out to will be different in each user's setup. So you'll have to break out the negative margins.

Once again, the only part of the page that needs to change is the CSS.

1. Locate the #ads rule inside the style tags in the head of the page, and change its width value to 180px. This makes the column 20 pixels wider than the width of the images inside it, to create a small gutter of space between it and the right column.

2. Locate the #wrapper rule, and modify it to match the following:

```
#wrapper {
    width: 41em;
    margin: 0 auto;
    padding-left: 180px;
    background: #FCC;
}
```

This reduced width matches the width of the right column of the page, which will remain elastic. The new padding creates an empty, fixed-width space on the left side of the wrapper for the left column to sit in. The background color is simply there so you can see where the div is lying on the page and make sure everything it aligning correctly.

You can see the empty space in the left side of the pink wrapper div in **Figure 6.26**. You now need to change the width of the banner div so it doesn't have that empty space to its left, and you also need to pull the sidebar into that empty space.

FIGURE 6.26 Padding creates a gap on the left side of the pink wrapper div, while the reduced width of the wrapper forces the columns below the green banner to stack instead of sit side by side.

3. Locate the #banner rule, and add a negative left margin equal to the width of the wrapper's padding to pull the left side of the banner over:

```
#banner {
    margin-left: -180px;
    background: #CFC;
}
```

FIGURE 6.27 The negative left margin on the banner pulls its left side out to overlap the wrapper's padding.

4. Go back to the #ads rule, and add the same margin-left value to pull that div over by its entire width:

```
#ads {
    float: left;
    width: 180px;
    margin-left: -180px;
    background: #FCF;
}
```

FIGURE 6.28 The nega-
tive left margin on the ads
`div` pulls it entirely over the
wrapper's padding, giving the
right column room to move
up directly underneath the
banner, where it started out.

That completes the new hybrid layout in all modern browsers. In IE 6,
however, the left column appears to be missing entirely, due to the
doubled float margin bug.

5. Add `display: inline;` to the `#ads` rule to fix the doubled float margin
   bug in IE 6.

Now you really are done! To test how each column now scales—or doesn't
scale—open the page in a browser and increase and decrease the text size.
(Make sure not to use the browser's zoom function to test this, as that makes
everything look elastic even if it's not.) The banner and right column should
expand and contract proportionally in size to the text, while the left column
should never change in size. Now the images in the left column will no longer get cut off when the text size is very small, because the column they're
in will never get smaller than 180 pixels (**Figure 6.29**).

FIGURE 6.29 The left
column now remains
the same width no mat-
ter what the text size, so
at small sizes the images
inside it don't get cut off.

Your page should look like Figures 6.28 and 6.29 (same page, just different
text sizes) in all major browsers. To compare your work to the completed
home page for this exercise, see the file home-end.html in the files you
extracted from ch6_exercise.zip.

7

Creating Spacing for Text

So far, most of the example pages you've seen as well as the exercise files you've worked on have had no spacing within or between columns; the text just sits up against the edges of the background colors on the columns. You might think that adding spacing for the text would be as easy as slapping a margin or some padding onto the divs, but it's not necessarily that simple. Adding spacing without making other adjustments elsewhere in the CSS could cause your layout to fall apart entirely. But never fear—I'll teach you how to work with margin and padding successfully in a variety of flexible layouts.

Matching Units of Measurement

■ **NOTE:** Each of the completed example files is available for download from this book's companion web site at www.flexiblewebbook.com. Download the file ch7_examples.zip to get the complete set. I'll let you know which file goes with which technique as we go along.

You'll have the easiest time adding spacing for text if you measure it in the same units that you've used for the widths of the columns (percentage values for liquid layouts, em values for elastic layouts). When you use the same units of measurements between widths and margins or padding, you're essentially just increasing the widths of each of those columns by however much margin or padding you add. Thus, just do what you would do any time you increase a column width: decrease the other column widths or increase the side margin that creates space for the now-wider column.

Spacing for Liquid Layouts

■ **NOTES:** The original file this CSS is adapted from is liquid_margins_twocol.html in the c4_examples.zip file.

The page showing this completed technique is liquid_margins_twocol_between.html in the ch7_examples.zip file.

In Chapter 4, we went over how to create a gap between the columns within a liquid layout. If you're using the matching-side-margins method, not floating all the columns, just increase the side margin that creates room for the float to some value larger than the width of that float (see Figure 4.6):

```
#content-main {
    float: right;
    width: 75%;
    background: #F0EE90;
}
#sidebar {
    margin-right: 80%;
    background: #FFA480;
}
```

If you're floating all of the columns (but not all in the same direction), just decrease the width of one or more of the columns:

```
#content-wrapper {
    float: right;
    width: 75%;
    background: #98F5E8;
}
#content-main {
    float: left;
    width: 67%;
    background: #F0EE90;
```

```
}
#content-secondary {
    float: right;
    width: 27%;
    background: #9BF598;
}
#sidebar {
    float: left;
    width: 20%;
    background: #FFA480;
}
```

Here, I've decreased the width of the content-secondary and sidebar columns from their earlier widths of 33 and 25 percent, respectively. The decreased width of the sidebar column creates a gap between itself and the content-wrapper column. Since their two widths no longer add up to 100 percent, and each is floated to an opposite side of the viewport, there has to be a gap between them. The same thing happens within the content-wrapper column: the decrease in the width of the content-secondary column creates a gap between itself and the content-main column. All of these gaps will be liquid in nature, because they're measured in percentages.

■ **NOTES:** The original file this CSS is adapted from is liquid_floats_threecol_wrapper.html in the c4_examples.zip file.

The page showing this completed technique is liquid_floats_threecol_wrapper_between.html in the ch7_examples.zip file.

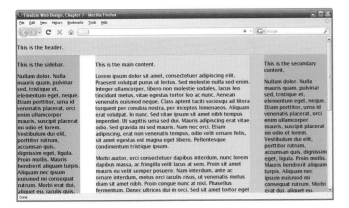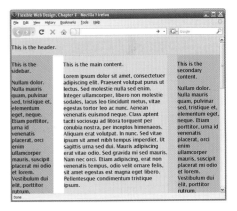

FIGURE 7.1 Decreasing the widths of opposing floats so they no longer add up to 100 percent creates gaps between those floats. These gaps change with the viewport size because they're measured in percentages.

Decreasing the widths of floats works when those floats are each going in opposite directions—since they don't add up to 100 percent, but are each aligned to opposite edges of their container, the extra space gets added in between them. But if you're floating divs in the same direction as each other, the extra space gets added onto the outside edge of the last float. To create space between them instead, you'll need to not only decrease the width of one or more of the columns, but also add a side margin to one of the columns that's equal to the space you want between them:

```
#content-main {
    float: right;
    width: 75%;
    background: #F0EE90;
}
#sidebar {
    float: right;
    width: 20%;
    margin-right: 4.9%;
    background: #FFA480;
}
```

■ **NOTE:** The page showing this completed technique is liquid_floats_twocol_between.html in the ch7_examples.zip file.

Since both columns will move as far to the right as they can, decreasing the width of the sidebar from 25 to 20 percent adds five percent of space to the left side of the sidebar, not to its right side, where it would sit between the sidebar and the main content column. Adding a `margin-right` value onto the sidebar—or a `margin-left` value onto the content-main `div`—moves the space in between the two. Although a value of five percent would exactly match the available space in this case, I've set the value here to 4.9 percent, to keep IE from dropping the sidebar column down due to rounding inconsistencies.

All of these methods work to create space between the columns, but they don't create any space between the edges of the columns and the viewport edges, nor do they create space within the colored background area of each column. We'll need to add more CSS to take care of each of these issues.

SPACE ON THE EDGE OF THE VIEWPORT

■ **NOTE:** The page showing this completed technique is liquid_margins_twocol_edges.html in the ch7_examples.zip file.

The easiest way to create space between the edges of the outermost columns and the viewport edges is to apply either margins or padding to the body element. Either property will work as well as the other in most browsers, but IE 6 misaligns the header and footer from the outermost columns slightly when using padding, so I recommend sticking with margin:

```
body {
    margin: 0 5%;
    padding: 0;
}
```

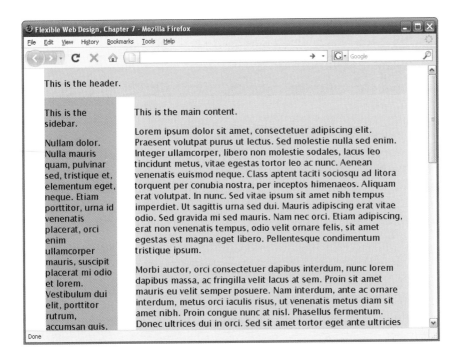

FIGURE 7.2 Left and right margins on the body element create space on either side of the layout within the viewport.

Change the 5% value to whatever you want the size of the gaps on both sides of the viewport to be. You could even create differently sized gaps on each side if you wanted to.

If you already have a wrapper `div` surrounding all the `div`s of your layout, an equally easy solution is to apply side margins to this wrapper. It works exactly the same as applying margins to the body element, but may work better in certain types of layouts, depending on what other CSS you're using on the body or wrapper `div`s. Either option is perfectly fine.

Neither option requires any changes to the widths or margins of the columns within the body or wrapper `div`s. Adding the side margins to these elements just decreases the available space for the interior columns—but those columns are still filling up 100 percent of that reduced space.

SPACE WITHIN THE COLUMNS

In most designs, adding space between the columns, instead of within them, is sufficient. This is because very often you don't assign background colors or images to individual columns, but rather to wrapper `div`s that surround multiple columns. The background on the wrapper simply "shines through" to the nested `div`s to give them their background. This is especially the case when you want to create the appearance of multiple columns being the same height as each other, because this is usually accomplished with the "faux columns" technique that uses a background on a wrapper instead of individual divs (you'll learn this technique in the next chapter).

But sometimes you'll have backgrounds placed directly on individual columns and need to make sure that the content within those columns doesn't run right up against the edges. In the examples shown throughout this book so far, there has been space within the top and bottom of each column, but not within the sides. This top and bottom space is due to the default margins on the paragraphs within the divs. Most text elements that are block-level elements have some amount of default top and bottom margin. So far, we've kept the default margins from escaping out of the top and bottom of each div—the phenomenon of margin collapsing we talked about in Chapter 4—by using one pixel of top and bottom padding on each of the divs.

Before you start adjusting the spacing within columns, it's best to do something about these default margins. Now that we're specifically taking care of spacing issues within divs, it's time to use a more robust method of preventing margin collapsing.

■ **NOTE:** All the examples from this point forward can be assumed to have this rule in them, unless otherwise stated.

A good method for adjusting the default spacing on text elements is to get rid of only the top margin on paragraphs and headings:

```
p, h1, h2, h3, h4, h5, h6 {
    margin-top: 0;
}
```

These elements all have both top and bottom margin by default, so getting rid of the top margins doesn't mean they'll no longer be spaced out from each other—the bottom margin will take over this job by itself.

Most likely, you'll have a paragraph or heading as the first piece of content within each div, so getting rid of their top margins will be sufficient to stop margin collapsing at the top of each div. If it's likely that you'll have other elements as the first piece of content, such as a list, you can add these elements to the grouped rule you just created, to also prevent their top margins from escaping out of their divs:

```
p, h1, h2, h3, h4, h5, h6, ul, ol {
    margin-top: 0;
}
```

A rule like this removes the possibility of margin collapsing occurring at the tops of your divs. You can then use padding on the divs themselves to control the amount of spacing within the top of each div (as we'll go over in a moment), which is much more reliable than relying on browser defaults to add this spacing for you.

However, this type of rule doesn't do anything to stop margin collapse from occurring at the bottom of the divs. For that, I recommend sticking with padding on the bottom of each div:

```
div {
    padding: 0 0 1px 0;
}
```

■ **NOTE:** All the examples from this point forward can be assumed to *also* have this rule in them, unless otherwise stated.

You can either stick with the single pixel of padding that we've been using all along, and depend on the bottom margins of the content within the divs to provide the spacing, or you can add a larger padding value. In either case, the amount of space within the bottom of each div will be equal to the size of the margin on the last element within that div—either the default margin if you haven't changed it, or the declared margin if you have—plus however much padding you've added on the bottom of the div. This combined value may be larger or smaller than the padding you declare at the top of each div. Usually, this inconsistency between the top and bottom spacing within a div isn't problematic; differences in spacing at the tops of divs, where you want all the content all lined up across the columns, is much more noticeable, but differences in spacing at the bottoms of divs, where each column ends at a different height, gets some leeway.

If you must have the exact same amount of padding at the bottom and the top of each div, you can remove the bottom margin on the last element within the div using the :last-child pseudo-class:

```
div :last-child {
    margin-bottom: 0;
}
```

This selector targets any element that is the last child element within any div—no matter what that last element is, it will get its bottom margin removed. This pseudo-class, however, is part of CSS 3, not the current specification, so it is not yet supported by IE. It does already work in many other browsers, such as Firefox, Safari, and Opera.

If you know what the last child element of the div is, of course, you can just remove the bottom margin on that element directly, without having to get into the :last-child pseudo-class. For instance, your footer might contain a single paragraph from which you can remove the margin using a simple descendant selector, or the last item in your main content area might already have a class on it that you can take advantage of.

REMOVING ALL THE MARGINS ON EVERYTHING

Another way of removing default margins to stop margin collapsing is to remove both the top and bottom margins on every single item that has them. CSS rules that do this are commonly called *reset styles*. The idea is to zero out all the defaults—including, but not limited to, those for margins—so that everything starts on a level playing field, and then add back in the actual values that you want. However, since you do at some point have to add margin back in somewhere—unless you're fine with all the paragraphs jamming right up against each other—using reset styles doesn't necessarily make dealing with margin collapsing any easier. You could use padding instead of margin to space text elements out from each other, but since adjacent vertical padding doesn't collapse together but instead doubles, that brings up its own set of challenges.

I personally find reset styles more trouble than they're worth, so we're not covering them here. It's largely a personal preference, though, so if you want to try them out and see if they work for you, you can go to http://meyerweb.com/eric/thoughts/2007/05/01/reset-reloaded to check out the reset style sheet from CSS guru Eric Meyer for inspiration in creating your own.

Once you get the spacing between the text elements set to your liking, you can move on to adding padding to the `div`s themselves. In our basic two-column layout, a grouped rule such as the following will work:

```
#header, #footer, #content-main, #sidebar {
    padding: 2% 2% 1px 2%;
}
```

■ **NOTE:** There's no reason why the padding value has to be the same on all four sides of a `div`. You can set each side to its own unique value if you wish.

If you are using the `:last-child` pseudo-class to get rid of bottom margin on the last element within each `div` and don't have to retain that one pixel of bottom padding to stop margin collapsing, or if you don't mind extra padding adding on to the bottom margin on the last element in each `div`, the rule can be even simpler:

```
#header, #footer, #content-main, #sidebar {
    padding: 2%;
}
```

The two percent measurement is relative to the width of each element's parent. Because all four of these `div`s share the same parent—the *body* element—all four `div`s will contain identically wide padding. If you want individual `div`s to have different amounts of padding, just apply the `padding` property to each `div` individually, assigning unique values to each.

Besides just adding the padding, you'll also need to change either the width of the floated `div` or the matching side margin on the non-floated `div` to accommodate the extra space:

```
#content-main {
    float: right;
    width: 71%;
    background: #F0EE90;
}
#sidebar {
    margin-right: 75%;
    background: #FFA480;
}
```

Here, I've decreased the width of the content-main `div` from 75 percent to 71 percent. Because padding is added on to width in the CSS box model, the total amount of space that the column will take up is still 75 percent of the viewport: 71 percent plus two percent on the left plus two percent on the right. So, the `margin-right` value of 75 percent doesn't need to change if you want space only inside the columns, not between them.

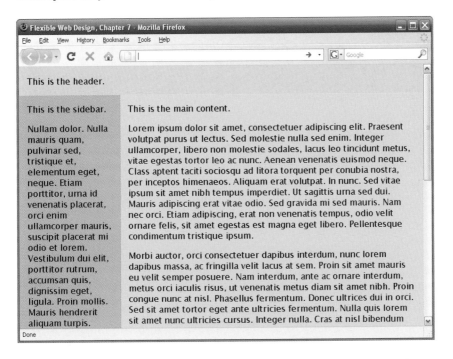

FIGURE 7.3 Padding added to the `div`s creates space inside the columns.

■ **NOTE:** The page showing this completed technique is liquid_margins_twocol_within.html in the ch7_examples.zip file.

An equally valid choice would have been to keep the width of content-main at 75 percent. With its four percent total padding added on, content-main would now take up 79 percent of the viewport, so you'd need to increase the margin-right value on the sidebar div to 79 percent to make enough room.

When your divs don't all share the same parent element, percentage padding values will be calculated from different bases and will end up appearing to be different sizes from one another. For instance, in our example three-column layouts that use a div named content-wrapper around two of the three columns, the two divs within the wrapper need to have larger padding values than the divs outside the wrapper if you want them to all appear the same size visually. If you give the divs inside the wrapper the same percentage values of padding, their padding will be calculated from the smaller size of the wrapper, not the bigger viewport, so those padding values will come out smaller too.

■ **NOTE:** The page showing this completed technique is liquid_floats_threecol_wrapper_within1.html in the ch7_examples.zip file.

Here's an example of CSS setting equal values of padding for divs both outside and inside the content-wrapper div (the width of each of the three columns is also decreased accordingly):

```
#header, #footer, #content-main, #content-secondary, #sidebar {
    padding: 2% 2% 1px 2%;
}
#content-wrapper {
    float: right;
    width: 75%;
    background: #98F5E8;
}
#content-main {
    float: left;
    width: 63%;
    background: #F0EE90;
}
#content-secondary {
    float: right;
    width: 29%;
    background: #9BF598;
}
#sidebar {
    float: left;
```

```
    width: 21%;

    background: #FFA480;

}
```

You can see in **Figure 7.4** that the main and secondary content columns, which are nested in the content-wrapper `div`, have slightly less padding than what appears on the sidebar, header, and footer `div`s. This is only a small difference, so you may be able to live with it.

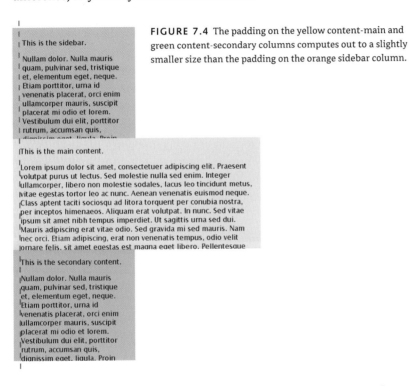

FIGURE 7.4 The padding on the yellow content-main and green content-secondary columns computes out to a slightly smaller size than the padding on the orange sidebar column.

If you must have all the padding amounts appear exactly the same size, you'll need to come up with the padding values for the nested columns using a formula similar to the one we went over in Chapter 4 for calculating widths of nested columns to make them appear the same size:

size of padding you want to match ÷ width of parent column = size of padding on nested column

If you want the padding on the two nested columns to match the size of the two percent padding on the sidebar, header, and footer `div`s, you'll need to divide 2 by 75 (the width of the content-wrapper `div`). This gives you a value of .0266, or about 2.7 percent. Increase the padding on the nested `div`s to this value, and decrease their widths by a matching amount:

```
#content-main {
    float: left;
    width: 61.6%;
    padding: 2.7% 2.7% 1px 2.7%;
    background: #F0EE90;
}
#content-secondary {
    float: right;
    width: 27.6%;
    padding: 2.7% 2.7% 1px 2.7%;
    background: #9BF598;
}
```

Then, change the grouped rule setting the two percent padding to include only the header, footer, and sidebar `div`s:

```
#header, #footer, #sidebar {
    padding: 2% 2% 1px 2%;
}
```

The padding within all the columns now appears equal visually (**Figure 7.5**).

■ **NOTE:** The page showing this completed technique is liquid_floats_ threecol_wrapper_ within2.html in the ch7_examples.zip file.

Unfortunately, these fractional width and padding values make this layout even more susceptible to rounding inconsistencies than it was before, so one-pixel gaps are even more likely to show up now than they were when we first went over this layout in Chapter 4. If this is a problem for your design, you can instead use the buffer `div`s technique that we'll go over later in the chapter.

ADDING PERCENTAGE PADDING TO THE NEGATIVE MARGIN LIQUID LAYOUT

You can add percentage padding values to the `div`s in the negative margin liquid layout without having to worry about these calculations for nested columns' padding. That's because the content-wrapper `div` in that layout is set to 100 percent of the viewport width, so even the content-main `div` nested within it is essentially calculating its padding from the viewport width, just as the non-nested `div`s are.

Even though it's much easier to figure out and apply padding values to the negative margin liquid layout than the non-negative margin layout we've gone over here, it also suffers from some one-pixel gaps once you add that padding. Stay tuned for other techniques that don't have this problem.

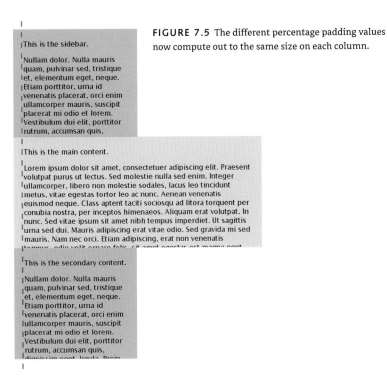

FIGURE 7.5 The different percentage padding values now compute out to the same size on each column.

Spacing for Elastic Layouts

Early in this chapter, I mentioned that ems are the easiest unit of measurement to use for adding spacing in elastic layouts. Adding margins and padding in ems to elastic layouts works just the same as adding margin and padding in percentages to liquid layouts. The only difference is that with ems you don't have to deal with the formula for calculating padding on nested divs; as long as the outer and inner divs both have the same font size, the ems will compute out the same.

So, to add space between columns in an elastic layout, use one of the following techniques:

- With the floats-with-matching-side-margins layout method, increase the side margin to some value larger than the width of the float. Change the width of the wrapper div (if present) or header and footer divs to match the larger combined width of all the columns (if you want the header and footer to match the columns in width).

- With the all-floats layout method, decrease the width of one or more of the columns. If the columns are not floating in opposite directions, you'll either need to switch one so they are, or you'll need to add a side margin between the adjacent floats in addition to the width change. Again, change the width of the wrapper div or header and footer divs to match the larger combined width.

To add space between the columns and the edges of the viewport, use one of the following techniques:

- Set side margins or padding on the body element (if you don't want the overall layout to be centered horizontally in the viewport).

- Use a wrapper div around all the divs, and set its side margins to auto (if you want the overall layout to be centered).

To add space within the columns, first set side padding on each of the divs, and then finish with one of the following options:

- With the floats-with-matching-side-margins layout method, increase the side margin or margins that face the floated div or divs to make extra room for the increased overall width of each float. Also, change the width of the wrapper div (if present) or header and footer divs to match the larger combined width of all the columns (if you want the header and footer to match in width).

- With either of the layout methods, decrease the width of one or more of the columns by the same amount of padding added.

- With the all-floats layout method, leave the widths of the columns alone but increase the width of the wrapper div or header and footer divs to match the larger combined width.

Mixing Units of Measurement

Adding margins and padding with units of measurements other than those used for the column widths—such as pixel padding on em columns or em margin between liquid columns—takes more work than simply increasing or decreasing widths to add on space for the new margins or padding. Mixing units of measurement between width, margin, and padding is like creating hybrid layouts: you lose the ability to easily add or subtract values from other elements, because each value is measured in a different unit.

For instance, if you have a floated column set to 10 ems wide, and you give it 20 pixels of padding on each side, how big a side margin should you set for the adjacent column to make room for the floated column? You don't know what 10 ems plus 20 pixels is, so you can't set a matching margin value.

In mixed-measurement cases, you can use one of the following techniques to add margins or padding while still keeping everything lined up and not overlapping:

* Assign margin and padding only on `div`s where no width is explicitly declared.

* Use margin or padding on the content within the `div`s instead of on the `div`s themselves.

* Nest an extra `div` within each `div` to act as a buffer, with the margin or padding on this inner `div`.

Adding Margin and Padding to Width-less `div`s

When you don't have a width declared on a `div`, there's obviously no pre-existing unit of measurement for the margin or padding measurement to clash with. Instead of being added on to the declared width, the margin or padding will just be taken out of the automatic width that the `div` assumes when it has no width declared.

For instance, none of the liquid layouts we've gone over have widths declared on the header or footer `div`s. Giving these `div`s margin or padding values in pixels or ems will not conflict with their default liquid behavior. For example:

```
#header, #footer {
    padding: 20px 20px 1px 20px;
}
```

ELASTIC SPACING IN LIQUID AND FIXED-WIDTH LAYOUTS

Ems make a great unit of measurement for margin and padding even when you're not dealing with elastic layouts. Just think about it: the purpose of providing margin and padding is to provide white space around text so it's easier to read. If the text is really small, you don't need very large spaces between columns of text to keep them from appearing jumbled together. But if the text is really large, you need much larger spaces between columns of text, because the spaces between the words are so much greater. Thus, it aids readability to have margin and padding grow as the text size grows—and that's just what em values do.

With 20 pixels of padding added inside each side (except the bottom) of the header and footer `div`s, they still remain liquid and still fill up the entire viewport—and no more. If they had widths of 100 percent declared, adding this pixel padding onto it would have made them exceed the width of the viewport by 40 pixels at all times, generating a horizontal scrollbar. Leaving a width off keeps this from happening.

Some of the column `div`s in the example layouts we've worked on throughout this book also don't have widths assigned to them. For instance, the sidebar `div` in the two-column liquid layout that uses a matching side margin next to the floated main content column doesn't have a width. You could assign it non-percentage padding easily:

```
#sidebar {
    margin-right: 75%;
    padding: 1.5em 1.5em 1px 1.5em;
    background: #FFA480;
}
```

Obviously, this is a pretty limited method—most of the `div`s in your layouts will have widths assigned to them. And even without widths present, you may not be able to apply both margin and padding successfully; for instance, we just applied non-percentage padding to a width-less sidebar `div`, but we couldn't add non-percentage margin to it because its side margin must match up with the width of the adjacent floated column, which is set in percentages. Still, it can be very useful for applying margins and padding to smaller, non-main-column elements, such as a feature box on your home page. There's no need to resort to more complicated methods when something simple like this will work, nor do you have to use the same spacing method on every single `div` within your page if different techniques work best for different pieces.

SPACE ON THE VIEWPORT EDGES

Remember earlier in the chapter when we added percentage margin to the body element to move a liquid layout away from the edges of the viewport? This technique works just as well when you don't match up the unit of measurement used for the margin on the body with the unit of measurement used on the overall layout. For instance, you could add `margin: 0 20px;` to your body rule and not adjust any of the percentages of the layout `div`s—they'd still take up 100 percent of the body; it's just that adding pixel margin subtracted out space from the body on each side.

Adding Margin and Padding to Content Instead of to divs

Although it doesn't work for adding spacing *between* divs, another way to add spacing *within* divs is to add it to the content within those divs instead of to the divs themselves.

Let's go back to our basic two-column liquid layout. If you wanted to add 20 pixels of space on the inside edges of each of the divs, you could first add 20 pixels of padding to the top of all the divs:

```
div {
    padding: 20px 0 1px 0;
}
```

It doesn't matter if the values for your top or bottom padding or margin are in units different from those used for the width of a div—only side padding or margin values affect width. Top or bottom padding or margin affects height, but we don't have any heights declared on any of our divs, so we don't need to make any adjustments to height when adding these 20 pixels of top padding to every div.

Once the top and bottom spacing is taken care of, you could also add side padding to all the paragraphs within the divs to move them away from the sides of the divs:

```
div p {
    padding: 0 20px;
}
```

> ■ **NOTE:** Margin would work just as well here to move the edges of the paragraphs away from the edges of the divs. Neither one is more correct than the other.

This adds consistent spacing within each of the divs without having to worry about recalculating widths or side margins (the page will look just like Figure 7.3). But right now the rule works only on paragraphs within the divs; if you were to add headings, lists, or other elements, they would still sit right up against the edges of the divs. To add the padding to every type of content inside the divs, you could use the universal selector:

```
div * {
    padding: 0 20px;
}
```

The *universal selector*—the asterisk—will target all elements, and since it's written here as a descendant of the div element, the rule above will target all content inside all divs, no matter how many levels deep. This is an easy and powerful rule, but also a risky one. Do you really want your lists indented the exact same 20 pixels from the side as the other content is, or might you want them indented slightly farther? Do you want floated images in your text to have 20 pixels of spacing on both sides, or just on the side that they're floated? What if you nest a paragraph inside a blockquote—both of these elements will have 20 pixels of padding added onto each side, so the blockquote will appear to be doubly indented. And if you nest divs within other divs, the nested divs will get the same 20 pixels of padding as all the other content, again potentially causing undesired doubled-up spacing.

A much safer way to pad all the content within columns is to specify exactly what pieces of content you want to have the padding, and how much for each, such as this:

```
p, h1, h2, h3, h4, h5, h6, dl {
    padding: 0 20px;
}
ul, ol, blockquote {
    margin-left: 0;
    padding: 0 20px 0 40px;
}
```

■ **TIP:** While there's no need to put each selector on a separate line, doing so when the selectors are more complicated than simple tags helps you remember to put a comma at the end of each one except the last, as well as to avoid typos in the selectors.

This alternative addresses some of the problems encountered with the universal selector rule, but not all. It doesn't keep padding from getting doubled up when one of these elements is nested inside another, such as a paragraph inside a blockquote.

To stop this, you have to add yet more CSS:

```
ul *,
ol *,
dl *,
blockquote * {
    padding: 0;
}
```

This rule uses the universal selector again to target all content within ul, ol, dl, and blockquote elements and set their padding to zero. Only these elements from our original padding rules can have other content nested within them, so only these elements need to have the padding on their nested children zeroed out.

■ **NOTE:** The page showing this completed technique is liquid_margins_twocol_within_content.html in the ch7_examples.zip file.

Obviously, this method of padding the content within the divs can involve a lot of CSS. Because of this, I wouldn't recommend using it as a site-wide method of padding all your divs. But it doesn't involve any complications in the (X)HTML, and the CSS doesn't have to be that complicated when you use this method only on smaller pieces of the page, such as a sidebar that you know will only ever contain paragraphs and h2 elements.

Adding Buffer divs

The most flexible and versatile way to add spacing between or within columns is to nest another div within each column div, and assign the margin or padding to each of these inner divs. I call these inner divs buffer, or padding, divs. Nesting divs like this doesn't come without its own costs, however; it adds several more divs to your (X)HTML just for presentational purposes, decreasing the semantic purity and cleanliness of your markup and adding to your page file sizes. But web design is all about compromises. If you're OK with this particular compromise—at least in certain situations—read on.

If you want every section on your page to have the same amount of padding within it, the best way to do this is with a CSS class:

```
.buffer {
    padding: 1.5em 1.5em 1px 1.5em;
}
```

Once you have the class defined, you need to nest the additional divs, and place that class on each inner div. For instance, the header div would now look like this:

```
<div id="header">
    <div class="buffer"><p>This is the header.</p></div>
</div>
```

The buffer div is immediately inside the div for which it's providing spacing. All of the content goes within the buffer div.

When the buffer divs are added to every structural div on the page, all of the page sections have uniform spacing (again, the page will look just like Figure 7.3).

If you want individual divs to have different amounts of spacing, you can still use a general CSS class to set the margin or padding that most divs will have, and then override it with descendant selectors on the necessary divs:

```
.buffer {
    padding: 1.5em 1.5em 1px 1.5em;
}
```

■ **NOTE:** The page showing this completed technique is liquid_margins_twocol_within_buffer.html in the ch7_examples.zip file.

```
#content-main .buffer,

#sidebar .buffer {

    padding: 2.5em 2.5em 1px 2.5em;

}
```

This sets the padding on all buffer divs to 1.5 ems, except for the padding on the content-main and sidebar divs, which will each have 2.5 ems of padding.

So far we've gone over how to use buffer divs to provide spacing within divs, but you can modify the CSS to have the buffer divs provide spacing between divs as well. To achieve this, you'll need to move the background color of every structural div onto its buffer div instead, as well as make sure you're using margin instead of padding on the buffer divs:

```
.buffer {

    margin: 1em;

}
#header .buffer,

#footer .buffer {

    background: #DDDDDD;

}
#content-main .buffer {

    background: #F0EE90;

}
#sidebar .buffer {

    background: #FFA480;

}
#content-main {

    float: right;

    width: 75%;

}
#sidebar {

    margin-right: 75%;

}
#footer {

    clear: both;

}
```

USING BUFFER divs WITH MATCHING UNITS OF MEASUREMENT

Although buffer divs are most useful when you're mixing units of measurement for the spacing with units used for the widths of the columns, it's also fine to use them when you're employing the same units of measurement throughout, such as percentage padding on the buffer divs for liquid columns or em padding on the buffer divs for elastic columns.

Earlier in this chapter you saw how fractional percentage padding values placed directly on liquid divs lead to a lot of rounding inconsistencies and gaps. Buffer divs can prevent this—but you'll still have to do plenty of algebra to figure out the correct relative values for each of the columns.

Since the inner divs (not the outer divs) now contain the background colors, and since the inner divs don't fill up the entire outer divs because of their margins, you end up with white space around each div (**Figure 7.6**). Once again, if you wanted different amounts of space between different divs—such as none on the sides of the header and footer, or less in between the two columns where the margins are currently doubling up—you could adjust the margin values within each individual descendant selector.

NOTE: The page showing this completed technique is liquid_margins_twocol_between_buffer.html in the ch7_examples.zip file.

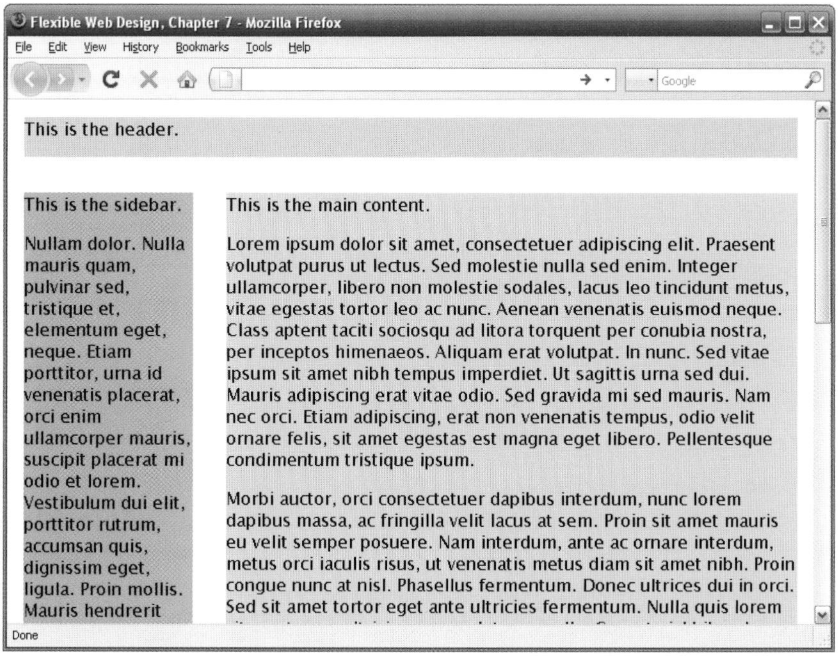

FIGURE 7.6 Giving the buffer divs margin instead of padding and moving the background colors onto the buffer divs instead of the outer divs creates space around each of the divs instead of within them.

If you wanted space both within and between each `div`, you could add padding onto these same buffer `div`s as well:

```
.buffer {
    margin: 1em;
    padding: 1.5em 1.5em 1px 1.5em;
}
```

Now each `div` has 1 em of space around it and 1.5 ems of space within it (**Figure 7.7**).

FIGURE 7.7 A single buffer `div` can provide space both outside and inside itself.

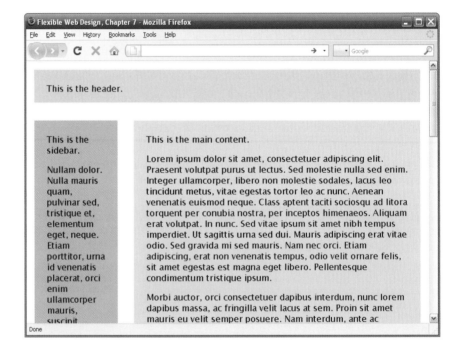

Site-Building Exercise: Adding Spacing to the Home and Inner Pages

In previous chapters' exercises, you've gotten all of the big layout elements for the Beechwood Animal Shelter pages in place, but we haven't yet placed the smaller elements in their precise spots or spaced things out from each other. This exercise will take care of most of the remaining placement and spacing issues in the two pages, using a variety of the techniques discussed earlier in the chapter.

You'll work with the exercise files from this book's companion web site at www.flexiblewebbook.com. Download and unzip the file ch7_exercise.zip.

Adding Spacing to the Header

Open the file programs-start.html in your text or code editor of choice. This is the same page as the final version of the Programs page you completed in Chapter 6.

So far, we haven't styled any of the content within the header div, so it all sits against the left side of the viewport. We want to get the header as a whole lined up with the two columns below it, as well as place the elements within the header in the correct spots in relation to each other.

1. Enter a new line below the opening tag for the header div, and type <div class="buffer"> to create a new buffer div.

2. Locate the closing div tag for the header div, immediately below the main navigation ul element. Enter a new line above it, and type </div> to close the buffer div you just created.

3. Add the following rule inside the style tags in the head of the page:

```
#header .buffer {
    position: relative;
    width: 90%;
    min-width: 40em;
    max-width: 65em;
    margin: 0 auto;
}
```

This copies the existing dimensions and margins from the wrapper div so that the header will always line up with the wrapper div below it (**Figure 7.8**). The only additional declaration added to this rule is position: relative;. This is needed because you'll be adding absolute positioning to the elements within the header in a moment, and you want those elements to position themselves relative to their default positions in the header's buffer div. Without relative positioning on the header's buffer div, the body element would serve as the positioning reference for the absolutely positioned elements.

■ **NOTE:** For a reminder of what the finished pages that you're working towards should look like, check out Figure 4.24 for the Programs page graphic comp and Figure 2.43 for the home page graphic comp.

■ **TIP:** You can put this new rule anywhere in the style section, but you'll have the best luck finding it again in the future if you keep it with other rules for the header.

FIGURE 7.8 The content of the header div now sits the same amount away from the edges of the viewport as does the wrapper div below it.

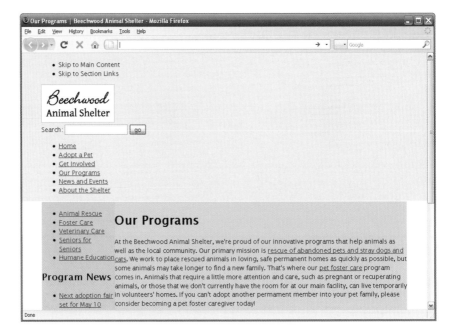

In order to move the elements within the header into their proper places, you'll need to add some id attributes and values to those elements so they can be targeted with CSS rules.

1. Locate the opening div tag for the buffer div inside the header. Immediately below it is an unordered list. Add id="nav-skip" to the opening ul tag.

2. Add a elements to the two list items within this ul to match the following:

   ```
   <li><a href="#content-main">Skip to Main Content</a></li>

   <li><a href="#section-links">Skip to Section Links</a></li>
   ```

3. Locate the second ul in the header div, immediately below the search form. Add id="nav-main" to the opening ul tag.

Now that the elements within the header have been uniquely identified, you can start moving each piece into place using CSS.

1. Back in the style section in the head of the page, add the following new rules:

   ```
   #header img {

       position: absolute;

       top: 20px;

       left: 0;
   ```

```
}
#header form {
    position: absolute;
    top: 20px;
    left: 190px;
}
#nav-skip {
    position: absolute;
    top: 20px;
    right: 0;
    margin: 0;
    padding: 0;
    list-style: none;
    text-align: right;
    font-size: 86%;
}
```

These rules position the logo image, the search form, and the skip links absolutely so that they are taken out of the float and won't interfere with the placement of the main navigation bar.

2. Add the following new rules to move the navigation bar into the correct spot within the header and space the individual list items out from each other:

```
#nav-main {
    float: left;
    margin: 79px 0 0 190px;
    padding: 0;
    list-style: none;
}
#nav-main li {
    float: left;
    margin: 0;
    padding: .5em .7em .4em .7em;
}
```

■ **NOTE:** You could also move this hack into the existing conditional comment for IE 6 on the Programs page. The home page doesn't have a conditional comment yet, though, so we'll keep it in the main styles for now.

3. Because nav-main is floated left and has a left margin, the IE 6 doubled float margin bug is triggered. Add `display: inline;` to the `#nav-main` rule to stop this.

Now that the header `div` contains only absolutely positioned and floated content—none of which is in the flow of the page—it collapses (**Figure 7.9**).

FIGURE 7.9 All of the elements within the header `div` are now in their correct spots, but the background color on the header has shrunk to a tiny band at the top of the header because the `div` itself has collapsed.

1. Add the following new rule to make the header `div` contain the floated main navigation bar:

   ```
   #header {
       display: table;
       width: 100%;
       margin-bottom: 30px;
   }
   ```

   The `display: table;` declaration is another simple float-containment method. Using `overflow: auto;` or floating the `div` would also work, but the overflow method would generate scrollbars on the header individually if someone had very large text on a smaller screen, and the floating method would cut off the background color of the header `div` at the right edge of the viewport, even if the content of the header `div` extended past that right edge.

   The bottom margin provides space between the bottom of the header and the wrapper `div` below.

This takes care of the header `div` in the Programs page, but you also need to deal with the header on the home page. Open the file home-start.html in your text or code editor of choice. This is the same page as the final version of the home page you completed in Chapter 6.

1. Copy all the HTML for the header `div` from your revised Programs page. Paste it over the existing HTML for the header `div` in home-start.html.

2. Inside the nav-skip unordered list, delete the second list item (since there are no section links to skip to on the home page).

3. In the remaining list item in the nav-skip list, change the link's `href` value from #content-main to #wrapper, since there is no `div` named content-main on the home page.

4. Copy all of the new CSS rules you created in your Programs page. Paste them into the `style` section in the `head` of home-start.html.

These changes make the header on the home page look and act just like the header on the Programs page (**Figure 7.10**). However, if you want the header on the home page to match up with the elastic wrapper below it, instead of being liquid, you'll need to make a few changes to the new CSS rules you pasted in.

FIGURE 7.10 The elements within the header are all placed correctly in relation to each other, but the header content as a whole doesn't match up in width with the content below it on the home page.

5. Locate the #header .buffer rule, and modify it to match the following:

```
#header .buffer {
    position: relative;
    width: 41em;
    margin: 0 auto;
    padding-left: 180px;
}
```

These styles copy those used by the wrapper div on the home page so that the two divs will always line up with each other.

6. Modify the left margin value on the #nav-main rule to account for the large amount of left padding now taking up space in the buffer div inside the header:

```
#nav-main {
    float: left;
    margin: 79px 0 0 10px;
    padding: 0;
    list-style: none;
}
```

These changes make the header div on the home page match up with the wrapper div below it (**Figure 7.11**).

FIGURE 7.11 The header div on the home page now matches the content below it in overall width.

CHANGING THE WRAPPING BEHAVIOR OF THE NAV BAR LINKS

You'll notice in Figure 7.11 that the last link in the nav bar has wrapped down onto a second line. This is correct behavior for the floated links if they can't all fit on one line. But if you want the individual words within each link to wrap instead, to make each link shorter, then replace the `float: left;` declaration in the `#nav-main li` rule with `display: table-cell;`. As I mentioned in Chapter 2, a value of `table-cell` for the `display` property makes the element it is applied to act just like a table cell—the links will grow and shrink as needed, but none will shrink past the width of their longest word, nor will they ever wrap. But, as I also mentioned in Chapter 2, IE 7 and earlier don't support the table-related `display` values. If you use `table-cell` on this nav bar, you'll probably still want to use the `float` declaration in IE 7 and earlier only, to provide a backup method for positioning the links.

Adding Spacing to the Footer

The footer is much simpler than the header—it contains only one element, a single paragraph, that you need to worry about providing spacing for. This paragraph can act like a buffer `div` within the footer without your having to make any additions to the HTML.

1. In the `style` section in the `head` of both pages, add a new rule for the paragraph within the footer:

```
#footer p {
    width: 90%;
    min-width: 40em;
    max-width: 75em;
    margin: 0 auto;
    font-size: 86%;
}
```

This makes the paragraph in the footer line up with the wrapper above it in the Programs page. It doesn't line up with the wrapper in the home page, but I don't see this as a problem that's worth fixing. Since the footer text has a smaller font size than the rest of the text on the page, you could not simply give it the same width and padding measurements as those used by the elastic wrapper and header—you'd have to make more changes to the CSS, as well as add another buffer `div` within the footer in the HTML.

Since the footer doesn't have nearly as much content as the header does, it doesn't seem as important to make it match up with the elastic wrapper on the home page if it's going to take all this extra work.

2. To give the footer text some space above and below it, add padding to the existing #footer rule:

```
#footer {
    clear: both;
    padding: 20px 0;
}
```

Dealing with Margin Collapsing

Up until now, the pages have had a simple rule giving one pixel of top and bottom padding to every div in order to stop the default margins on text elements from escaping from their containers. Before making any other spacing changes to the content of either the Programs or home page, it's time to switch to another margin-collapsing-prevention method that will work better with the other spacing changes you'll make. Make the following changes to both pages.

1. Add the following grouped rule to get rid of all the default top margins on the main text elements:

```
p, h1, h2, h3, h4, h5, h6 {
    margin-top: 0;
}
```

2. Add the following rules to provide further text formatting:

```
h1, h2 {
    font-family: Cambria, "Palatino Linotype", Palatino, serif;
}
h1 {
    margin-bottom: 0;
    font-size: 200%;
}
h2 {
    margin-bottom: .5em;
    font-size: 136%;
}
```

ORGANIZING STYLES

You may want to add these new rules to the bottom of your style sheet, separated out from all the rest of the layout-related styles you've written so far. Using
CSS comments is a good way to divide up your style sheet into thematically
related chunks so you can quickly find the style you're looking for later when you
need to modify it. I recommend keeping rules for generic paragraphs, headings,
and blockquotes under a CSS comment like /*TEXT*/. You can also create com-
mented sections called /*LISTS*/, /*TABLES*/, and so forth.

3. Locate and delete the following rule near the top of the style section in
   the head of each page:

   ```
   div {
       padding: 1px 0;
   }
   ```

Adding Spacing to the Content of the Programs Page

It's now time to space out the columns and content of the Programs page
separately from the very different home page.

1. Locate <h1>Our Programs</h1> in the HTML. Cut it from its current location, and paste it directly under the opening div tag for the wrapper div.

2. Type <div id="title"> immediately before the h1 element and </div>
   immediately after it. The resulting HTML for the start of the wrapper div
   should look like this:

   ```
   <div id="wrapper">
       <div id="title">
           <h1>Our Programs</h1>
       </div>
       <div id="content-wrapper">
           <div id="content-main">
               <p>At the Beechwood Animal Shelter, we're...
   ```

3. Add a new CSS rule for this new div that matches the following:

   ```
   #title {
       padding: 1.5em;
       background: #7ABA65;
   }
   ```

4. Add a buffer `div` immediately inside the content-main `div` and surrounding all its content:

```
<div id="content-main">

    <div class="buffer">

        <p>At the Beechwood Animal Shelter, we're ...

        ... small group tours of our facilities.</p>

    </div>

</div>
```

5. Add a new CSS rule for this new `div` that matches the following:

```
#content-main .buffer {

    padding: 30px 1.5em 1px 2em;

}
```

The main content area is now nicely spaced out (**Figure 7.12**). The sidebar will take a little more work because it has more elements in it. You'll first need to add a little more structure to its HTML in order to uniquely identify and separately style its different components.

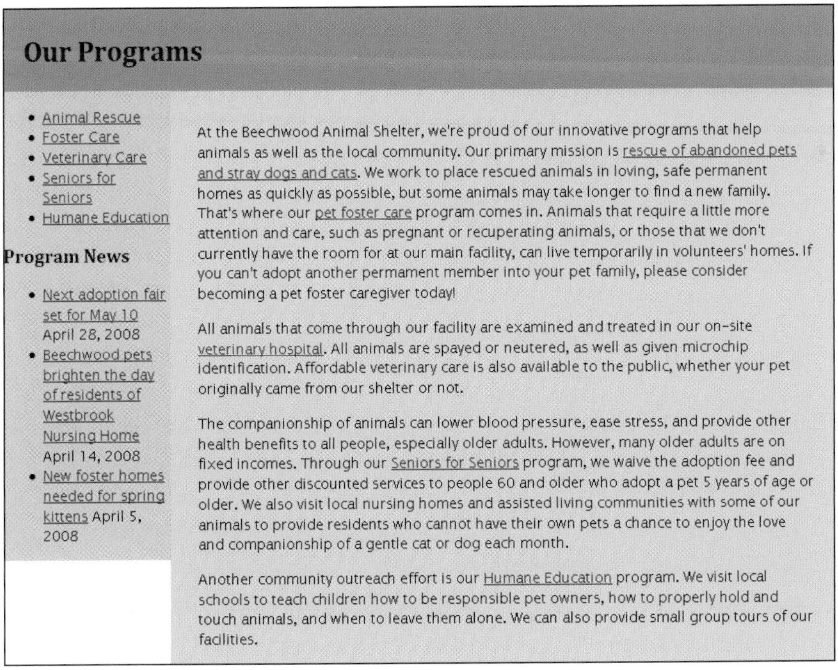

FIGURE 7.12 The new title `div` and the content-main `div` now both have spacing within them.

6. Locate `<div id="nav-secondary">` in the HTML. Add `id="section-links"` to the opening `ul` tag that immediately follows it.

7. Locate `<h2>Program News</h2>` a few lines down. Enter a new line above it, and type `<div id="news">`.

8. Locate the closing `ul` tag a few lines further down. Enter a new line beneath it, and type `</div>` to close the news `div` you just created.

9. Go back to the `style` section in the `head`. Add the following new rule to get rid of the default left margin and padding as well as the bullets on the section-links `ul` element:

```
#section-links {
    margin: 30px 0 0 0;
    padding: 0;
    list-style: none;
}
```

This rule adds 30 pixels of spacing to the top of the list to move it down from the top of the column, but it doesn't add any spacing to the left of the list. That will be added to the links within the list instead. This is because we want a solid block of color behind each list item, with a border above and below it. It's best to put this color on the *a* elements, because you can then easily change the background color when anyone hovers over or tabs to any *a* element.

10. Add the following new rule to add spacing to the links within the unordered list:

```
#section-links a {
    display: block;
    padding: .5em 1.5em .8em 1.5em;
    border-bottom: 1px solid #FFF;
    background: #F2F4F7;
}
```

Padding set in ems will work well to ensure the links always have enough room around them—no matter their font size—to be readable and easy to click. Background color and borders have been added here as well as the spacing, because without them you can't really tell if you have the amount of spacing you want.

11. Now that the links have their borders, go back to the `#section-links` rule, and add a border to its top to make sure the very top link doesn't miss out on its top border:

```
#section-links {
    margin: 30px 0 0 0;
```

```
    padding: 0;
    border-top: 1px solid #FFF;
    list-style: none;
}
```

12. IE 6 and earlier will add space between each of the links because they are set to display: block. To fix this, add the following new rule inside the conditional comment style section in the head:

```
#section-links li {
    display: inline;
}
```

This takes care of the spacing for the section links in the nav-secondary div (**Figure 7.13**). Now we'll work on the news div immediately below it.

13. Add the following new rule to provide spacing within all four sides of the news div:

```
#news {
    padding: 1.5em;
}
```

FIGURE 7.13 The section links list as a whole has been moved away from the top of the column, and the links within it are nicely spaced out from each other.

14. Add the following new rules to remove the default spacing on the list within the news div and set new spacing values of its own:

```
#news ul {
    margin: 0;
    padding: 0;
    list-style: none;
}
#news li {
    margin: 0 0 .8em 0;
}
```

15. Add the following new rule to move the date on each news item down onto its own line:

```
#news span {
    display: block;
}
```

These changes complete all of the spacing work you need to do on the Programs page (**Figure 7.14**). To compare your work to the completed

Programs page for this exercise, see the file programs-end.html that you extracted from ch7_exercise.zip.

FIGURE 7.14 All of the elements on the Programs page are now nicely aligned and spaced out from each other.

FIGURE 7.14 All of the elements on the Programs page are now nicely aligned and spaced out from each other.

Adding Spacing to the Content of the Home Page

The home page will require completely different CSS to provide spacing for its columns and content. You'll start by providing spacing within and around the banner div.

1. Add the following new rule inside the style section in the head of the home page:

    ```
    #banner p {
        width: 17em;
        margin: 0;
        font: 129% Cambria, "Palatino Linotype", Palatino, serif;
        line-height: 1.4;
    }
    ```

The width set on the paragraph makes the text within the banner div take up only a small portion of the overall div, leaving plenty of space within which the eventual background image can display.

2. To provide space around the paragraph in the banner, as well as create a gap under the banner div, modify the existing #banner rule to match the following:

```
#banner {
    margin: 0 0 20px -180px;
    padding: 2em 0 6em 20px;
    background: #CFC;
}
```

These changes complete the spacing work for the banner div (**Figure 7.15**).

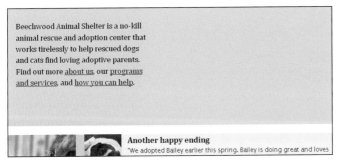

FIGURE 7.15
The text within the green banner div has the proper amount of space around it, and there is a gap under the banner div as a whole.

3. Add the following new rule to create a gap between the two images in the left ads column:

```
#ads img {
    margin-bottom: 20px;
}
```

4. Add a margin-bottom value to the existing #story rule to create a gap beneath the happy ending div:

```
#story {
    float: right;
    width: 41em;
    margin-bottom: 20px;
    background: #FFC;
}
```

You're now ready to move on to the adopt-pets div. The first item to take care of within it is the "Adopt me!" heading. This text isn't shown anywhere in the graphic comp; instead, an image of a pet collar tag saying "Adopt me!" is shown on the right side of the div. You're going to turn the text that currently exists in the page into this pet-tag image using a CSS image-replacement technique.

Image replacement is the general name given to any CSS technique that uses images to replace the text shown on the page. The purpose of this is to keep the text in the (X)HTML so that it will be accessible to search engines, screen readers, and other user agents that don't use images, while having a more visually interesting rendition of the content display to those who browse the web viewing images. The image-replacement technique we're going to use here is called the Phark Method, but there are many, many more to choose from, each with their own pros and cons. A good rundown of the most popular options is available on the CSS-Tricks blog at http://css-tricks.com/nine-techniques-for-css-image-replacement.

5. Add the following new rule to replace the text in the h2 element in the adopt-pets div with the pet-tag image:

```
#adopt-pets h2 {
    width: 105px;
    height: 116px;
    background: url(images/adopt-header.png);
    text-indent: -9999px;
}
```

This rule works by first setting the desired image as the background of the element containing the text. You set the width and height of the element to exactly match the size of the background image so that all of it shows, but nothing more. Finally, an extremely large negative text-indent value moves the text within the element off the left side of the screen so it (the text) can't be seen.

You can see in **Figure 7.16** that the "Adopt me!" text is gone and the pet-tag image is left in its place. Now you need to move the image into the correct spot on the page.

FIGURE 7.16 The "Adopt me!" text has been replaced with the background image of the pet tag.

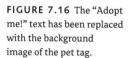
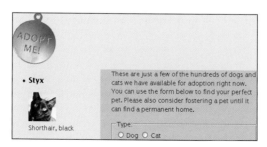

6. Modify the #adopt-pets h2 rule you just created to float the h2 over to the right side of its div and put some space around it:

```
#adopt-pets h2 {
    float: right;
    width: 105px;
    height: 116px;
    margin: -10px -40px 10px 10px;
    background: url(images/adopt-header.png);
    text-indent: -9999px;
}
```

The negative margin values on the top and right pull the image outside of the div to overlap its borders, matching the placement shown in the graphic comp (**Figure 7.17**). The positive margin values on the left and bottom provide spacing between the image and the adjacent text.

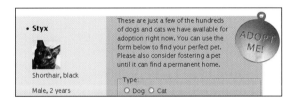

FIGURE 7.17 Floating the h2 containing the pet-tag image to the right, as well as giving it negative margins, places it correctly in relation to the other elements inside the adopt-pets div.

There are a couple of problems in IE 6 and earlier, however: they cut off the portion of the image that extends outside the edges of the div, and the image itself doesn't have a transparent background (**Figure 7.18**). You'll need to add a conditional comment to the home page to hold some IE 6-specific hacks.

FIGURE 7.18 In IE 6, the pet tag image has a gray background and is cut off at the edge of the purple search form.

7. Immediately below the closing style tag in the head of the page, add the following conditional comment:

```
<!--[if IE 6]>
<style>
#adopt-pets h2 {
    position: relative;
```

■ NOTE: The filter declaration in this rule has been split onto two lines simply for spacing issues in the book, but you can put it all on one line in your own CSS. It works either way.

```
        background-image: none;
        filter: progid:DXImageTransform.Microsoft.AlphaImageLoader
            (src="images/adopt-header.png", sizingMethod="crop");
    }
    </style>
    <![endif]-->
```

The position: relative; declaration is what fixes the cut-off portion of the negatively margined image. The rest of the rule fixes the lack of alpha transparency in the PNG background image by removing that background image and replacing it with a Microsoft-proprietary property called filter.

This conditional comment targets only IE 6, not IE 5.x, since we aren't concerned with fully supporting IE 5.x in this book. If you wish, you can easily make it target all versions of IE up to and including 6 by changing <!--[if IE 6]> to <!--[if lte IE 6]>.

Now that you've taken care of the image replacement, you can turn your attention to the other pieces of content within the adopt-pets div.

8. Modify the existing #adopt-pets ul rule to give it the desired amount of spacing and get rid of the default bullets:

```
#adopt-pets ul {
    float: left;
    width: 12em;
    margin: 0;
    padding: 1.5em;
    list-style: none;
}
```

Be sure to decrease the width from 14 ems to 12 ems as shown. Although you've added an extra 3 ems of space with the 1.5 ems of padding on each side of the list, you're only decreasing the width by 2 ems. The new width of 12 ems, combined with the 3 ems of padding, totals to 15 ems, the exact size of the existing left margin on the pet search form. The old width of 14 ems left one em of space between the list and the form, but now the 1.5 ems of right padding on the list is providing that spacing.

The elements within the list of featured pets are still not placed correctly—the name of each pet still sits above its photo instead of to its right, for instance—but you'll take care of these remaining issues in Chapter 9, after you've learned about creating teaser thumbnail lists. We're just worried about providing spacing for the list as a whole right now; you'll deal with the spacing and placement of the elements inside this list later.

LIMITATIONS OF THE ALPHAIMAGELOADER FILTER

The AlphaImageLoader filter that you've applied in the conditional comment is one way to get alpha-transparent background images working in IE 6 and earlier, but it can't do everything a regular background image can do. It's really just displaying a static image behind the text, so the image can't be tiled or positioned like background images can be. Also, the filter is much more resource-intensive than regular images, and can cause IE to become sluggish if used multiple times on the same page. Finally, links and form elements laid over images brought in with the filter may stop working, depending on the other CSS in the page.

To avoid some of these problems, turn to a JavaScript solution instead, such as:

+ IE PNG Fix by Angus Turnbull of TwinHelix (www.twinhelix.com/css/iepngfix)

+ Unit PNG Fix by Unit Interactive (http://labs.unitinteractive.com/unitpngfix.php)

+ SuperSleight by Drew McLellan (http://24ways.org/2007/supersleight-transparent-png-in-ie6)

9. Add padding to the existing #search-pets rule to provide spacing at its top, bottom, and right sides:

```
#search-pets {
    margin-left: 15em;
    padding: 1.5em 1.5em 1.5em 0;
    background: #CCF;
}
```

The spacing on the left side is being taken care of by the list of featured pets to its left.

These changes complete all of the spacing work you need to do on the home page (**Figure 7.19**). To compare your work to the completed home page for this exercise, see the file home-end.html that you extracted from ch7_exercise.zip.

FIGURE 7.19 All of the elements on the home page are now nicely aligned and spaced out from each other.

8

Adding Background Images and Color

The main challenge that arises with adding background images to flexible layouts is ensuring those images will stretch or tile to cover an entire area of unknown dimensions. In this chapter, you'll learn how to combine background images with background color to extend their range. You'll also learn how to adapt the popular "faux columns" equal-height columns technique to use in liquid and elastic layouts.

Blending Background Images

A great way to extend the area that a background image will cover is to blend the background image into a matching background color or one or more additional background images so that the pieces appear to be one large background with no seams. This is useful in all types of layouts—flexible and fixed-width—but is especially helpful in flexible layouts, since the area a background image might have to cover is even more variable in dimension.

Creating Gradients

■ **NOTE:** Each of the completed example files is available for download from this book's companion web site at www.flexiblewebbook. com. Download the file ch8_examples.zip to get the complete set. I'll let you know which file goes with which technique as we go along.

A common use for blending background images into background color is when you want to create the appearance of a gradient background.

Gradient backgrounds are a great example of the type of blending of background image and color that I'm talking about. Even if the area you want the gradient to cover is huge, there's no need to create an enormous image of a gradient to use as your background. Instead, create one small piece that can be tiled, and then use a background color that exactly matches the ending color on the gradient to fill in the rest of the space.

■ **NOTE:** The page showing this completed technique is gradient.html in the ch8_examples.zip file.

For instance, what if you wanted the background on the main content area of your familiar two-column liquid layout to start out gold and gradually fade to yellow, as in **Figure 8.1**? There's no need to create an extremely tall and wide image to fill the space. You can create a small slice, like the one shown in **Figure 8.2**, and tile it to the right and left:

```
#content-main {
    float: right;
    width: 75%;
    background: #F0EE90 url(gradient.jpg) repeat-x;
}
```

■ **NOTE:** The image shown in Figure 8.2 really needs to be only one pixel wide in order to tile correctly—I've just made it a little wider so you can actually see it!

I've left the background color we've always used, #F0EE90, in place to fill in whatever space the background image doesn't take up; you can see this non-image space in **Figure 8.3**. Because the color #F0EE90 exactly matches the color at the bottom of the gradient, there appears to be no seam between the image and the color.

To tile a gradient background image—or any background image, for that matter—to the right and left only, use repeat-x as the background-repeat value. To tile a background image up and down, use repeat-y.

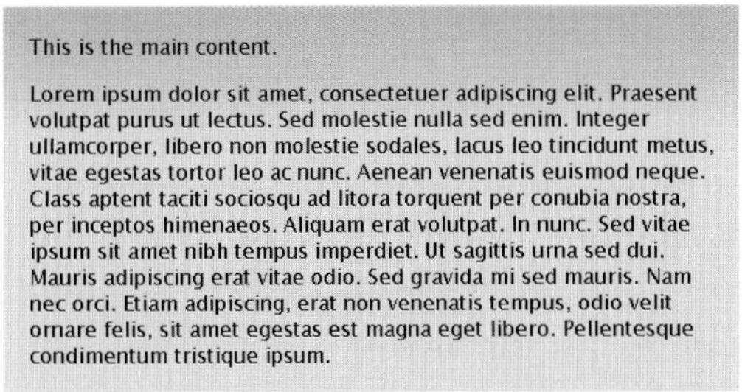

This is the main content.

Lorem ipsum dolor sit amet, consectetuer adipiscing elit. Praesent volutpat purus ut lectus. Sed molestie nulla sed enim. Integer ullamcorper, libero non molestie sodales, lacus leo tincidunt metus, vitae egestas tortor leo ac nunc. Aenean venenatis euismod neque. Class aptent taciti sociosqu ad litora torquent per conubia nostra, per inceptos himenaeos. Aliquam erat volutpat. In nunc. Sed vitae ipsum sit amet nibh tempus imperdiet. Ut sagittis urna sed dui. Mauris adipiscing erat vitae odio. Sed gravida mi sed mauris. Nam nec orci. Etiam adipiscing, erat non venenatis tempus, odio velit ornare felis, sit amet egestas est magna eget libero. Pellentesque condimentum tristique ipsum.

FIGURE 8.1 A gradient background image on a variable width and height area.

FIGURE 8.2 A small slice of a gradient image, like this one, can be tiled horizontally for the background of a variable width box.

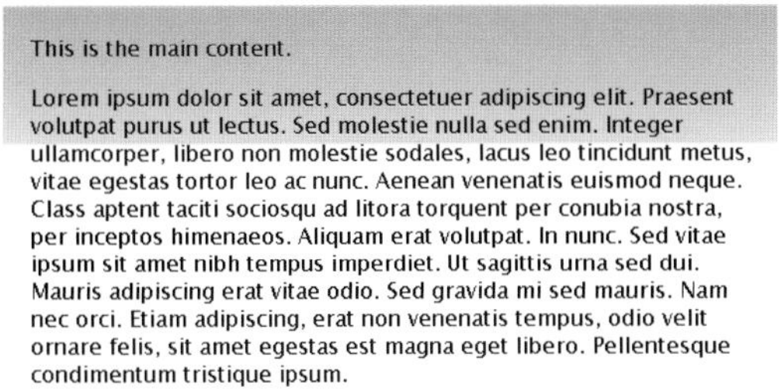

This is the main content.

Lorem ipsum dolor sit amet, consectetuer adipiscing elit. Praesent volutpat purus ut lectus. Sed molestie nulla sed enim. Integer ullamcorper, libero non molestie sodales, lacus leo tincidunt metus, vitae egestas tortor leo ac nunc. Aenean venenatis euismod neque. Class aptent taciti sociosqu ad litora torquent per conubia nostra, per inceptos himenaeos. Aliquam erat volutpat. In nunc. Sed vitae ipsum sit amet nibh tempus imperdiet. Ut sagittis urna sed dui. Mauris adipiscing erat vitae odio. Sed gravida mi sed mauris. Nam nec orci. Etiam adipiscing, erat non venenatis tempus, odio velit ornare felis, sit amet egestas est magna eget libero. Pellentesque condimentum tristique ipsum.

FIGURE 8.3 The gradient background image tiles only to the right and left, leaving a large space below it empty for background color to fill if added.

Another way to blend gradients into background colors is by fading the gradient into full transparency. This comes in very handy when you want to blend a gradient into another background image instead of a background color.

For instance, let's say we wanted to put drop shadows on both sides of the wrapper on our two-column layout, and these drop shadows needed to lay over a patterned background image on the body element. The first step is to create an alpha-transparent PNG image of the drop shadow for each side of the wrapper. Both images need to be partially transparent throughout and fade to full transparency on either end (**Figure 8.4**).

FIGURE 8.4 The source graphics for the left and right parts of the drop shadow image are partially transparent throughout. Transparency is indicated by the checked pattern in Adobe Fireworks and Adobe Photoshop.

In the page itself, we need to wrap all the divs in two wrappers instead of just one. Here's what the div structure would look like:

```
<div id="wrapper1">

    <div id="wrapper2">

        <div id="header"></div>

        <div id="content-main"></div>

        <div id="sidebar"></div>

        <div id="footer"></div>

    </div>

</div>
```

We need two wrappers because we don't know how wide the overall layout will be. If you had a fixed-width layout, you could have a single wrapper holding a single background image. This background image would have a drop shadow on each side and simply be tiled downward to fill in the fixed-width space. In a liquid or elastic layout, there's no way to know how far apart the two drop shadows will be, so you need to create two separate images and place each on a separate wrapper `div`.

With the two wrappers in the HTML, place the left drop shadow on one and the right drop shadow on the other, both set to tile vertically using `repeat-y`. The right background image will also need to be aligned to the right side of its container using a value of `right` in the `background` shorthand property:

```
#wrapper1 {
    width: 80%;
    margin: 0 auto;
    background: url(drop_shadow_left.png) repeat-y;
}
#wrapper2 {
    background: url(drop_shadow_right.png) repeat-y right;
}
```

To make sure that the content within the wrappers doesn't cover the background images, give each `div` padding on the same side as its background image:

```
#wrapper1 {
    width: 80%;
    margin: 0 auto;
    padding: 0 0 0 20px;
    background: url(drop_shadow_left.png) repeat-y;
}
#wrapper2 {
    padding: 0 20px 0 0;
    background: url(drop_shadow_right.png) repeat-y right;
}
```

■ **NOTE:** The page showing this completed technique is drop_shadows.html in the ch8_examples.zip file.

Each drop shadow image now tiles down the page on either side of the content (**Figure 8.5**). No matter what background image or color is on the `body` element, the drop shadow will allow it to partially show through, creating the real appearance of a shadow laid over another surface.

TILING TRANSPARENCY IN IE 6 AND EARLIER

Remember the fix using the AlphaImageLoader filter in Chapter 7's exercise section for the lack of support for alpha-transparent PNGs in IE 6 and earlier? Well, don't try to apply that fix to this example—it won't work if you tile or position the background image, as we're doing here. In fact, most JavaScript fixes for alpha-transparent PNGs in IE don't even work when tiling or positioning is thrown into the mix. Luckily, there is one script that does have support for this: IE PNG Fix v.2.0 by Angus Turnbull of TwinHelix. It's in alpha at the time of this writing, but I've gotten it to work successfully on this example page at least. Download the script at www.twinhelix.com/css/iepngfix.

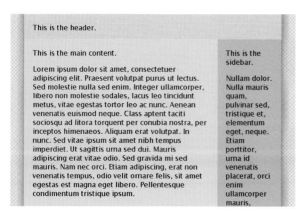

FIGURE 8.5 A separate alpha-transparent PNG tiles down each side of the page and allows the pattern on the body element to partially show through, creating the appearance of a shadow behind the content area of the page.

Creating Rounded Corners

Rounded corners are one of the most popular CSS tricks—there are dozens and dozens of different ways to create them. Some methods blend background images into background colors, others blend multiple background images into each other, and still others use no images at all but simply CSS tricks or even JavaScript to create round corners on the fly. There's no one technique that is ideal for all types of sites. We'll cover one of the more basic techniques here, but if you want to experiment with others and look for the one that best fits your requirements, check out the "CSS Rounded Corner 'Roundup'" at the Smiley Cat Web Design blog (www.smileycat.com/miaow/archives/000044. php). The techniques are sorted into tables, so you can quickly identify the attributes you're looking for (such as how many images it uses, if it works for liquid, and so on) and find matching techniques.

The most basic type of rounded corner box has a solid background color, no borders, and sits on top of another solid background color area. This type of box can be made by using four images, one for each corner, and blending them into the background color.

First, you need to create the four images for the corners (**Figure 8.6**). Each image must have a solid background color not only inside the curve, but outside it as well. The solid color on the outside of each curve needs to match the background color of the area on top of which the rounded corner box is going to sit. For instance, our images in Figure 8.6 have white outside the curved orange portion because the sidebar that we're going to be adding these corners to will be sitting on top of the white background of the body element.

FIGURE 8.6 The four rounded corner images have solid color both inside and outside the curves.

Each image needs to go on a separate block element, so you may have to nest additional divs inside the main div for your box. For instance, if we wanted to add rounded corners to the sidebar in our liquid layouts, here is what the div structure might look like:

```
<div id="sidebar">
    <div class="top-right">
        <div class="bottom-left">
            <div class="bottom-right">
                <p>This is the sidebar.</p>
                ...
            </div>
        </div>
    </div>
</div>
```

You then place each corner image as a background on each of the divs. Each image must be set to no-repeat and positioned to the appropriate side of the box:

```
#sidebar {
    background: #FFA480 url(tl.gif) no-repeat;
}
#sidebar .top-right {
    background: url(tr.gif) no-repeat top right;
}
#sidebar .bottom-left {
    background: url(bl.gif) no-repeat bottom left;
}
```

```
#sidebar .bottom-right {
    padding: 20px;
    background: url(br.gif) no-repeat bottom right;
}
```

The solid white portion of each image covers up the non-rounded corners of the sidebar div. Because each nested div fills its parent div completely, the nested divs' background images perfectly line up with the background color on the sidebar div, creating the appearance of one solid block (**Figure 8.7**).

■ **NOTE:** The page showing this completed technique is rounded_corners.html in the ch8_examples.zip file.

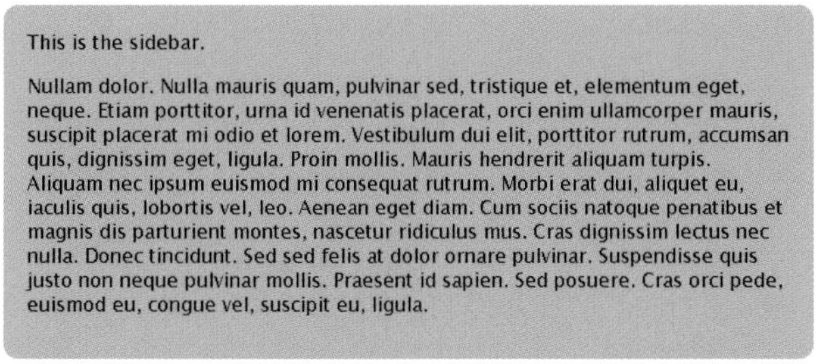

This is the sidebar.

Nullam dolor. Nulla mauris quam, pulvinar sed, tristique et, elementum eget, neque. Etiam porttitor, urna id venenatis placerat, orci enim ullamcorper mauris, suscipit placerat mi odio et lorem. Vestibulum dui elit, porttitor rutrum, accumsan quis, dignissim eget, ligula. Proin mollis. Mauris hendrerit aliquam turpis. Aliquam nec ipsum euismod mi consequat rutrum. Morbi erat dui, aliquet eu, iaculis quis, lobortis vel, leo. Aenean eget diam. Cum sociis natoque penatibus et magnis dis parturient montes, nascetur ridiculus mus. Cras dignissim lectus nec nulla. Donec tincidunt. Sed sed felis at dolor ornare pulvinar. Suspendisse quis justo non neque pulvinar mollis. Praesent id sapien. Sed posuere. Cras orci pede, euismod eu, congue vel, suscipit eu, ligula.

FIGURE 8.7 Each rounded corner image blends in with the background color on the outermost div and covers its square corners.

CSS3 ENHANCEMENTS TO ROUNDED CORNER TECHNIQUES

It stinks that we have to add multiple divs to hold multiple background images, but some day it won't be like this. The next version of CSS, CSS3, allows you to apply multiple background images to a single element and position each one separately. Unfortunately, only Safari, Konqueror, and Google Chrome support this piece of CSS 3 at the time of this writing—and even once the other browsers adopt it, it will probably be a while before we designers can use it widely, as older browsers don't disappear overnight.

Another CSS3 property that can help you create rounded corner boxes is border-radius, which will automatically round your corners for you—no images necessary! This property is already supported by Firefox, Safari, Konqueror, and Google Chrome (though you may have to use browser-specific prefixes, like -moz-border-radius, to get it to work).

The tutorial "Rounded Corner Boxes the CSS3 Way" by Andy Budd demonstrates how to use both of these CSS3 properties (http://24ways.org/2006/rounded-corner-boxes-the-css3-way).

AVOID PADDING ON THE OUTER divs

Make sure that when you use this technique you don't have a rule giving one pixel of top or bottom padding to all of the divs in order to stop margin collapsing. If you do, each of the nested divs will be nudged in slightly from its parent, but you can work around the misalignment in a couple ways.

Your first option is to set the padding back to zero on each of the divs, except the innermost one, on which you can leave the padding since it contains no other divs that will get misplaced by its padding.

Your second option is to use negative margins to pull each nested div back up to its proper place. If you had one pixel of only bottom padding on each div—no top padding—you wouldn't need to set any negative margins on the divs forming the top two corners of the box, because they'd both be aligned perfectly at the top. For the bottom two corner divs, you'd need to use a negative two-pixel margin-bottom value on the second nested div (the one holding the bottom-left image) and a negative one-pixel margin-bottom value on the third nested div (the one holding the bottom-right image).

If you have other block elements within the sidebar that you can be sure will always be at the top or bottom of your box, you can simplify the HTML by "hanging" a corner image on each of these. For instance, let's say our sidebar always started with an h2 element and had no other h2 elements within it. You could get rid of the top-right div:

```
<div id="sidebar">
  <div class="bottom-left">
    <div class="bottom-right">
      <h2>This is the sidebar.</h2>
      ...
    </div>
  </div>
</div>
```

Then, change the #sidebar .top-right selector to #sidebar h2 instead to place the top-right corner background image on the h2:

```
#sidebar {
  background: #FFA480 url(tl.gif) no-repeat;
```

```
}

#sidebar h2 {

    background: url(tr.gif) no-repeat top right;

}

#sidebar .bottom-left {

    background: url(bl.gif) no-repeat bottom left;

}

#sidebar .bottom-right {

    padding: 20px;

    background: url(br.gif) no-repeat bottom right;

}
```

This places the corner image on the heading, but the padding on the bottom-right div indents the heading on its right side, so its background image doesn't align with the background color on the sidebar div (**Figure 8.8**).

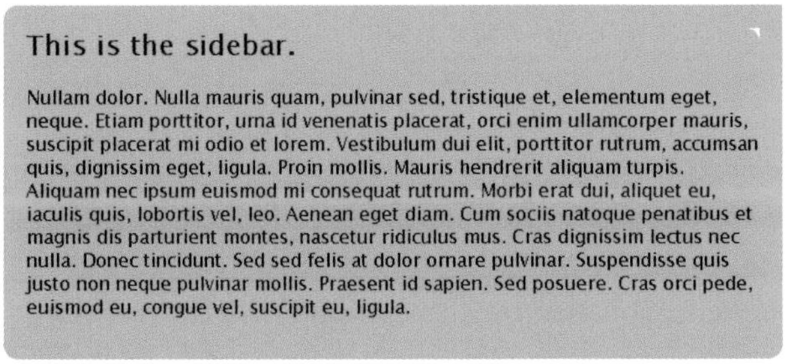

This is the sidebar.

Nullam dolor. Nulla mauris quam, pulvinar sed, tristique et, elementum eget, neque. Etiam porttitor, urna id venenatis placerat, orci enim ullamcorper mauris, suscipit placerat mi odio et lorem. Vestibulum dui elit, porttitor rutrum, accumsan quis, dignissim eget, ligula. Proin mollis. Mauris hendrerit aliquam turpis. Aliquam nec ipsum euismod mi consequat rutrum. Morbi erat dui, aliquet eu, iaculis quis, lobortis vel, leo. Aenean eget diam. Cum sociis natoque penatibus et magnis dis parturient montes, nascetur ridiculus mus. Cras dignissim lectus nec nulla. Donec tincidunt. Sed sed felis at dolor ornare pulvinar. Suspendisse quis justo non neque pulvinar mollis. Praesent id sapien. Sed posuere. Cras orci pede, euismod eu, congue vel, suscipit eu, ligula.

FIGURE 8.8

The right corner image is misaligned because the heading it is placed on is indented from the sides of the box.

There are a couple different ways to fix this. One option is to get rid of the padding on the bottom-right div and instead use padding or margin on all the individual elements within the sidebar to move the content away from the sides. Another option is to keep the padding on the bottom-right div but use negative margins on the h2 to pull its top and right edges up and over, and then give it its own padding on those sides to make up for this:

```
#sidebar h2 {

    margin-top: -20px;

    margin-right: -20px;

    padding: 20px 20px 0 0;

    background: url(tr.gif) no-repeat top right;

}
```

SAME TECHNIQUE, DIFFERENT LOOK

This type of rounded corner technique—where you position a non-repeating background image to one side of a box and blend it into that box's background color—can be used for all sorts of effects besides creating rounded corners. One of these additional effects is blending a photo with a faded edge into a background color, as you saw examples of in Figures 2.16 and 2.17. You'll get a chance to create this sort of effect in the exercise section at the end of the chapter.

These changes move the heading's background image into place while still giving the heading text space around it (**Figure 8.9**).

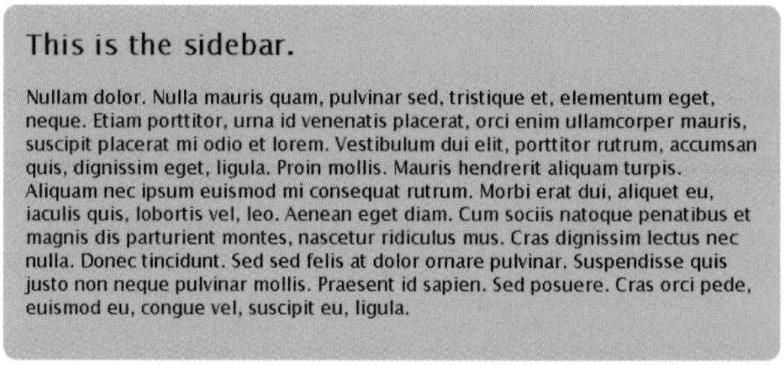

FIGURE 8.9 Negative margins pull the heading's right and top edges over so its corner image can be aligned with the edges of the box.

> **This is the sidebar.**
>
> Nullam dolor. Nulla mauris quam, pulvinar sed, tristique et, elementum eget, neque. Etiam porttitor, urna id venenatis placerat, orci enim ullamcorper mauris, suscipit placerat mi odio et lorem. Vestibulum dui elit, porttitor rutrum, accumsan quis, dignissim eget, ligula. Proin mollis. Mauris hendrerit aliquam turpis. Aliquam nec ipsum euismod mi consequat rutrum. Morbi erat dui, aliquet eu, iaculis quis, lobortis vel, leo. Aenean eget diam. Cum sociis natoque penatibus et magnis dis parturient montes, nascetur ridiculus mus. Cras dignissim lectus nec nulla. Donec tincidunt. Sed sed felis at dolor ornare pulvinar. Suspendisse quis justo non neque pulvinar mollis. Praesent id sapien. Sed posuere. Cras orci pede, euismod eu, congue vel, suscipit eu, ligula.

There are many variations on this technique, including using different elements to place the backgrounds on, nesting the extra elements differently or not at all, positioning the elements holding the backgrounds differently, and using different numbers of background images, to name a few. The basic idea is that you create multiple images of rounded corners, apply them to multiple elements inside a single div, and blend the images into a background color. Again, to see some of the other variations, go to www.smiley-cat.com/miaow/archives/000044.php.

Creating Curved Edges

Rounded corner techniques aren't really just about rounded corners—you can actually use them for any sort of graphic effect you want on the edges of a box. For instance, you could create a box with a ragged edge like the one shown in Figure 2.7 by piecing together multiple background images and selectively positioning and tiling them to form the appearance of one large background image.

One type of graphic edge effect that's worth going over separately is creating a curved edge, such as the one shown in Figure 2.8. Let's say we wanted to curve the top of the main content area in our two-column layout, as well as give it a slight glow effect (**Figure 8.10**). As long as there is a straight portion of the curve that can be tiled, we can make this into a flexible box.

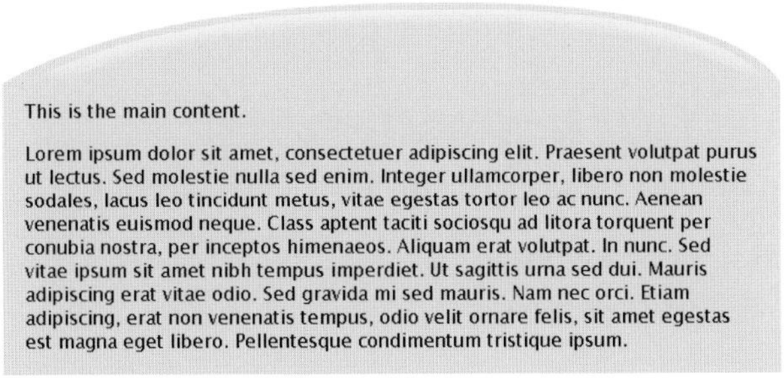

This is the main content.

Lorem ipsum dolor sit amet, consectetuer adipiscing elit. Praesent volutpat purus ut lectus. Sed molestie nulla sed enim. Integer ullamcorper, libero non molestie sodales, lacus leo tincidunt metus, vitae egestas tortor leo ac nunc. Aenean venenatis euismod neque. Class aptent taciti sociosqu ad litora torquent per conubia nostra, per inceptos himenaeos. Aliquam erat volutpat. In nunc. Sed vitae ipsum sit amet nibh tempus imperdiet. Ut sagittis urna sed dui. Mauris adipiscing erat vitae odio. Sed gravida mi sed mauris. Nam nec orci. Etiam adipiscing, erat non venenatis tempus, odio velit ornare felis, sit amet egestas est magna eget libero. Pellentesque condimentum tristique ipsum.

FIGURE 8.10
The graphic, curved top of the main content column that we want to make flexible.

After creating the curve image in your graphics program of choice, you'll need to find that small piece in the middle where the curve levels out. Slice a vertical strip containing this straight-edged piece. Then, slice the other two ends into their own separate images (**Figure 8.11**).

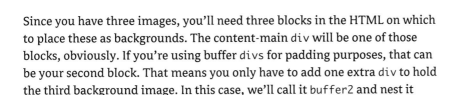

Since you have three images, you'll need three blocks in the HTML on which to place these as backgrounds. The content-main `div` will be one of those blocks, obviously. If you're using buffer `div`s for padding purposes, that can be your second block. That means you only have to add one extra `div` to hold the third background image. In this case, we'll call it `buffer2` and nest it inside the first buffer `div`:

FIGURE 8.11 The curve image needs to be sliced into three images: a left piece, a right piece, and the piece in the middle that has a straight edge.

```
<div id="content-main">
  <div class="buffer">
    <div class="buffer2">
      <p>This is the main content.</p>

      ...

    </div>
  </div>
</div>
```

■ **NOTE:** Just as with the rounded corner example, if you have some block element that you know will always be at the top of the box you're trying to put the curve on, you can use this as one of the "hooks" for your background images and forgo having to add another div.

It's now time to apply the background images to these three `div`s. Apply the middle portion to the outermost `div`, and tile it horizontally:

```
#content-main {
    float: left;
    width: 75%;
    background: #F0EE90 url(curve_middle.png) repeat-x;
}
```

The next `div`, buffer, can hold either the left or right part of the curve image. We'll set the left part on it, and set it to not tile at all:

```
#content-main .buffer {
    background: url(curve_left.png) no-repeat;
}
```

You'll also need to override any padding set on all buffer `div`s earlier in the CSS:

```
#content-main .buffer {
    padding: 0;
    background: url(curve_left.png) no-repeat;
}
```

If you don't get rid of the padding on the second `div`, the third `div` won't have its top or sides lined up with the previous two `div`s, so you won't be able to align all three background images either.

Last but not least, apply the right curve image to the third `div`, buffer2, and set it to not tile as well. You'll also need to align it to the right side of the `div`:

```
#content-main .buffer2 {
    background: url(curve_right.png) no-repeat right top;
}
```

Since the two buffer `div`s are nested directly in the content-main `div`, all three `div`s fill up exactly the same space and their background images all align perfectly, creating the appearance of one large curve (**Figure 8.12**). The right piece of the curve basically slides back and forth along the length of the main content area as the window changes in size, covering up more or less of the tiled straight piece in the middle.

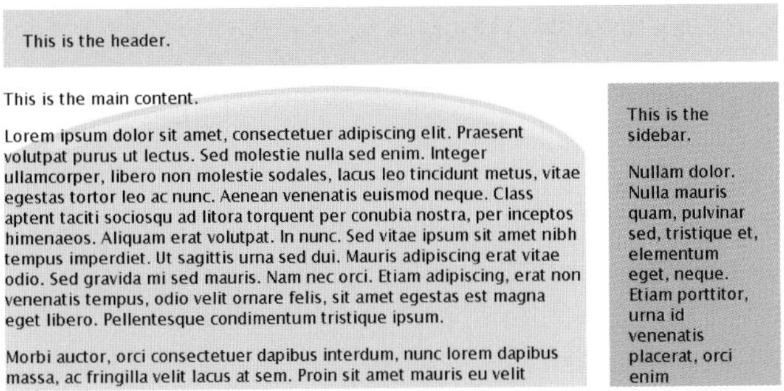

This is the header.

This is the main content.

This is the sidebar.

Lorem ipsum dolor sit amet, consectetuer adipiscing elit. Praesent volutpat purus ut lectus. Sed molestie nulla sed enim. Integer ullamcorper, libero non molestie sodales, lacus leo tincidunt metus, vitae egestas tortor leo ac nunc. Aenean venenatis euismod neque. Class aptent taciti sociosqu ad litora torquent per conubia nostra, per inceptos himenaeos. Aliquam erat volutpat. In nunc. Sed vitae ipsum sit amet nibh tempus imperdiet. Ut sagittis urna sed dui. Mauris adipiscing erat vitae odio. Sed gravida mi sed mauris. Nam nec orci. Etiam adipiscing, erat non venenatis tempus, odio velit ornare felis, sit amet egestas est magna eget libero. Pellentesque condimentum tristique ipsum.

Nullam dolor. Nulla mauris quam, pulvinar sed, tristique et, elementum eget, neque. Etiam porttitor, urna id venenatis placerat, orci enim

Morbi auctor, orci consectetuer dapibus interdum, nunc lorem dapibus massa, ac fringilla velit lacus at sem. Proin sit amet mauris eu velit

This is the header.

This is the main content.

This is the sidebar.

Lorem ipsum dolor sit amet, consectetuer adipiscing elit. Praesent volutpat purus ut lectus. Sed molestie nulla sed enim. Integer ullamcorper, libero non molestie sodales, lacus leo tincidunt metus, vitae egestas tortor leo ac nunc. Aenean venenatis euismod neque. Class aptent taciti sociosqu ad litora torquent per conubia nostra, per inceptos himenaeos. Aliquam erat volutpat. In nunc. Sed vitae ipsum sit amet nibh tempus imperdiet. Ut sagittis urna sed dui. Mauris adipiscing erat vitae odio. Sed gravida mi sed mauris. Nam nec orci. Etiam adipiscing, erat non venenatis tempus, odio velit ornare felis, sit amet egestas est magna eget libero. Pellentesque condimentum tristique ipsum.

Nullam dolor. Nulla mauris quam, pulvinar sed, tristique et, elementum eget, neque. Etiam porttitor, urna id venenatis placerat, orci enim ullamcorper mauris, suscipit placerat mi odio et lorem.

Morbi auctor, orci consectetuer dapibus interdum, nunc lorem dapibus massa, ac fringilla velit lacus at sem. Proin sit amet mauris eu velit semper posuere. Nam interdum, ante ac ornare

FIGURE 8.12
The right part of the curve slides back and forth to cover up more or less of the tiled straight piece in the middle.

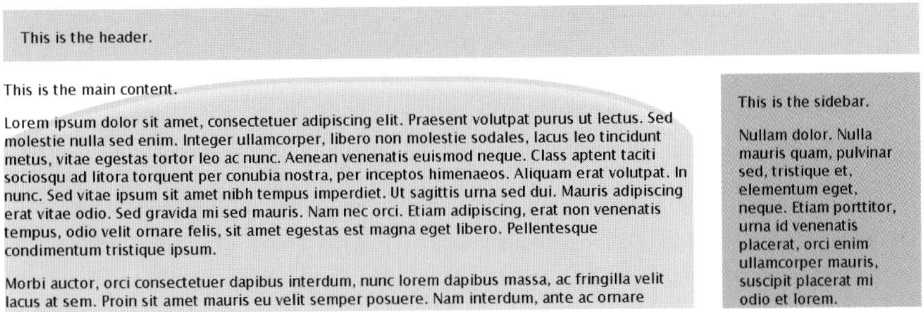

Of course, you'll want to make sure the text inside the main content area doesn't overlap the curved background images, so add padding to the inner-most `div`:

```
#content-main .buffer2 {
    padding: 80px 20px 20px 20px;
    background: url(curve_right.png) no-repeat right top;
}
```

You'll also need to make sure that the main content area never gets smaller than the combined width of the two side pieces of the curve. If it does, they will not align, and the curve will have a distinct break in the middle. To avoid this, add a `min-width` value to the content-main `div`:

```
#content-main {
    float: left;
    width: 75%;
    min-width: 603px;
    background: #F0EE90 url(curve_middle.png) repeat-x;
}
```

NOTE: The page showing this completed technique is curve.html in the ch8_examples.zip file.

Creating the Appearance of Equal-Height Columns

Perhaps the most common task CSS designers want to accomplish with background images and color is making two or more columns equal in height so that their backgrounds extend exactly the same amount down the page and they're nicely aligned on the bottom. As opposed to table cells, which are connected through table rows, individual divs have no connection to each other, so side-by-side divs will not match each other in height by default.

It's possible to get divs to act like table cells and match each other in height using display: table-cell or other table-related display values. But, as I mentioned in Chapter 2, IE doesn't support these values, so unless you're willing to let IE users see unequal-height columns, you need to use some other technique.

Luckily, in early 2004 Dan Cederholm came up with a way to create the appearance of equal-height columns without the columns actually having identical heights. He called this technique "faux columns" in his article by the same name at A List Apart (www.alistapart.com/articles/fauxcolumns), and both the name and the technique have held up to this day. In the article, Dan shows that you can use a background image on the wrapper for the columns that contains strips of color where you want each column to be. When you tile this background image down the wrapper, it creates the appearance of multiple, equal-height columns. You then simply float the columns in the wrapper over the matching spots on the background image.

This is quite a simple technique for fixed-width sites, but gets a little trickier when you want to apply it to liquid or elastic sites. It's still quite possible, however, and I'll show you how to do it. We'll start with how to use faux columns on hybrid liquid-fixed sites, since this is an intermediate step (in difficulty) between fixed-width faux columns and liquid faux columns.

NON-FAUX-COLUMN TECHNIQUES FOR EQUAL-HEIGHT COLUMNS

Using background images on wrappers isn't the only way to create equal-height columns. Georg Sortun has written up one of these alternate techniques at www.gunlaug.no/contents/wd_additions_22.html as well as linked to some other methods. Each method has its own shortcomings and complexities. I find the traditional faux columns method the most reliable, and pretty straightforward, so that's what we're going to stick with in this book.

Faux Columns for Liquid-Fixed Hybrid Layouts

It's almost as easy to create faux columns for a two-column liquid-fixed hybrid layout as for a fully fixed-width layout.

Figure 8.13 shows the layout we'll be applying faux columns to. The orange sidebar has a fixed width of 200 pixels, and the yellow main content area fills in the rest of the space.

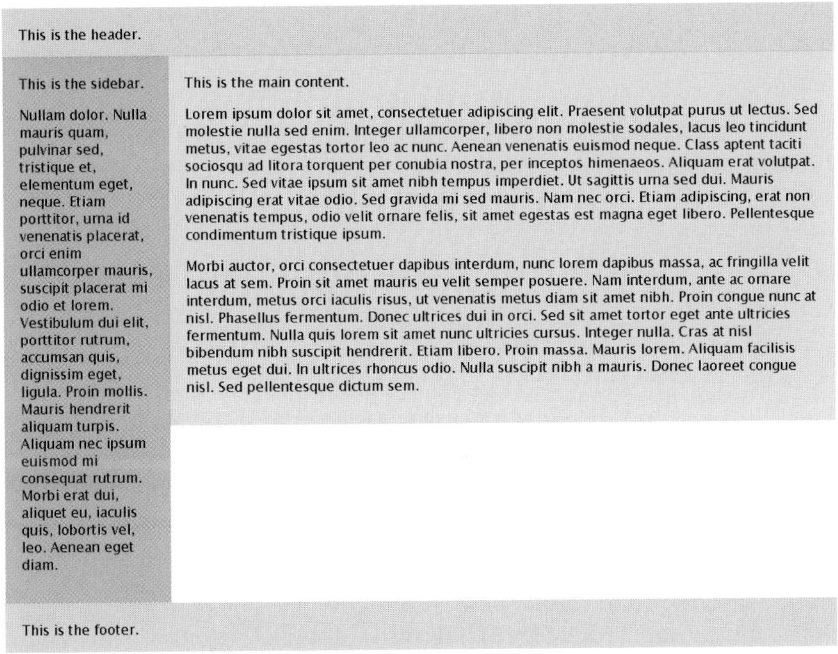

FIGURE 8.13 This two-column layout doesn't have faux columns, so each column is only as high as its content dictates.

The first step is to apply a wrapper `div`:

```
<div id="wrapper">

    <div id="header"></div>

    <div id="sidebar"></div>

    <div id="content-main"></div>

    <div id="footer"></div>

</div>
```

You can wrap this wrapper `div` either around all the `div`s on the page, as I've done here, or just around the columns you want to have equal height (in this case, the sidebar and content-main `div`s). If you do decide to apply the wrapper around all the `div`s, make sure that the header and footer will each have a background of their own to cover up the tiled background you'll be applying to the wrapper `div`.

■ **NOTE:** You could also forgo the wrapper `div` and just use the body element as your holder for the tiling background image. Using a wrapper `div` simply gives you a little more flexibility for other styling effects you may want to add later.

Next, add a CSS rule for the wrapper div to make sure it contains its children floats and doesn't collapse. In this case, floating the div works just fine:

```
#wrapper {
    float: left;
}
```

FIGURE 8.14 The background for the fixed-width column matches the column in width but needs only a small amount of height.

You're now ready to make your background image. If the liquid column is simply going to have a solid color background, you have it easy—just create a background image for the *other* column, the fixed-width one, set to exactly its width (**Figure 8.14**). The height can be small, as you'll tile the image up and down.

Back in the CSS, first remove the background colors from the sidebar and content-main divs. Then, add your background image to the wrapper div and set it to repeat-y so it will tile vertically:

```
#wrapper {
    float: left;
    background: url(fauxcolumns_fixed.jpg) repeat-y;
}
```

This fills the entire left side of the wrapper div with the background image from top to bottom, so even when the main content column is longer than the sidebar, the sidebar still appears to stretch all the way down to the footer (**Figure 8.15**).

■ **NOTE:** If your fixed-width column is on the right side of the viewport, add right to the background shorthand property to position the background image on the right side of the wrapper instead of the default left.

To create the background color for the main content area, all you have to do is apply its background color to the wrapper div:

```
#wrapper {
    float: left;
    background: #F0EE90 url(fauxcolumns_fixed.jpg) repeat-y;
}
```

This color then fills in all the space in the wrapper not covered by the wrapper's background image, so even when the sidebar is longest, the main content area appears to stretch down to the footer (**Figure 8.16**).

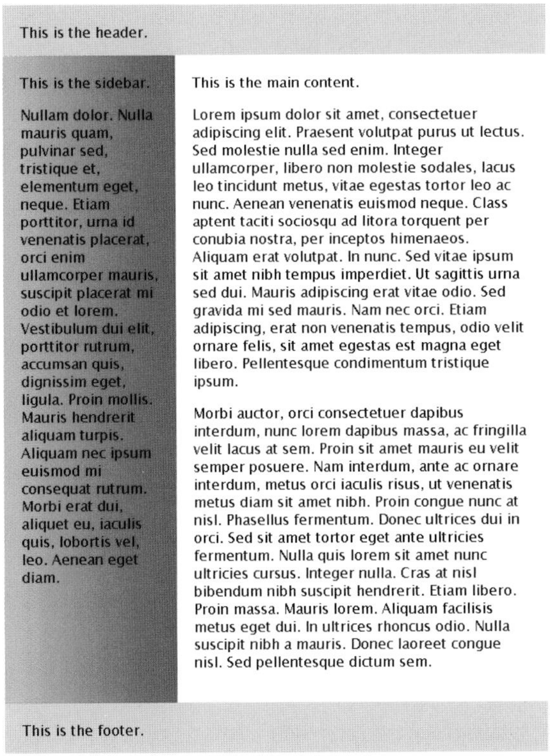

FIGURE 8.15 The background image behind the sidebar fills the gap between the end of the sidebar's content and the footer, creating the appearance that the sidebar is the same height as the main content column.

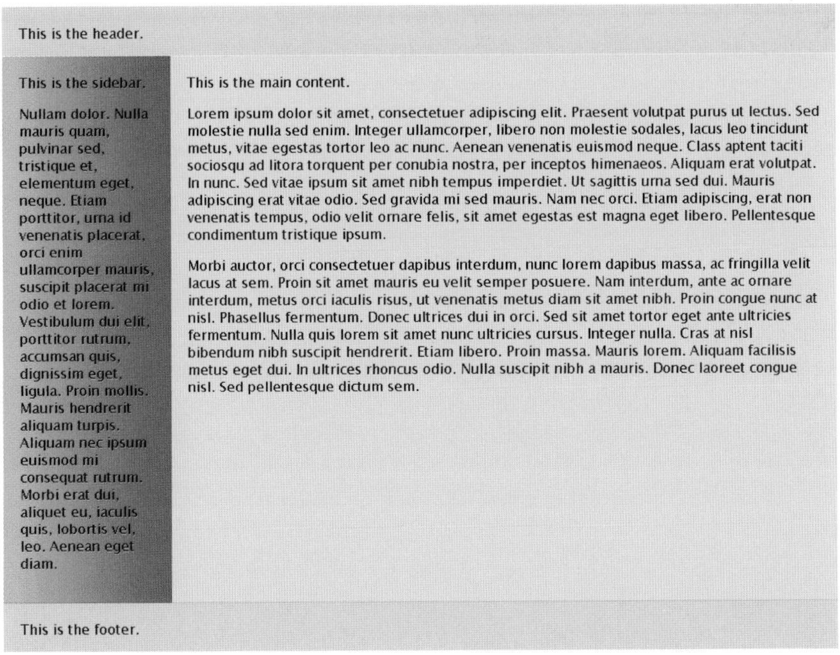

FIGURE 8.16 The background color on the wrapper div fills whatever space the background image on the wrapper doesn't, creating the appearance of a main content column that stretches all the way down to the footer.

■ **TIP:** If you want a gap between the two columns' backgrounds, simply keep some white space in your background image slice in between the two columns' background patterns.

What if you don't want just a solid background color for the liquid column? You don't know what the combined width of the two columns will be, so you can't create a background image for the wrapper `div` to match that width—but you don't have to! All you need to know is that the liquid area fills the entire rest of the viewport. So, make an image as wide as you think your overall layout might grow to—if you have a pixel `max-width` set on your overall layout, use this for the width. The image shown in **Figure 8.17** is 2000 pixels wide, just to be safe. Create a fixed-width area on the left (or whichever side your fixed-width column is on) matching the width of your fixed-width column. Fill the rest of the image with the background pattern for the liquid column.

FIGURE 8.17 The background image for the wrapper `div` contains a fixed-width area on the left for the sidebar, and the rest of the extremely wide image is filled with the background pattern for the main content column.

Then, simply place this background image on the wrapper and set it to tile vertically, just as before:

```
#wrapper {
    float: left;
    background: #F0EE90 url(fauxcolumns_liquid-fixed.png)
    repeat-y;
}
```

■ **NOTE:** The page showing this completed technique is fauxcolumns_liquid-fixed.html in the ch8_examples.zip file.

This background image now fills the entire wrapper `div` from top to bottom and side to side, so the main content area gets a pattern behind it as well (**Figure 8.18**). I've left the background color in place even though it's not strictly necessary anymore; any time you use a background image, it's a good idea to have a backup background color to make sure your text is still readable even if the user has images turned off or for some reason the image fails to load.

WHAT ABOUT ELASTIC-FIXED HYBRID LAYOUTS?

Creating faux columns for elastic-fixed hybrid layouts works exactly the same way: create a very wide background image with a fixed-width piece for the fixed column and fill the rest of the image with the color or pattern for the elastic column. Tile this background image down the wrapper `div`.

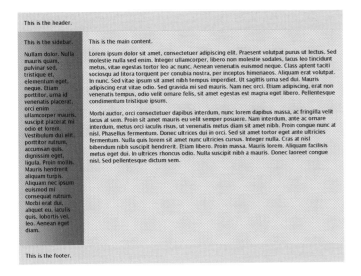

FIGURE 8.18 No matter which column contains the longest content, the background pattern for each always stretches all the way down to the footer, so the columns always appear equal in height.

Faux Columns for Fully Liquid Layouts

Creating faux columns when all columns are liquid takes a bit more work than liquid-fixed hybrids, but the trick is all in how you set up the background image.

TWO COLUMNS

The two-column liquid layout we've been working with for most of our examples has a sidebar on the left that takes up 25 percent of the viewport and a main content column on the right taking up the remaining 75 percent. If we want the sidebar to have that same orange-to-red gradient shown in Figure 8.14, then, logically, we need this gradient to take up the left 25 percent of the image and the yellow crosshatched background for the main content area to take up the right 75 percent of the image.

Using the same 2000-pixel-wide image, the left 25 percent is 500 pixels wide, so I've stretched the sidebar's gradient to cover the left 500 pixels of the image. The remaining 75 percent (1500 pixels) will have the yellow crosshatched background pattern.

However, we don't want our left column width fixed at 500 pixels as it is in this background image. If we place it on the wrapper as is, it won't adjust in size as the actual columns do when the window is resized.

FIGURE 8.19 If the background image is aligned on the left side of the wrapper, the portion of the image on the left will always be 500 pixels wide, and won't align with the sidebar laying over it.

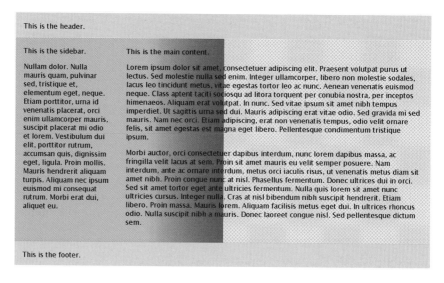

The trick is in the `background-position` property. This property controls where the background image is placed in its container. When you use pixels or other fixed units to position the background image, the top left corner of the image is moved to that point in the box. However, when you use percentages, you position a point within the image itself, not the top left corner. This point is moved to the corresponding percentage point location in the box. So, if you set `background-position` to 40% 20%, the point 40 percent across and 20 percent down the image is placed 40 percent across and 20 percent down the box.

FIGURE 8.20 The colored area represents the background image of the box; the dimmed-out portions are those that sit outside the bounds of the box and cannot be seen. The points 40 percent across and 20 percent down both the box and the image are aligned by using `background-position: 40% 20%`.

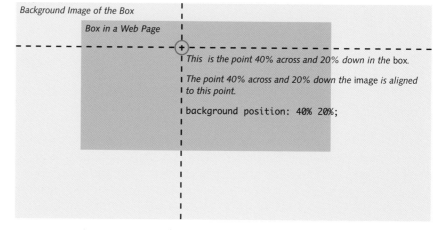

In our case, we want the gradient part of the background image to take up only 25 percent of the viewport. The spot where the two columns will meet is 25 percent over from the left edge of the screen, and this is also where we want the edge of the two colors to be. So, we want to tell the browser to find the spot in the background image that is 25 percent from the left, and position this spot 25 percent across the page to make it correspond with the meeting point of the two columns:

```
#wrapper {
    float: left;
    background: #F0EE90 url(fauxcolumns_liquid.png) repeat-y 25%
0;
}
```

With this simple change, the background image now lines up perfectly with the two columns no matter what size the viewport is (**Figure 8.21**).

NOTE: The page showing this completed technique is fauxcolumns_liquid_twocol.html in the ch8_examples.zip file.

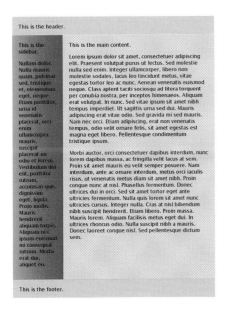
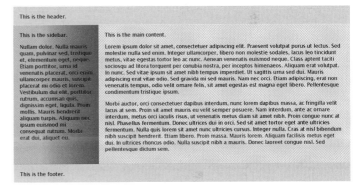

FIGURE 8.21 More or less of the background image shows as the viewport changes in size, yet it always stays aligned with the spot in between the two columns.

THREE COLUMNS

What if you want to have three columns, all liquid and all equal height? In this case, a single shifting background image would not work, because the center portion needs to grow and shrink in width. Instead, you need to create multiple background images that can overlay one another to create the effect. Thus, you'll need two container elements, each with a tiling background image—one with the image for the left column and the other with the image for the right.

The three-column liquid layout we created in Chapter 4 already has one wrapper div, named content-wrapper, around the two right columns. You could add another wrapper around all the divs on the page, or you could just use the body element to hold the first tiling background image:

```
body {
    margin: 0;
    padding: 0;
    background: #F0EE90 url(fauxcolumns_liquid.png) repeat-y 25% 0;
    font-family: "Lucida Sans Unicode", "Lucida Grande", sans-serif;
}
```

You'll then need to make sure to remove all the background colors from the columns so the background image on the body can be seen. This first tiling background image creates the appearance of the left column (**Figure 8.22**).

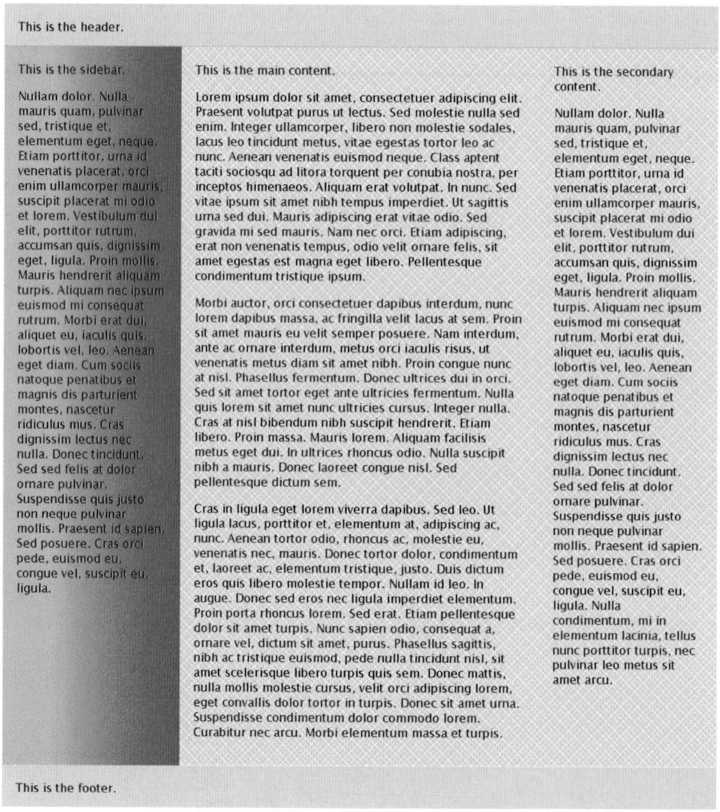

FIGURE 8.22 The first background image creates the delineation between the left and middle columns.

This is the header.

This is the sidebar.

Nullam dolor. Nulla mauris quam, pulvinar sed, tristique et, elementum eget, neque. Etiam porttitor, urna id venenatis placerat, orci enim ullamcorper mauris, suscipit placerat mi odio et lorem. Vestibulum dui elit, porttitor rutrum, accumsan quis, dignissim eget, ligula. Proin mollis. Mauris hendrerit aliquam turpis. Aliquam nec ipsum euismod mi consequat rutrum. Morbi erat dui, aliquet eu, iaculis quis, lobortis vel, leo. Aenean eget diam. Cum sociis natoque penatibus et magnis dis parturient montes, nascetur ridiculus mus. Cras dignissim lectus nec nulla. Donec tincidunt. Sed sed felis at dolor ornare pulvinar. Suspendisse quis justo non neque pulvinar mollis. Praesent id sapien. Sed posuere. Cras orci pede, euismod eu, congue vel, suscipit eu, ligula.

This is the main content.

Lorem ipsum dolor sit amet, consectetuer adipiscing elit. Praesent volutpat purus ut lectus. Sed molestie nulla sed enim. Integer ullamcorper, libero non molestie sodales, lacus leo tincidunt metus, vitae egestas tortor leo ac nunc. Aenean venenatis euismod neque. Class aptent taciti sociosqu ad litora torquent per conubia nostra, per inceptos himenaeos. Aliquam erat volutpat. In nunc. Sed vitae ipsum sit amet nibh tempus imperdiet. Ut sagittis urna sed dui. Mauris adipiscing erat vitae odio. Sed gravida mi sed mauris. Nam nec orci. Etiam adipiscing, erat non venenatis tempus, odio velit ornare felis, sit amet egestas est magna eget libero. Pellentesque condimentum tristique ipsum.

Morbi auctor, orci consectetuer dapibus interdum, nunc lorem dapibus massa, ac fringilla velit lacus at sem. Proin sit amet mauris eu velit semper posuere. Nam interdum, ante ac ornare interdum, metus orci iaculis risus, ut venenatis metus diam sit amet nibh. Proin congue nunc at nisl. Phasellus fermentum. Donec ultrices dui in orci. Sed sit amet tortor eget ante ultricies fermentum. Nulla quis lorem sit amet nunc ultricies cursus. Integer nulla. Cras at nisl bibendum nibh suscipit hendrerit. Etiam libero. Proin massa. Mauris lorem. Aliquam facilisis metus eget dui. In ultrices rhoncus odio. Nulla suscipit nibh a mauris. Donec laoreet congue nisl. Sed pellentesque dictum sem.

Cras in ligula eget lorem viverra dapibus. Sed leo. Ut ligula lacus, porttitor et, elementum at, adipiscing ac, nunc. Aenean tortor odio, rhoncus ac, molestie eu, venenatis nec, mauris. Donec tortor dolor, condimentum et, laoreet ac, elementum tristique, justo. Duis dictum eros quis libero molestie tempor. Nullam id leo. In augue. Donec sed eros nec ligula imperdiet elementum. Proin porta rhoncus lorem. Sed erat. Etiam pellentesque dolor sit amet turpis. Nunc sapien odio, consequat a, ornare vel, dictum sit amet, purus. Phasellus sagittis, nibh ac tristique euismod, pede nulla tincidunt nisl, sit amet scelerisque libero turpis quis sem. Donec mattis, nulla mollis molestie cursus, velit orci adipiscing lorem, eget convallis dolor tortor in turpis. Donec sit amet urna. Suspendisse condimentum dolor commodo lorem. Curabitur nec arcu. Morbi elementum massa et turpis.

This is the secondary content.

Nullam dolor. Nulla mauris quam, pulvinar sed, tristique et, elementum eget, neque. Etiam porttitor, urna id venenatis placerat, orci enim ullamcorper mauris, suscipit placerat mi odio et lorem. Vestibulum dui elit, porttitor rutrum, accumsan quis, dignissim eget, ligula. Proin mollis. Mauris hendrerit aliquam turpis. Aliquam nec ipsum euismod mi consequat rutrum. Morbi erat dui, aliquet eu, iaculis quis, lobortis vel, leo. Aenean eget diam. Cum sociis natoque penatibus et magnis dis parturient montes, nascetur ridiculus mus. Cras dignissim lectus nec nulla. Donec tincidunt. Sed sed felis at dolor ornare pulvinar. Suspendisse quis justo non neque pulvinar mollis. Praesent id sapien. Sed posuere. Cras orci pede, euismod eu, congue vel, suscipit eu, ligula. Nulla condimentum, mi in elementum lacinia, tellus nunc porttitor turpis, nec pulvinar leo metus sit amet arcu.

This is the footer.

We now need to place a background image on content-wrapper that will lay over the background image on the body and create the appearance of the right column. This one needs to have the rightmost 25 percent (500 pixels) filled with the pattern for the right column. The rest of the image needs to be transparent so the background on the body element can show through.

■ **NOTE:** The page showing this completed technique is fauxcolumns_liquid_threecol.html in the ch8_examples.zip file.

Set this image on the content-wrapper div, and align its 75 percent point 75 percent across the box, creating a 25-percent-wide right column:

```
#content-wrapper {

    float: left;

    width: 100%;

    background: url(fauxcolumns_liquid_rightcol.png) repeat-y 75% 0;

}
```

Now all three columns have their own backgrounds, each appearing to be equal in height to whichever column is longest at any given time (**Figure 8.24**).

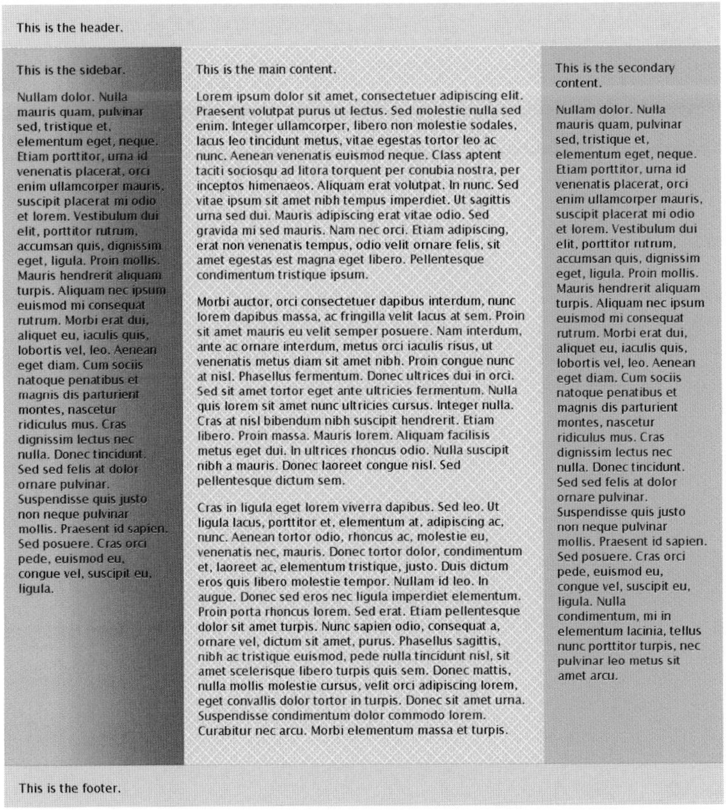

FIGURE 8.23 The background image for the third column needs to have a large transparent area, indicated here by the checkered pattern, to allow the background image of the left and middle columns to show through.

FIGURE 8.24 The final three-column, faux column layout, with the second background laid on top of the first.

Faux Columns for Elastic Layouts

Faux columns for fully elastic layouts actually work exactly the same way as those for liquid layouts. Even though you're declaring widths in ems instead of percentages, each em measurement equates to some percentage of its parent element. For instance, a 10-em sidebar inside a 50-em wrapper div is 20 percent of the wrapper.

Here are the steps for creating an elastic faux column layout:

1. Figure out what percentage of its container each column takes up. If a column doesn't have an elastic container (for instance, the sidebar is placed directly inside the body element, which is liquid, not elastic), just make sure you add one in the form of a wrapper div with an elastic width set. If the percentage comes out to a fraction, you may want to adjust your em values to get everything to a full integer in order to avoid cross-browser rounding inconsistencies.

2. For each container, create a background image that shows two colors or patterns, each of which should take up the percentage of the image that its corresponding column will take up inside its container.

3. Make sure that the second background image, if using one to create a third column, is completely transparent in the percentage portion that will be taken up by the previous two columns.

4. Tile a background image down each container element. Use a percentage value in the background-position property that matches the percentage width of the left column inside the container.

■ **NOTE:** The page showing this completed technique is fauxcolumns_elastic_threecol.html in the ch8_examples.zip file.

Site-Building Exercise: Adding Backgrounds to the Home and Inner Pages

■ **NOTE:** For a reminder of what the finished pages that you're working towards should look like, check out Figure 4.24 for the Programs page graphic comp and Figure 2.43 for the home page graphic comp.

The home and Programs pages of the Beechwood Animal Shelter site are nearly complete now in terms of their layout, but a big reason why they don't yet look much like their graphic comps is that we haven't applied the proper background colors and graphics. By the end of this exercise, you'll have most of the backgrounds in place and have the pages looking much more polished.

You'll work with the exercise files from this book's companion web site at www.flexiblewebbook.com. Download and unzip the file ch8_exercise.zip.

Adjusting Backgrounds and Colors
for the Header of Both Pages

The first set of changes you'll make, mainly for the header area, will be identical for both the home and Programs pages, so open both home-start.html and programs-start.html in your text or code editor of choice. These are the same pages as the final versions of the pages you completed in Chapter 7. You can either make all the following changes in one page and then paste them into the other, or make each change in each file as you go along. If you're going to copy them from one file to the other, you will probably want to keep all the new rules together so you know what you added and what you need to copy. You can reorder them into a more logical sequence once you've made the transfer.

1. Locate the following rule near the top of the style section in the head of each page:

   ```
   #header, #footer {
       background: #EFEFEF;
   }
   ```

   Delete this entire rule to remove the placeholder background colors on the header and footer divs.

2. Add a background image and bottom border to the existing #header rule:

   ```
   #header {
       display: table;
       width: 100%;
       margin-bottom: 30px;
       border-bottom: 6px solid #85A7E4;
       background: #60240C url(images/bg-header.gif) repeat-x;
   }
   ```

   The background image, which is just the pale blue portion of the header, is set to tile horizontally using repeat-x. There is also a background color set that matches the brown of the bottom bar on the header. When the two are combined with each other as well as with the bottom border, it creates the striped appearance we're after while still enabling the brown bar of the header to be flexible in height.

   These changes take care of the background of the header, but the text within it needs its color changed as well (**Figure 8.25**).

FIGURE 8.25 The background color of the header is correct, but the links within it aren't.

Although we don't want the links in the header to be brown, the rest of the links throughout the page should be. We'll address that now, with a general color rule and an exception.

3. Create a new rule setting the color on all *a* elements to the same brown used in the main navigation bar:

```
a {
    color: #60240C;
}
```

4. Override this color for the links inside both nav-skip and nav-main by creating the following new rules:

```
#nav-skip a {
    color: #86B0E3;
}
#nav-main a {
    color: #FFF;
    font-weight: bold;
    text-decoration: none;
}
```

FIGURE 8.26 The links' color has been changed to better match the background of the header.

These new rules take care of most of the styling for the nav bar, but they introduce a problem in the home page in IE 6: when you first load the page, everything in the header except for the nav bar has vanished. Resizing the text makes it reappear. (This doesn't occur on the Programs page.) The trigger is the `font-weight: bold;` declaration. It seems to make the entire nav bar grow in size slightly—though why that should make the other content in the header disappear is simply another one of IE's great mysteries.

5. To fix the disappearing header content in IE 6 on the home page, add a new rule for nav-main inside the existing IE 6-only conditional comment at the end of the `head`, setting the left margin to 7 pixels:

```
#nav-main {
    margin-left: 7px;
}
```

Reducing the margin from 10 pixels to 7 seems to give IE 6 the extra room it wants to accommodate the slightly expanded nav bar, and the header content will now show at all times.

The final task to style the header's content is applying the subtle gradient backgrounds to the individual links in the main navigation bar. Each link has a gradient on the left and the right, and since we don't know how much space will be needed in between the two on any given link, we can't make both sides into a single image. And since each side will therefore need to be a separate image, we'll need two separate elements to hold each background. You can use the li element for one and the *a* element for the other.

6. Modify the existing #nav-main li rule to match the following:

```
#nav-main li {
    float: left;
    margin: 0;
    padding: 0;
    background: url(images/nav-main-left.jpg) repeat-y;
}
```

The background will tile vertically, so no matter how tall the link grows because of enlarged text, the background image will still fill the space. The padding, which worked so well when there were no background images on the links, has now been removed; you want each *a* element inside the li elements to fill the entire li, not be indented from its edges.

7. Modify the #nav-main *a* rule you created earlier to match the following:

```
#nav-main a {
    display: block;
    padding: .5em 10px;
    background: url(images/nav-main-right.jpg) repeat-y right;
    color: #FFF;
    font-weight: bold;
    text-decoration: none;
}
```

This sets the right gradient image on the links inside the list items, aligns those images to the right, and makes the images tile vertically. The padding spaces the links out from one another and keeps the text from completely overlapping the gradient on each side of its box. Setting the links to be blocks instead of inline elements, as they are by default, ensures that this padding on the links will push out the bounds of the list items they're nested in; padding on inline elements does not do this.

FIGURE 8.27 Subtle gradient images that blend in with the brown background of the header are applied to each link in the main navigation bar.

Home   Adopt a Pet   Get Involved   Our Programs   News and Events   About the Shelter

The header is now completely styled. If you haven't yet copied these changes from one page into the other, be sure to do that now, except for the new rule in the IE 6 conditional comment on the home page—that should remain on the home page only.

Adjusting Backgrounds for the Programs Page

The main background on the content area of the Programs page is a gradient in the left sidebar; we want this background to stretch to the footer even when the main content column is longer. This means we need to use a faux-columns technique.

CREATING THE FAUX COLUMNS BACKGROUND IMAGE IN ADOBE FIREWORKS

NOTE: If you don't have Fireworks, just use your preferred graphics program—the steps should be basically the same. Or, simply cheat and use the background image that's provided in ch8_exercise.zip!

The first step to creating faux columns is creating the proper background image. We didn't cover making the background image slice for the content area of the Programs page back in Chapter 3, when we were making our other slices, because you first needed to know how liquid faux columns work in order to set up the background image correctly. You'll make that background image now in Fireworks.

1. Open the graphic comp file comp.png from the ch3_exercise.zip file. In the Pages panel, select the page named "inner" to view the Programs page design.

2. Click on the sidebar's background gradient to select it, and then use Edit > Copy to copy this shape.

3. Choose File > New, and create a new document that is 2000 pixels wide, 20 pixels high, and has a resolution of 96 pixels per inch. Set the canvas color to white.

4. Paste the shape you copied from comp.png into the new document.

5. Align the shape so its right edge is 400 pixels from the left side of the canvas (**Figure 8.28**). You can drag it into place, or use the Property inspector to set its X value to 200—since the shape itself is 200 pixels wide, this will place its right edge at 400 pixels.

   400 pixels is 20 percent of 2000, which corresponds with the 20 percent width set on the nav-secondary div in the actual page.

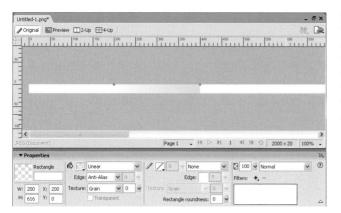

FIGURE 8.28 The gradient's left edge is placed 200 pixels over from the left edge of the canvas, and its right edge is placed 400 pixels over.

■ **NOTE:** Technically, the document only has to be one pixel high. But I like to make my background image slices a little bigger in order to keep the browser from having to make so many passes for tiling in the background, and also just so I can see what I'm working with.

6. Select the Rectangle tool from the Tools panel. Draw a rectangle that is 200 pixels wide, 20 pixels tall, and aligned at the top left corner of the canvas (both X and Y values in the Property inspector should be zero).

7. With the rectangle you just drew still selected, click on the Fill category drop-down menu in the Property inspector to change the fill to Solid (**Figure 8.29**).

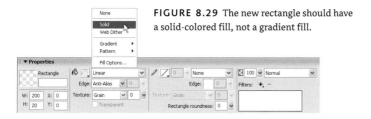

FIGURE 8.29 The new rectangle should have a solid-colored fill, not a gradient fill.

8. Click on the Fill Color box in the Property inspector to open the color pop-up window. Type #FCFDFD in the hex color code box (**Figure 8.30**).

This color matches the leftmost color in the gradient so the two rectangles will appear to blend together seamlessly.

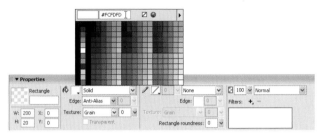

FIGURE 8.30 Set the color of the new rectangle in the color pop-up window.

9. In the Optimize panel, set the image to export as a JPEG with Quality set to 80.

10. Choose File > Save As, and save the image as bg-inner.png.

As a last step, you can export the web-ready image as bg-inner.jpg, but this file is already present in the images folder of the ch8_exercise.zip file.

APPLYING THE BACKGROUNDS TO THE PAGE

Go back to the Programs page in your text or code editor, and complete the following steps to apply its remaining backgrounds.

1. Add the background image you just created to the existing #wrapper rule in the style section of the page:

```
#wrapper {
    overflow: auto;
    width: 90%;
    min-width: 40em;
    max-width: 65em;
    margin: 0 auto;
    background: url(images/bg-inner.jpg) repeat-y 20% 0;
}
```

The image is set to tile vertically using repeat-y. Its 20 percent point is aligned with the spot 20 percent across the wrapper div, which exactly matches the edge of the nav-secondary div. The overflow: auto; declaration makes sure that this background image is seen—without it, the wrapper div would not stretch down to contain the floated nav-secondary div.

2. Remove the `background` properties from the `#content-main` and `#nav-secondary` rules to let the background image on the wrapper `div` show through.

3. Add a tiling background image to the `#section-links a` rule that will blend in with the background color that is already in place:

```
#section-links a {
    display: block;
    padding: .5em 1.5em .8em 1.5em;
    border-bottom: 1px solid #FFF;
    background: #F2F4F7 url(images/bg-section-links.jpg)
repeat-y right;
    font-weight: bold;
    text-decoration: none;
}
```

The `font-weight` and `text-decoration` rules merely format the text to more closely match what's shown in the comp.

4. As one final text formatting tweak, add `color: #666;` to the existing `#news span` rule.

This completes the changes to the two main columns of the Programs page (**Figure 8.31**). You now need to style the title `div`.

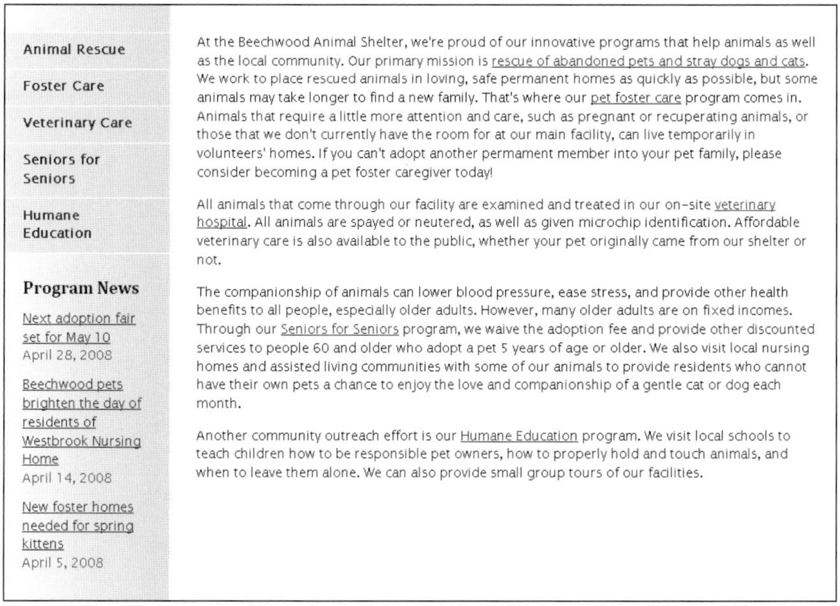

Animal Rescue

Foster Care

Veterinary Care

Seniors for Seniors

Humane Education

Program News

Next adoption fair set for May 10
April 28, 2008

Beechwood pets brighten the day of residents of Westbrook Nursing Home
April 14, 2008

New foster homes needed for spring kittens
April 5, 2008

At the Beechwood Animal Shelter, we're proud of our innovative programs that help animals as well as the local community. Our primary mission is rescue of abandoned pets and stray dogs and cats. We work to place rescued animals in loving, safe permanent homes as quickly as possible, but some animals may take longer to find a new family. That's where our pet foster care program comes in. Animals that require a little more attention and care, such as pregnant or recuperating animals, or those that we don't currently have the room for at our main facility, can live temporarily in volunteers' homes. If you can't adopt another permanent member into your pet family, please consider becoming a pet foster caregiver today!

All animals that come through our facility are examined and treated in our on-site veterinary hospital. All animals are spayed or neutered, as well as given microchip identification. Affordable veterinary care is also available to the public, whether your pet originally came from our shelter or not.

The companionship of animals can lower blood pressure, ease stress, and provide other health benefits to all people, especially older adults. However, many older adults are on fixed incomes. Through our Seniors for Seniors program, we waive the adoption fee and provide other discounted services to people 60 and older who adopt a pet 5 years of age or older. We also visit local nursing homes and assisted living communities with some of our animals to provide residents who cannot have their own pets a chance to enjoy the love and companionship of a gentle cat or dog each month.

Another community outreach effort is our Humane Education program. We visit local schools to teach children how to be responsible pet owners, how to properly hold and touch animals, and when to leave them alone. We can also provide small group tours of our facilities.

FIGURE 8.31 The backgrounds and colors for the two main columns on the Programs page are now in place.

5. Add the dog photo header-programs.jpg as a background to the existing #title rule:

```
#title {
    min-height: 129px;
    padding: 1.5em;
    background: #7ABA65 url(images/header-programs.jpg)
no-repeat top right;
}
```

The new background value sets the dog image on the div, prevents it from tiling, and positions it in the top right corner. Because you've left the background color in the rule as well, the image will blend seamlessly with the color used across the rest of the div. The min-height value matches the height of the dog photo so that the entire image will always show.

Now that the background image is in place on the title div, the spacing within the div needs to be adjusted. We want the heading text within the div to sit near the bottom of the div and grow upwards into the div as it increases in size. You'll need to use absolute positioning to achieve this.

6. Remove the padding declaration and add position: relative; to the #title rule.

This will allow the heading text to be positioned relative to this div.

7. Add a new rule for the h1 inside the title div that matches the following:

```
#title h1 {
    position: absolute;
    left: 20px;
    bottom: 20px;
}
```

8. To create a small amount of white space between the bottom of the title div and the two columns below it, add a white bottom border to the title div that will cover up a bit of the tiling background on the wrapper div:

```
#title {
    position: relative;
    min-height: 129px;
    border-bottom: 6px solid #FFF;
    background: #7ABA65 url(images/header-programs.jpg)
no-repeat top right;
}
```

This completes all the background image work for the Programs page (**Figure 8.32**). In fact, the Programs page now matches the comp and is completely finished; you won't work on it any more in this book!

FIGURE 8.32 All of the backgrounds and colors for the entire Programs page are in place, so it matches the original graphic comp.

To compare your work to the completed Programs page for this exercise—and the entire book—see the file programs-end.html in the files you extracted from ch8_exercise.zip.

Adjusting Backgrounds for the Home Page

The background image shown in the banner on the home page is going to use a variable cropping technique that you won't learn how to do until Chapter 9, so for this exercise, the main background you need to worry about on the home page is the one for the adopt-pets div.

1. Remove the placeholder background colors from the #wrapper, #ads, #story, and #search-pets rules. All of these divs will just have the white background of the body showing through.

2. Modify the background on the existing #adopt-pets rule to match the following:

   ```
   #adopt-pets {
       float: right;
       width: 41em;
       background: #FAFAFC url(images/bg-adopt-pets.jpg) repeat-x;
   }
   ```

   This sets the gradient background on the div, tiles it horizontally, and sets a background color that matches the bottom color of the gradient so the image and color will blend together seamlessly.

3. Add color: #60240C; to the existing #adopt-pets ul rule.

4. Add the following new rules to style the pet search form:

   ```
   #search-pets fieldset {
       margin: 0 0 .8em 0;
       padding: .4em 0 0 0;
       border: none;
       border-top: 1px solid #ADC4ED;
   }
   #search-pets legend {
       color: #000;
       font-weight: bold;
   }
   #search-pets label {
       margin-right: .5em;
   }
   ```

   This takes care of the form styling in most browsers. IE, however, places the legend elements farther to the right than the other browsers do, leaving a piece of fieldset border poking out to the left of each legend.

5. Add margin: -7px; to the #search-pets legend rule to pull the legend elements over in IE. This doesn't move the legend text at all in other browsers, so it doesn't have to be placed in an IE-only conditional comment—though you certainly could hide it that way if you wanted to.

And with that, you're done! To compare your work to the completed home page for this exercise, see the file home-end.html in the files you extracted from ch8_exercise.zip.

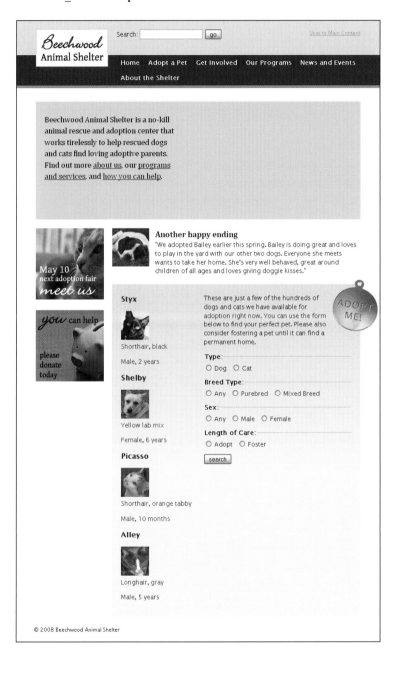

FIGURE 8.33 The backgrounds and colors for the adopt-pets div on the home page are now in place.

9

Creating Flexible Images

No matter how perfectly you build your liquid or elastic layout, it's not going to work if you don't make the content within it flexible too. Text is easy—it wraps by default. Images are where it gets tricky. Luckily, as you saw in Chapter 2, there are lots of creative ways to make your images—content images as well as decorative graphic elements—flexible to either the viewport or the text size. In this chapter, you'll learn the CSS behind those flexible image examples.

Dynamically Changing Images' Screen Area

■ **NOTE:** Each of the completed example files is available for download from this book's companion web site at www.flexiblewebbook.com. Download the file ch9_examples.zip to get the complete set. I'll let you know which file goes with which technique as we go along.

Since the area available for an image to display within a flexible layout changes on the fly, your images may need to as well. While fixed-width images *can* work within flexible layouts—as long as they're not too large, or you have matching minimum widths in place—there are lots of ways you can dynamically change the screen area that an image takes up.

Foreground Images that Scale with the Layout

One way to dynamically alter the footprint of an image is to make it literally scale. You saw an example of an image that scales with the text in Figure 2.18, and an example of an image scaling with the changing dimensions of its parent element in Figure 2.19. Both are elegant effects that are deceptively simple to create.

Both liquid and elastic scaling images start out with a regular img element in the (X)HTML:

```
<img src="styx.jpg" alt="my cat Styx">
```

Notice that this img element has no width or height attributes, as it normally would. You control the dimensions with CSS instead.

■ **NOTE:** This rule will make all images 50 percent as wide as their parents. In a real page, you would probably add an id or class to the specific image you wanted to scale and use that id or class as the selector in the CSS.

For a liquid image, create a CSS rule to set the image's width to a percentage value:

```
img {
    width: 50%;
    }
```

No height value is necessary; the browser determines the height that will proportionately constrain the image's dimensions. If you were more concerned about making the height of your image stay proportional to its parent's height than you were with width, you could use the height property in the CSS and leave off the width property. Just make sure not to use the two together.

As with all percentage dimensions, the percentage width value you choose is relative to the width of the parent element. As you change the width of the parent element, the image scales to match (**Figure 9.1**).

If you want the image to scale with the text size instead of the width of the parent element, simply change the `width` value in the CSS to an em value:

```
img {
    width: 20em;
}
```

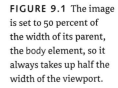

FIGURE 9.1 The image is set to 50 percent of the width of its parent, the body element, so it always takes up half the width of the viewport.

As we discussed in Chapter 2, any time a browser scales an image, there's going to be some distortion, but you can keep it minimal by starting out with a very large image so the browser will usually be scaling it down.

FIGURE 9.2 The image is set to 20 ems, so it will always be roughly 40 text characters wide.

■ **TIP:** If the image must stay above a certain size to remain "readable," add a pixel min-width value too.

■ **NOTE:** The page showing this completed technique is scale.html in the ch9_examples.zip file.

FIGURE 9.3 The image does not stay proportional to the text size once it reaches its maximum width of 500 pixels.

To assure that the browser *always* scales the image down, not up, you can set a maximum width on the image that matches its set pixel width:

```
img {
    width: 20em;
    max-width: 500px;
}
```

Now the image will scale only until it grows to 500 pixels wide; thereafter it will act as any other fixed-width image (**Figure 9.3**).

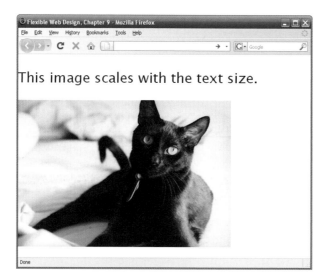

SIMULATE IMAGE SCALING WITH JAVASCRIPT

If you don't want the browser to scale your images at all, yet you want them to change in size based on the amount of space available, you can use JavaScript to swap in differently sized versions of the same image. The JavaScript detects the user's viewport size and chooses the appropriate version of the image to show. This works in the same way that resolution-dependent layouts (discussed in Chapter 1) swap in different CSS files based on viewport size.

A live site that uses image-swapping to simulate scaling is Art & Logic (www.artlogic.com). There are five illustrations under the banner on the home page. Try narrowing or widening your browser window; the images don't scale in real time in most browsers, but as soon as you stop moving the window, they jump to a different size to match the available new space.

Hiding and Revealing Portions of Images

Another way to change the amount of screen area an image takes up is to dynamically change how much of the image is shown at any given time. The image itself doesn't change in size—the amount of space in which it's allowed to show does, and the rest of the image just remains hidden outside of that space. I call this "variable cropping," and you saw an example of it in Figure 9.2.

You can create a variable cropping effect with either background or foreground images. Both look the same, but each is specially suited to different situations.

VARIABLE CROPPING WITH BACKGROUND IMAGES

Putting the image that you want to dynamically crop in the background is ideal when the image is purely decorative. This technique lets you keep the image in the CSS with the other decorative images, so if you later change the look of the site, all the decorative images can be changed in a single style sheet instead of having to replace multiple img elements across multiple pages of the site. By keeping the decorative image as a CSS background, you're also making it likely that the image won't print when the user prints the page—background printing is turned off by default in all major browsers—so the user can save ink by printing only content.

To use a CSS background image, you'll first need an element on which to place the background. This example will use a div:

```
<div id="background"></div>
```

The div is completely empty; it contains no content, but exists simply to hold a background image. If you have a more semantic element you can hang the background on instead, use it. For instance, perhaps the image you want to dynamically crop sits above an h3 element and matches it in width. You could add the image as a background to the h3 element and give the h3 enough top padding to make sure its text sits below the image, not on top of it.

Next, create a rule for this div that sets the image as its non-tiling background:

```
div#background {
    background: url(styx.jpg) no-repeat;
    border: 2px solid #000;
}
```

I've added a border on to this div as well so you can easily see where its edges lie. Right now, with no content within the div, it will collapse to zero height. Add dimensions to the div to prop it open:

```
div#background {

    width: 50%;

    height: 330px;

    background: url(styx.jpg) no-repeat;

    border: 2px solid #000;

}
```

■ **TIP:** To dynamically change the height of the image as well as or instead of the width, use a flexible value for the height property .

The width is set to some flexible dimension—either a percentage, as I've done here, or an em value to make it elastic—so that the div can change in width to show more or less of the image. The height is set to the pixel height of the image so that the entire height of the image will show at all times.

The div will now always be 50 percent as wide as the viewport; its background image doesn't change in size, but gets cropped to a varying degree from the right side (**Figure 9.4**).

FIGURE 9.4 As the width of the browser window decreases, the black-bordered div narrows and cuts off more and more of the right side of its background image.

However, this particular image would look better cropped from the left side, as the cat's face is on the right side of the photo. To specify from where the image gets cropped, use the background-position property, or its shorthand in the background property, to change the alignment of the image within the div:

```
div#background {

    width: 50%;

    height: 330px;

    background: url(styx.jpg) no-repeat right;

    border: 2px solid #000;

}
```

The image is now anchored to the right side of the div, so more or less of its left side shows as the div changes in size (**Figure 9.5**).

This is all the CSS necessary to get the basic variable cropping technique working, but you can add a few other enhancements if you like. For instance, right now, once the `div` exceeds the width of the image, empty white space shows within the `div`. There are a few ways you could handle this. You could add a background color to the `div` as well that would fill up whatever space the image cannot; if you blend the edge of the image into this background color, the effect can look seamless, as in Figures 2.16 and 2.17. Or, you could add a maximum width to the `div` so it can never grow larger than the image. You could also add minimum widths, as well as maximum and minimum heights, to ensure that the `div` can never grow or shrink past particular points in the image.

FIGURE 9.5 With the background anchored to the right side of the `div`, more of the left side of the image is cut off when the browser window is narrowed.

■ **NOTE:** The page showing this completed technique is crop_background.html in the ch9_examples.zip file.

VARIABLE CROPPING WITH FOREGROUND IMAGES

If the image that you want to dynamically crop is functional content, you'll want to keep it as a foreground image by placing it in the (X)HTML using the `img` element. You can ask yourself these questions to determine if the image is content, not decoration:

◆ Does the image convey information that I ought to put as text in an `alt` attribute?

◆ Do I want to make sure the image always prints because without it the printout wouldn't make sense or be complete?

◆ Do I want to link the image?

If the answer to any of these questions is yes, the image is content and should be kept in the (X)HTML. CSS background images can't achieve any of these goals—at least not without some complicated workarounds and hacks, all of which are quite silly, considering how easily a simple `img` element can achieve all this.

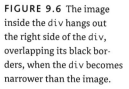

■ **NOTE:** The img element has an alt attribute providing the text equivalent of the image. You can't do this with a CSS background image.

As with the background-image version of the variable cropping technique, you'll need some block element in the (X)HTML to hold the image. We'll use a div again; this time it won't be empty, but will instead contain the img element:

```
<div id="foreground">
    <img src="styx.jpg" alt="my cat Styx" width="500"
height="330">
</div>
```

Just as before, the div needs to have a flexible width and a height set to the pixel height of the image:

```
div#foreground {
    width: 50%;
    height: 330px;
    border: 2px solid #000;
}
```

So far, all we have is a regular div holding a regular image—there's nothing yet that makes this a variable cropping technique. If the image is bigger than the div, it doesn't get cropped, but simply overflows (**Figure 9.6**).

FIGURE 9.6 The image inside the div hangs out the right side of the div, overlapping its black borders, when the div becomes narrower than the image.

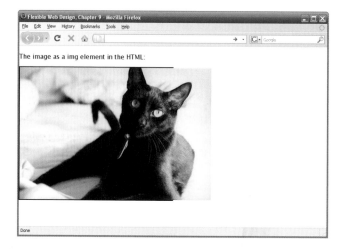

To get the cropping effect, add overflow: hidden; to the CSS rule:

```
div#foreground {
    overflow: hidden;
    width: 50%;
    height: 330px;
    border: 2px solid #000;
}
```

Now whatever portion of the image would overflow out of the `div` is hidden from view (**Figure 9.7**).

FIGURE 9.7
With `overflow` set to `hidden`, the extra portion of the image is now hidden from view.

Once again, though, it would be better for this image to be cropped from the left side, not the right. We can't use the `background-position` property this time because it's not a background image. To change how a foreground image is anchored within its parent, you can float the image:

```
div#foreground img {
    float: right;
}
```

This anchors the image to the right side of the `div`, so more or less of its left side shows as the `div` changes in size. Using a foreground image results in an effect that looks exactly like using a background image (seen in Figure 9.5), but the foreground image has alternative text, and you could also easily add a link to it.

■ **NOTE:** The page showing this completed technique is crop_foreground. html in the ch9_examples. zip file. You can also view both background and foreground techniques together on the page crop.html.

Creating Sliding Composite Images

Perhaps you don't want either end of your image dynamically cropped off—there may be important content on each side that you want to always keep in view. You could scale the entire image instead, which would keep the entire width of the image always visible, but it would also change the vertical space the image takes up, and perhaps you don't want this either. This is the perfect time to try using what I call a composite image.

Creating what appears to be a single image out of multiple pieces that slide over and away from each other takes a little more work on the graphics side than the variable width image techniques we've gone over so far. The real-web-site example of this composite image technique shown in Figures 2.23 and 2.24 used two images to create the effect; you can use an unlimited number of images, but we'll keep it simple and use two for our own alien-invasion example as well.

One image is going to be at least partially overlapping the other, so at least the topmost image needs to have a transparent background. (You may choose to make the lower image transparent too, to allow parts of the main page background to show through, for instance.) You can use either a GIF with index transparency or a PNG with alpha transparency. PNGs are more versatile, since they can lay over any other color or pattern without the skinny colored edge that shows around GIF images when they're placed over something that's a different color than they were optimized for. PNGs can also have variable degrees of transparency, instead of each pixel being either 100 percent transparent or 100 percent opaque.

We'll use an alpha-transparent PNG for our top image in this example. **Figure 9.8** shows our flying saucer image in Adobe Fireworks; the checkerboard background indicates the transparent areas of the image. **Figure 9.9** shows the image that the flying saucer will be laid on top of—a photo of the Chicago skyline—which can be saved as an ordinary JPG.

FIGURE 9.8 The flying saucer image has large areas of partial or total transparency through which the skyline image will be visible.

FIGURE 9.9 The skyline image is completely separate from the flying saucer image.

Once you have your images made, you need two block elements to place each on as a background image. One block element needs to be nested inside the other. In a real page, you'd want to make use of block elements that were already in place as much as possible, such as existing wrapper and header divs. For this simple example, we'll use two empty divs:

```
<div id="outer"><div id="inner"></div></div>
```

Next, you need to create rules placing each image as a non-repeating background on each div, with the image you want on the bottom used for the background of the outer div:

```
#outer {
    background: url(skyline.jpg) no-repeat;
}
#inner {
    background: url(ufo.png) no-repeat;
}
```

Since the `divs` are empty, they also need dimensions added to them to stop them from collapsing entirely, as well as to create the flexible behavior that we want:

```
#outer {
    width: 100%;
    max-width: 1000px;
    height: 300px;
    background: url(skyline.jpg) no-repeat;
}
#inner {
    width: 100px;
    height: 250px;
    background: url(ufo.png) no-repeat;
}
```

Both of the images now show on the page, with the flying saucer layered over the skyline (**Figure 9.10**). However, the flying saucer never moves when the window changes in size—it's always pinned to the top left corner of the skyline photo. That's because the `div` for which it's a background begins in that corner, and non-repeating, non-positioned background images display in the top left corner by default.

■ **NOTE:** Remember that IE 6 and earlier do not support alpha-transparent PNGs, so the flying saucer image will have a solid gray background in those browsers. Use the `alphaimageloader` hack described in the exercise section of Chapter 7 to fix this.

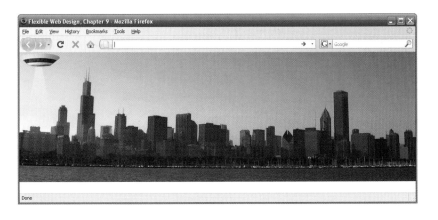

FIGURE 9.10 The flying saucer image is layered over the skyline image to create the appearance of a single image, but the flying saucer isn't yet in the place we want it.

There are a couple ways to fix this: use the `background-position` property to change where the flying saucer displays within the `div`, or move the entire `div`. Either option is fine, but the latter seems a little easier to understand and implement—at least to me—so that's what we'll use here.

We'll move the `div` using absolute positioning; floating would work as well. First, add `position: relative;` to the `#outer` rule to make that `div` act as the containing element for the absolutely positioned inner `div`. Then, add `position: absolute;` as well as `top` and `right` values to the `#inner` rule:

```
#inner {
    position: absolute;
    top: 50px;
    right: 50px;
    width: 100px;
    height: 250px;
    background: url(ufo.png) no-repeat;
}
```

■ **NOTE:** The page showing this completed technique is composite.html in the ch9_examples.zip file.

Now the flying saucer image will always be 50 pixels away from both the top and right edges of the skyline photo. Because the outer `div` has a flexible width, its right edge moves as the window is resized, which in turn makes the flying saucer image move as well (**Figure 9.11**).

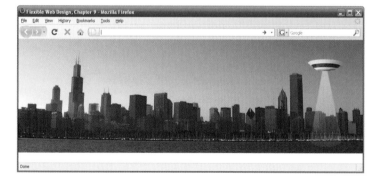

FIGURE 9.11 The flying saucer image now appears to move as the browser window changes in size.

Creating Flexible Collections of Images

You now know several ways to make individual images flexible to either their parent's dimensions or text size, but what about when you need a whole group of images to be flexible as a whole? Let's go over how to make two of the most common types of image collections—teaser thumbnail lists and image galleries—flexible too.

Teaser Thumbnail Lists

A teaser thumbnail list is my own personal name for the design convention of a list where each item is made up of a title, short description, and thumbnail image. Figure 2.22 is one example of a teaser thumbnail list, as is the list of featured pets on the home page of our fictional Beechwood Animal Shelter site (Figure 2.43). These types of lists can be built in many different ways, but many techniques result in lists that are not flexible or not as accessible to the end user as they could be.

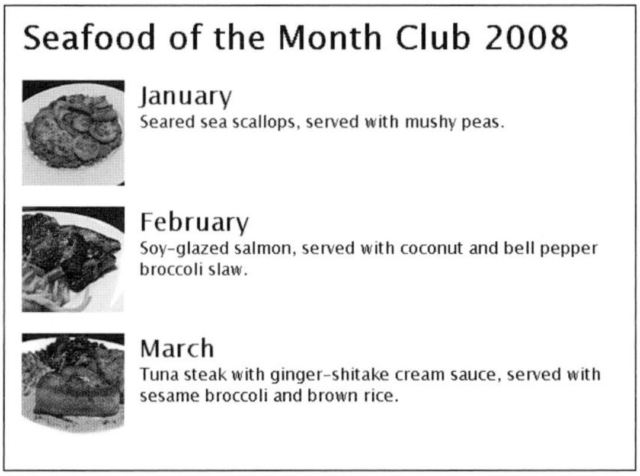

Seafood of the Month Club 2008

January
Seared sea scallops, served with mushy peas.

February
Soy-glazed salmon, served with coconut and bell pepper broccoli slaw.

March
Tuna steak with ginger-shitake cream sauce, served with sesame broccoli and brown rice.

FIGURE 9.12 Each teaser thumbnail list item is made up of a title, short description, and thumbnail image.

Figure 9.12 shows the teaser thumbnail list I'll be using as an example throughout this section. I've chosen the following HTML as the most semantic way of marking up each of the elements of this design component:

```
<h1>Seafood of the Month Club 2008</h1>
<ul>
  <li>
    <h2>January</h2>
    <img src="january.jpg" alt="" width="100" height="100">
    <p>Seared sea scallops, served with mushy peas.</p>
  </li>
  <li>
    <h2>February</h2>
    <img src="february.jpg" alt="" width="100" height="100">
```

```
      <p>Soy-glazed salmon, served with coconut and bell pepper
  broccoli slaw.</p>
    </li>
    <li>
      <h2>March</h2>
      <img src="march.jpg" alt="" width="100" height="100">
      <p>Tuna steak with ginger-shitake cream sauce, served with
  sesame broccoli and brown rice.</p>
    </li>
  </ul>
```

You'll note that the img elements follow the h2 heading elements, even though Figure 9.12 shows the images appearing on the same line as the headings. You'll need to find a way to get the images to move up to sit beside the headings, even though they come later in the source. Luckily, you're already an expert at doing just that—you have several negative margin layouts you can use to achieve such an effect. A teaser thumbnail list is essentially nothing more than a two-column layout. This particular one has a fixed-width left "sidebar" and a liquid right "main content area," so any negative margin technique that works for two-column, hybrid liquid-fixed layouts will work here.

To turn this into a negative margin "layout," the basic steps are:

1. Create an empty space on the left side of the list.

2. Use negative margins to pull each image into that space.

3. Float all the elements within each list item so they can sit side by side.

We'll create the empty space on the left side of the list using a left margin on the ul element that is equal to the width of the images (100 pixels) plus the width of the gap we want between each image and its accompanying text (15 pixels):

```
ul {
    margin: 0 0 0 115px;
    padding: 0;
    list-style: none;
}
```

This rule also gets rid of some of the default list styling, including the bullets. The rest of the default list styling that needs to be overridden is on the list items:

```
li {
```

```
    margin: 0 0 20px 0;
    padding: 0;
}
```

This removes the default left margin and padding that some browsers add to li elements, as well as adds 20 pixels of space below each list item to space them out from each other.

EASIER TEASER THUMBNAIL LIST CREATION OPTIONS

If you're still feeling a little uneasy about creating negative margin layouts, there are a few easier ways to create teaser thumbnail lists that achieve the same visual effect:

◆ Remove the images from the (X)HTML altogether and simply use CSS background images to place the thumbnails next to each heading-paragraph pair. This is a perfectly acceptable option—*if the thumbnails are purely decoration*. If you want the images to show even when the user has CSS off or unavailable, as well as when the user prints the page, you should keep them in the (X)HTML. Doing so also allows you to add alternative text and links to the images—not important if they're just decoration, but essential if they're content.

◆ You can keep the images in the (X)HTML and still avoid a negative margin technique by placing the image before the heading within each list item. This markup isn't quite as ideal as placing the headings first—after all, the headings should head or precede the images and text they describe. But the markup is still quite clean and fairly semantic, and it does allow you to use a simple floats-with-matching-side-margins technique: just float the images to the left, and give the headings and paragraphs left margin values that exceed the images' width.

◆ Another way to keep the images in the (X)HTML but use the most semantic markup of headings-first is to use the same unit of measurement for both the thumbnails and the blocks of text beside them. The example we're going over here is essentially a hybrid layout: the thumbnails are fixed-width and the text beside them is liquid. This is the most common type of teaser thumbnail list. But you could make the thumbnails scalable instead. This would allow you to use a simple float-all-the-columns layout method: float the images to the left and the headings and paragraphs to the right, all with matching units of measurement. You'll get to try this method in the exercise section at the end of the chapter.

FIGURE 9.13 A large empty space on the left side of the list stands ready to receive the thumbnails.

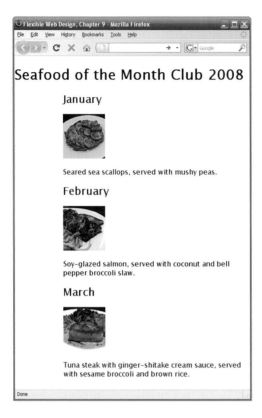

You can now pull the image into the empty space on the left:

```
img {
    float: left;
    margin-left: -115px;
}
```

This positions the images correctly horizontally, but not vertically (**Figure 9.14**). To get them to move up and sit beside the headings, the headings have to be floated, as do the paragraphs:

```
h2 {
    float: right;
    width: 100%;
    margin: 0;
}
p {
    float: right;
```

```
    width: 100%;
    margin: 0;
}
```

FIGURE 9.14 Negative left margins pull the images to the left, but don't pull them up to sit beside the headings.

The width: 100%; declarations ensure that each piece of text fills up the entire width to the right of the images, instead of each element shrinkwrapping to its content, as floats without declared widths do naturally.

The images have now moved up to sit beside the headings, but they overlap each other (**Figure 9.15**). This is because the list items contain only floated content now, which is out of the flow, and have thus collapsed down to zero height.

FIGURE 9.15 Floating the text elements to the right allows the images to sit beside the headings, but the list items will not expand to hold the full height of the thumbnails when everything inside the list items is floated.

■ **NOTE:** The page showing this completed technique is teaser.html in the ch9_examples.zip file.

To address this, we need to use a float containment method to get each list item to encompass all of the floated elements within it. Floating the li elements themselves is one easy way to do this:

```
li {
    float: left;
    width: 100%;
    margin: 0 0 20px 0;
    padding: 0;
}
```

The list items are now properly spaced out from each other, whether the text within them is shorter or longer than the thumbnail images (**Figure 9.16**).

The only problem is that floating the list items made the images disappear in IE 6 and earlier. To fix this, add position: relative; to both the li and img rules:

```
li {
    float: left;
    width: 100%;
    margin: 0 0 20px 0;
    padding: 0;
    position: relative;
}
img {
    float: left;
    margin-left: -115px;
    position: relative;
}
```

FIGURE 9.16 No matter which is longer—thumbnail or accompanying text—the list items remain spaced out from each other.

Thumbnail Image Galleries

Although images are usually fixed in width, you can line them up side by side and still create a block of image thumbnails that can change in total width. You saw an example of this in Figure 2.41, where the thumbnails wrapped onto a variable number of lines to accommodate the liquid width of the content area. Another way to create a flexible image gallery is to make all of the thumbnails scale, using one of the scalable image techniques you learned at the start of the chapter. Let's go over both options.

WRAPPING THE THUMBNAILS

The two behaviors you want thumbnails in a flexible image gallery to achieve—sitting side by side and wrapping onto more lines as needed—are both native behaviors of floats. So, the only thing you need to do to make thumbnails wrap is to float each one in the same direction.

You could just place the images straight into the (X)HTML with no container, and float each of the img elements. But a more semantic way to mark up a group of images is to use an unordered list, which offers you more styling possibilities as well. Put each img into an li element:

```
<ul>
    <li><img src="january.jpg" alt="January" width="100" height="100">
</li>
    <li><img src="february.jpg" alt="February" width="100" height="100">
</li>
    <li><img src="march.jpg" alt="March" width="100" height="100">
</li>
    <li><img src="april.jpg" alt="April" width="100" height="100">
</li>
    <li><img src="may.jpg" alt="May" width="100" height="100">
</li>
    <li><img src="june.jpg" alt="June" width="100" height="100">
</li>
    <li><img src="july.jpg" alt="July" width="100" height="100">
</li>
</ul>
```

Next, remove the default list styling:

```
ul {
    margin: 0;
    padding: 0;
    list-style: none;
}
li {
    margin: 0;
    padding: 0;
}
```

Now, simply float the `li` elements all to the left, and give them some margin on their right and bottom sides to space them out from each other:

```
li {
    float: left;
    margin: 0 10px 10px 0;
    padding: 0;
}
```

■ **NOTE:** The page showing this completed technique is gallery_wrap.html in the ch9_examples.zip file.

That's all you need to do to create a basic, wrapping thumbnail image gallery (**Figure 9.17**). The perfect number of thumbnails always sits on each line, no matter the viewport width, so you don't get a horizontal scrollbar or a really large gap on the right. If you didn't want the gallery to take up the entire width of its parent, simply assign a width to the `ul` element; as long as the width is a percentage or em value, the list will still be flexible and the thumbnails will still wrap.

FIGURE 9.17 The number of thumbnails on each line adjusts to the space available in the viewport.

You may have noticed that all of the thumbnails in this example share the same dimensions. Variable widths on thumbnails are not a problem, but variable heights make this wrapping thumbnail technique fail. **Figure 9.18** shows the same page with the height of some of the thumbnails increased. When the thumbnails wrap, they move as far over to the left as they can go. But when one of the thumbnails in the previous row hangs down farther than the rest, it impedes the new row of thumbnails from moving any further to the left, and big gaps can be left in the rows.

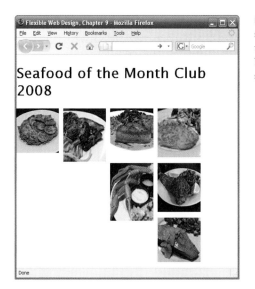

FIGURE 9.18 The extra height on the second thumbnail blocks the fifth thumbnail from moving all the way to the left, leaving a gap in the second row. The same problem happens in the third row.

There are a couple ways you can modify the basic technique to work with variable height thumbnails. The simplest is to assign a fixed height to the li elements that matches the height of the tallest thumbnail. This makes all the li elements match in height, instead of depending on the size of the images inside them to dictate their heights, so there are no taller list items sticking down any more that might block the wrapping thumbnails.

If you can't assign a fixed height to the li elements, though, perhaps because your thumbnails are pulled into the page dynamically and you don't know what the largest height will be, there's still hope. You'll need to use something other than floats to get the thumbnails sitting side by side—and that something is display: inline-block.

An inline block mixes the attributes of block and inline elements. It's placed on the same line as adjacent content, like inline elements are, but you can assign it width, height, margin, and padding, just like a block element.

Since inline block elements sit side by side by default, when you apply a display value of inline-block to the li elements, you can get rid of the float declaration:

```
li {
    display: inline-block;
    margin: 0 10px 10px 0;
    padding: 0;
}
```

In browsers that support `inline-block`, that's all you need to do to keep the thumbnails from hanging up on each other when they wrap (**Figure 9.19**). If you want the thumbnails aligned along their top edges, as they were when we used floats, simply add `vertical-align: top;` to the `li` rule.

FIGURE 9.19 When the thumbnails are turned into inline blocks, instead of floats, they no longer hang up on one another.

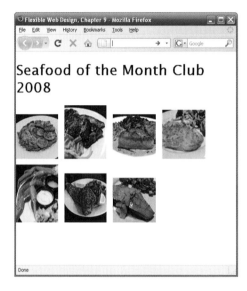

In browsers that don't support `inline-block`, the thumbnails will just display straight down, each on its own line. These browsers include versions of IE earlier than 8 and versions of Firefox earlier than 3. Let's take care of the IE problem first.

IE 7 and 6 support `inline-block` only on elements that are inline by default, so you can trick these browsers into making `inline-block` work by setting the list items to `display: inline`. Hide this rule inside a conditional comment that only IE 7 and earlier can read:

```
<!--[if lte IE 7]>
<style type="text/css">
li {
    display: inline;
}
</style>
<![endif]-->
```

■ NOTE: Browser-proprietary values will make your CSS fail validation checks. But they don't hurt any browsers that can't understand them, so don't worry about the lack of validation—validation is just a means to an end, not necessarily an end unto itself.

This fixes the problem in IE; now onto Firefox.

Versions of Firefox prior to 3 lacked support for `inline-block` but had their own proprietary values, `-moz-inline-box` and `-moz-inline-stack`, for the

display property that worked almost identically. Add either of these values
to the li rule:

```
li {
    display: -moz-inline-box;
    display: inline-block;
    margin: 0 10px 10px 0;
    padding: 0;
    vertical-align: top;
}
```

■ **TIP:** Add the proprietary value before the proper value, as done here, so that the browser will use the latter one when it's able to support it.

This fixes the problem in Firefox 2 without hurting any other browsers,
including Firefox 3—they all just ignore the -moz-inline-box value. If you
have links wrapped around the images, however, you'll have just a bit more
work to do. Firefox 2 will position the images incorrectly and not make the
entire image clickable when you nest a elements inside the li elements. To
fix this, turn the a elements into blocks:

```
li a {
    display: block;
}
```

■ **NOTE:** The page showing this completed technique is gallery_wrap_irregular.html in the ch9_examples.zip file.

Again, this doesn't hurt other browsers.

SCALING THE THUMBNAILS

If you want the thumbnails in your image gallery to scale instead of—or
in addition to—wrapping, you need to add the scalable foreground image
technique (that we went over earlier in the chapter) to the basic wrapping
thumbnail gallery CSS.

The first step in making scalable foreground images, you may remember, is to
remove the width and height dimensions from the img elements in the (X)HTML:

```
<ul>
    <li><img src="january.jpg" alt="January"></li>
    <li><img src="february.jpg" alt="February"></li>
    <li><img src="march.jpg" alt="March"></li>
    <li><img src="april.jpg" alt="April"></li>
    <li><img src="may.jpg" alt="May"></li>
    <li><img src="june.jpg" alt="June"></li>
    <li><img src="july.jpg" alt="July"></li>
</ul>
```

Next, add a percentage or em width onto the `li` elements:

```
li {
    float: left;
    width: 18%;
    margin: 0 10px 10px 0;
    padding: 0;
}
```

■ NOTE: The page showing this completed technique is gallery_scale.html in the ch9_examples.zip file.

Finally, add a rule for the `img` elements that sets their widths to 100 percent so they always fill up the variable size of their parent list items:

```
img {
    width: 100%;
}
```

The thumbnails now scale with the browser window (**Figure 9.20**).

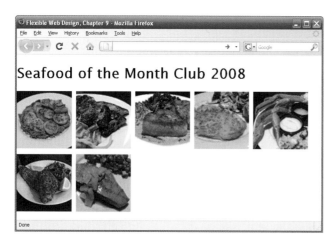 

FIGURE 9.20 The thumbnails still wrap to a small degree, but now their primary method of adjusting to the viewport is to scale with it.

If you want to avoid the blurriness or pixelation that happens when browsers scale images past their native dimensions, you can add a maximum width onto the images that matches their pixel widths:

```
img {
    width: 100%;
    max-width: 100px;
}
```

When the thumbnails reach this `max-width` value, they will stop scaling. The list items, however, will not, so the images will appear to move farther apart from each other, still filling up the available space (**Figure 9.21**).

FIGURE 9.21 Once the thumbnails reach their maximum widths, they will stop scaling, but will still adjust to the viewport size by moving farther apart to fill the space.

Site-Building Exercise: Adding Flexible Images to the Home Page

In the last chapter, you completed all the work on the Programs page. The home page needs only a little more work to get it matching the comp (shown back in Figure 2.43)—the banner image needs to be added as a variably cropped background image, and the list of featured pets needs to be turned into a flexible teaser thumbnail list.

You'll work with the exercise files from this book's companion web site at www.flexiblewebbook.com. Download and unzip the file ch9_exercise.zip.

Adding the Variable Cropping Banner Image

Open the file home-start.html in your text or code editor of choice. This is the same page as the final version of the home page you completed in Chapter 8.

1. Locate the #banner rule inside the style tags in the head of the page, and modify it to match the following:

```
#banner {
    margin: 0 0 20px -180px;
    padding: 2em 0 6em 20px;
    background: #864316 url(images/banner.jpg) no-repeat 0 40%;
    color: #fff;
}
```

This places a background image on the banner that will exceed the width and height of the banner at most text sizes. The portion of the background image that will show within the banner is controlled by the `background-position` values within the `background` shorthand property. Both the width and height of the banner will change as the text size does, creating a background image that is dynamically cropped both horizontally and vertically.

In addition to setting a dynamically cropping background image, this rule removes the placeholder background color and replaces it with a brown that matches the predominant color in the background image. This means that if images are not available or the text is increased to a very large size, the banner will still have some color to it that the text can show up against. Here, the text color is set to white.

2. As a final coloring tweak, add a rule for the links within the banner setting their color to white:

```
#banner a {
    color: #fff;
}
```

The banner now has perfectly legible text and links at a variety of text sizes (**Figure 9.22**).

FIGURE 9.22 The banner grows in size with the text, revealing more or less of its background image.

Creating the Teaser Thumbnail List

The list of featured pets to adopt is already present on the home page and marked up with the most semantic HTML, but is not yet styled to look like a teaser thumbnail list. If you want the thumbnail images to be fixed in width, with the text blocks beside them elastic, you'd need to use the negative margin method described earlier in this chapter. But if you want the thumbnails to be elastic as well, you can use an even easier method—basically, just replicate a typical float-all-the-columns layout.

1. To create the left columns of the list, add a new rule to float the images inside the list to the left:

```
#adopt-pets ul img {
    float: left;
    width: 3em;
}
```

2. To create the right columns of the list, add new rules for the h3 and p elements, floating them to the right:

```
#adopt-pets ul h3 {
    float: right;
    width: 8.5em;
    margin: 0;
    font-size: 100%;
}
#adopt-pets ul p {
    float: right;
    width: 8.5em;
    margin: 0;
}
```

> **NOTE:** Dreamweaver's Design View doesn't do so well with these rules; in fact, it doesn't display the teaser images or the text—just another reminder that in web design, the browser is the final judge.

The list already has a width of 12 ems set on it. With the thumbnails taking up 3 ems and the text taking up 8.5, there will be .5 ems of space left between each thumbnail and its associated text, without any need to set an explicit margin between the two "columns."

Note that the h3 element has its font size set to 100 percent so that its text will inherit the list's text size and match the text size of the paragraphs. If the headings and paragraphs didn't match in text size, you couldn't use the same em width values for both—they would compute out to different pixel sizes.

> **NOTE:** Opera doesn't behave consistently when displaying the gap between images and text in this setup—don't ask me to describe it, but if you would like to try to hack it into submission, check out www.nealgrosskopf.com/tech/thread.asp?pid=20.

3. To space out each pet listing from the next, add a new rule for the `li` elements:

```
#adopt-pets li {
    float: left;
    margin: 0 0 1em 0;
    padding: 0;
}
```

Floating the `li` elements makes them contain their children floats; without this, they would collapse, and the bottom margin would be useless.

The images of the pets are correctly positioned next to their descriptions, and they stay proportional to that text as it grows in size.

This completes the teaser thumbnail list. In fact, all the image work needed for the home page is now done—you've finished the page (**Figure 9.23**).

FIGURE 9.23 The completed home page, at two different text sizes.

To compare your work to the completed home page for this exercise—and the entire book—see the file home-end.html that you extracted from ch9_exercise.zip.

Index

Credits

FIGURES

Figures 1.4 and 2.33 Jason Santa Maria, www.jasonsantamaria.com

Figures 1.6 and 2.18 Simple Bits, www.simplebits.com

Figures 2.1 and 2.2 www.greg-wood.co.uk

Figures 2.3 and 2.4 Dynamix New Media, www.dynamixnewmedia.com

Figure 2.5 The Lippincott, www.thelippincott.net, designed by The Archer Group, Wilmington, DE, www.archer-group.com

Figure 2.6 Scrapbook Your Memories, http://scrapbookyourmemories.myshopify.com

Figures 2.7 and 2.41 www.simonwiffen.co.uk, designed and produced by Simon Wiffen

Figure 2.8 Neurotic, www.neuroticweb.com

Figure 2.9 Eton Digital, www.etondigital.com

Figures 2.10 and 2.11 Usolab, www.usolab.com

Figure 2.12 Sesame Communications, www.sesamecommunications.com

Figure 2.13 © Erskine Design LLP, www.erskinecorp.com

Figures 2.14 and 2.15 Dartmouth College, www.dartmouth.edu

Figure 2.16 Air Adventure Australia, www.airadventure.com.au, designed by www.jimmyweb.net

Figure 2.17 Defacto, www.defacto-cms.com

Figure 2.19 www.liberatutti.it, author Marco Mattioli, owner of Compraweb

Figure 2.20 MCR Foundation, www.mcrfoundation.com, designed by Parallel Creative Group, site by Coptix

Figure 2.21 Borealis, www.borealisoffsets.com, created by smashLAB

Figure 2.22 Todd Silver Design, www.toddsilverdesign.net, designed by Todd Silver

Figures 2.23 and 2.24 Ronin Snowboards, www.roninsnowboards.com, created by Bartek Czerwinski, Spoiltchild Design

Figure 2.25 Bokardo, http://bokardo.com

Figures 2.26 and 2.27 Cafédirect plc, www.cafedirect.co.uk

Figure 2.28 UX Magazine, www.uxmag.com

Figure 2.29 © The Open University, www.open.ac.uk/cpd/

Figure 2.30 e-days, www.e-days.co.uk

Figure 2.31 tap tap tap, www.taptaptap.com

Figure 2.32 Web Designer Wall, www.webdesignerwall.com, creator Nick La, N.Design Studio, www.ndesign-studio.com

Figure 2.34 StylizedWeb, www.stylizedweb.com

Figure 2.35 Django, www.djangoproject.com, designed by Wilson Miner

Figures 2.36 and 2.39 Webdesign UK, www.wduk.co.uk, creator Léo Ludwig

Figure 2.37 Courtesy of SPARC (Sport & Recreation New Zealand), www.sparc.org.nz

Figure 2.38 Cody Lindley, www.codylindley.com

Figure 2.40 Indelebile, www.indelebile.net, creator Ciro Visciano

Figure 4.13 Inmersio, www.inmersio, designed by Paulo Tromp

Figure 6.23 The Accessible Art Fair Geneva, http://accessibleart.ch, designed by d/vision, http://dvision.es

PHOTOGRAPHS

In the Beechwood Animal Shelter home page, selected photos came from:

Gray cat: Taken by Flickr user .Jennifer Leigh., licensed under Creative Commons Attribution 2.0 Generic (http://creativecommons.org/licenses/by/2.0/deed.en)

Puppy in box: "peekaboo," taken by Flickr user dryfish, licensed under Creative Commons Attribution 2.0 Generic (http://creativecommons.org/licenses/by/2.0/deed.en)

Piggy bank: "Baby Piggy Bank," taken by trungson, licensed under Creative Commons Attribution-Share Alike 2.0 Generic (http://creativecommons.org/licenses/by-sa/2.0/deed.en)

In the Chapter 9 composite image example, the photos came from:

City: "Chicago Skyline," taken by Mike Novales, licensed under Creative Commons Attribution 2.0 Generic (http://creativecommons.org/licenses/by/2.0/deed.en)

Flying saucer: "UFO-OVNI," taken by Flickr user Piutus, licensed under Creative Commons Attribution 2.0 Generic (http://creativecommons.org/licenses/by/2.0/deed.en)

Safari
Books Online

Get free online access to this book!

And sign up for a free trial to Safari Books Online to get access to thousands more!

With the purchase of this book you have instant online, searchable access to it on Safari Books Online! And while you're there, be sure to check out the Safari on-demand digital library and its Free Trial Offer (a separate sign-up process)—where you can access thousands of technical and inspirational books, instructional videos, and articles from the world's leading creative professionals with a Safari Books Online subscription.

Simply visit www.peachpit.com/safarienabled and enter code ZRHZRBI to try it today.